Lecture Notes in Computer Science 7909

Commenced Publication in 1973
Founding and Former Series Editors:
Gerhard Goos, Juris Hartmanis, and Jan van Leeuwen

T0185894

Keith Duddy   Gerti Kappel (Eds.)

Theory and Practice
of Model Transformations

6th International Conference, ICMT 2013
Budapest, Hungary, June 18-19, 2013
Proceedings

 Springer

Volume Editors

Keith Duddy
Queensland University of Technology
4000 Brisbane, QLD, Australia
E-mail: keith.duddy@qut.edu.au

Gerti Kappel
Vienna University of Technology
1040 Vienna, Austria
E-mail: gerti@big.tuwien.ac.at

ISSN 0302-9743   e-ISSN 1611-3349
ISBN 978-3-642-38882-8   e-ISBN 978-3-642-38883-5
DOI 10.1007/978-3-642-38883-5
Springer Heidelberg Dordrecht London New York

Library of Congress Control Number: 2013939603

CR Subject Classification (1998): D.2, F.3, D.3, K.6

LNCS Sublibrary: SL 2 – Programming and Software Engineering

Typesetting: Camera-ready by author, data conversion by Scientific Publishing Services, Chennai, India

Printed on acid-free paper

Springer is part of Springer Science+Business Media (www.springer.com)

Preface

This volume contains the papers presented at the International Conference on Model Transformation (ICMT 2013), the sixth conference in the series, and the first to be held at the new parent event "Software Technologies: Applications and Foundations" (STAF Conferences, www.stafconferences.info). STAF was formed after the end of the successful precursor event, TOOLS federated conferences. This year's STAF event covered the conferences TAP (International Conference on Tests and Proof) and SC (International Conference on Software Composition) next to ICMT and the three workshops BIGMDE (International Workshop on Big MDE), VOLT (International Workshop on the Verification of Model Transformations), and TTC (Transformation Tool Contest). ICMT 2013 and all other STAF 2013 events were graciously hosted at Budapest University of Technology and Economics during June 17–20, 2013, and we thank the General Chair, Dániel Varró, and his team for their organizational skills and great hospitality in Hungary.

ICMT is the premier forum for contributions advancing the state of the art in the field of model transformation and aims to bring together researchers and practitioners alike from all areas of model transformation. Model transformation encompasses a variety of technical spaces, including modelware, grammarware, dataware, and ontoware, a variety of model representations, e.g., based on different types of graphs, and a variety of transformation paradigms including rule-based transformations, term rewriting, and manipulations of objects in general-purpose programming languages, to mention just a few.

The study of model transformation includes foundations, structuring mechanisms, and properties, such as modularity, composability, and parameterization of transformations, transformation languages, techniques, and tools. An important goal of the field is the development of high-level model transformation languages, providing transformations that are amenable to higher-order model transformations or tailored to specific transformation problems. To have an impact on software engineering in general, methodologies and tools are required to integrate model transformation into existing development environments and processes.

This year's program consisted of 13 full papers and five tool and application demonstrations, the latter being supported by an extended abstract in the proceedings. Since ICMT 2013 could attract 58 full submissions this implies an acceptance rate of 22%. The papers covered the spectrum of approaches and technologies mentioned above, and were presented in five sessions that represent the broad scope of ICMT: (a) New Programming Models, (b) Tools and Applications, (c) Transformation Engineering, (d) Testing, and (e) Evolution and Synchronization. We were also fortunate to have a keynote talk by Andreas Zeller (Saarland University) on "Mining Models from Generated System Tests."

And after the traditional conference format, we were pleased to see at our sister event, the Transformation Tool Contest, the diverse tools and approaches in our field in action.

ICMT 2013 was made possible by the collaboration of many people. We were supported by a great team, most notably Publication Chair and EasyChair manager par excellence Manuel Wimmer, Publicity Chair Philip Langer, who got the message out to the transformation community, and Ludovico Iovino, who kept our website up to date. The Steering Committee was very helpful and provided advice when we needed it. We would like to thank all the members of the ICMT 2013 Program Committee for the tremendous effort they put into their reviews and deliberations, and all the additional reviewers for their invaluable contributions. Finally, special thanks go to all the researchers and students who contributed with their work and participated in the conference – without them, ICMT 2013 would not have taken place. We hope that you find the papers in these proceedings as stimulating as we did.

April 2013   Keith Duddy
                                                                            Gerti Kappel

Organization

General Chair

Dániel Varró   Budapest University of Technology and Economics (Hungary)

Program Chairs

Keith Duddy   Queensland University of Technology (Australia)

Gerti Kappel   Vienna University of Technology (Austria)

Publication Chair

Manuel Wimmer   Vienna University of Technology (Austria)

Publicity Chair

Philip Langer   Vienna University of Technology (Austria)

Web Chair

Ludovico Iovino   Università degli Studi dell'Aquila (Italy)

Steering Committee

Jean Bézivin   University of Nantes (France)
Jordi Cabot   INRIA-École des Mines de Nantes (France)
Martin Gogolla   University of Bremen (Germany)
Jeff Gray   University of Alabama (USA)
Zhenjiang Hu   National Institute of Informatics Tokyo (Japan)
Juan de Lara   Universidad Autónoma de Madrid (Spain)
Richard Paige   University of York (UK)
Alfonso Pierantonio (Chair)   Università degli Studi dell'Aquila (Italy)
Laurence Tratt   King's College London (UK)
Antonio Vallecillo   University of Málaga (Spain)
Eelco Visser   Delft University of Technology (The Netherlands)

Program Committee

Jordi Cabot	INRIA-École des Mines de Nantes (France)
Antonio Cicchetti	Mälardalen University (Sweden)
Tony Clark	Middlesex University (UK)
Benoît Combemale	IRISA, Université de Rennes 1 (France)
Krzysztof Czarnecki	University of Waterloo (Canada)
Juan de Lara	Universidad Autónoma de Madrid (Spain)
Davide Di Ruscio	Università degli Studi dell'Aquila (Italy)
Jürgen Ebert	University of Koblenz-Landau (Germany)
Alexander Egyed	Johannes Kepler University Linz (Austria)
Gregor Engels	University of Paderborn (Germany)
Claudia Ermel	Technische Universität Berlin (Germany)
Robert France	Colorado State University (USA)
Jesús García-Molina	Universidad de Murcia (Spain)
Dragan Gašević	Athabasca University (Canada)
Martin Gogolla	University of Bremen (Germany)
Jeff Gray	University of Alabama (USA)
Esther Guerra	Universidad Autónoma de Madrid (Spain)
Reiko Heckel	University of Leicester (UK)
Zhenjiang Hu	National Institute of Informatics Tokyo (Japan)
Marouane Kessentini	Missouri University of Science and Technology (USA)
Dimitris Kolovos	University of York (UK)
Jochen Kuester	IBM Research Zurich (Switzerland)
Ivan Kurtev	University of Twente (The Netherlands)
Thomas Kühne	Victoria University of Wellington (New Zealand)
Leen Lambers	Hasso-Plattner-Institut, Universität Potsdam (Germany)
Tihamer Levendovszky	Vanderbilt University (USA)
Ralf Lämmel	University of Koblenz-Landau (Germany)
Richard Paige	University of York (UK)
Alfonso Pierantonio	Università degli Studi dell'Aquila (Italy)
Ivan Porres	Åbo Akademi University (Finland)
Werner Retschitzegger	Johannes Kepler University Linz (Austria)
Bernhard Rumpe	RWTH Aachen University (Germany)
Andy Schürr	Darmstadt University of Technology (Germany)

Steffen Staab	University of Koblenz-Landau (Germany)
Jim Steel	University of Queensland (Australia)
Perdita Stevens	University of Edinburgh (UK)
Markus Stumptner	University of South Australia (Australia)
Eugene Syriani	University of Alabama (USA)
Jesús Sánchez Cuadrado	Universidad Autónoma de Madrid (Spain)
Gabriele Taentzer	Philipps-Universität Marburg (Germany)
James Terwilliger	Microsoft Corporation (USA)
Massimo Tisi	INRIA-École des Mines de Nantes (France)
Laurence Tratt	King's College London (UK)
Mark Van Den Brand	Eindhoven University of Technology (The Netherlands)
Pieter Van Gorp	Eindhoven University of Technology (The Netherlands)
Hans Vangheluwe	University of Antwerp (Belgium) and McGill University (Canada)
Eelco Visser	Delft University of Technology (The Netherlands)
Janis Voigtländer	University of Bonn (Germany)
Hironori Washizaki	Waseda University Tokyo (Japan)
Haiyan Zhao	Peking University (China)
Albert Zündorf	Kassel University (Germany)

Additional Reviewers

Al-Refai, Mohammed	Engelen, Luc
Anjorin, Anthony	Feuser, Johannes
Arendt, Thorsten	George, Tobias
Asadi, Mohsen	Golas, Ulrike
Bak, Kacper	Gröner, Gerd
Blouin, Arnaud	Hermann, Frank
Bosnacki, Dragan	Hildebrandt, Stephan
Branco, Moises	Hölldobler, Katrin
Brosch, Petra	Horn, Tassilo
Brüseke, Frank	Iovino, Ludovico
Burgueño, Loli	Koch, Andreas
Corley, Jonathan	Lauder, Marius
Cosentino, Valerio	Lindel, Stefan
Dajsuren, Yanja	Martens, Wim
Dang, Duc-Hanh	Navarro Perez, Antonio
Demuth, Andreas	Rajan, Ajitha
Diskin, Zinovy	Reder, Alexander
Dyck, Johannes	Scharf, Andreas
Ehrig, Hartmut	Schölzel, Hanna

Schulze, Christoph
Seidl, Martina
Soltenborn, Christian
Sun, Wuliang
Truscan, Dragos

Varanovich, Andrei
Varró, Gergely
Wachsmuth, Guido
Wieber, Martin

Mining Models from Generated System Tests

Andreas Zeller

Saarland University
Saarbrücken, Germany
zeller@cs.uni-saarland.de
http://www.st.cs.uni-saarland.de

Abstract. Modern Analysis and Verification techniques can easily check advanced properties in complex software systems. Specifying these models and properties is as hard as ever, though. I present techniques to extract models from legacy systems based on dynamic analysis of automatically generated system tests – models that are real by construction, and sufficiently complete and precise to serve as specifications for testing, maintenance, and proofs.

Table of Contents

Transformation Engineering

Testing

Streaming Model Transformations: Scenarios, Challenges and Initial Solutions

Jesús Sánchez Cuadrado and Juan de Lara

Universidad Autónoma de Madrid, Spain
{Jesus.Sanchez.Cuadrado,Juan.deLara}@uam.es

Abstract. Several styles of model transformations are well-known and widely used, such as batch, live, incremental and lazy transformations. While they permit tackling advanced scenarios, some applications deal with models that are only available as a possibly infinite stream of elements. Hence, in *streaming transformations*, source model elements are continuously produced by some process, or very large models are fragmented and fed into the transformation engine. This poses a series of issues that cannot be tackled using current transformation engines. In this paper we motivate the applicability of this kind of transformations, explore the elements involved, and review several strategies to deal with them. We also propose a concrete approach, built on top of the Eclectic transformation tool.

Keywords: Model transformations, Streaming transformations, Transformation engines, Scalability.

1 Introduction

Model-Driven Engineering (MDE) is increasingly being used to tackle problems of raising complexity, in scenarios for which current model transformation technology was not originally conceived [6,27]. One such scenario is transforming models that are only available as a stream of model elements. While data stream processing has been investigated in the databases [1,20] and XML [15] technical spaces, its application to MDE has been little investigated so far [10].

A streaming model transformation is special kind of transformation in which the whole input model is not completely available at the beginning of the transformation, but it is continously generated. Hence, it must be processed incrementally, as elements arrive to the transformation process. For instance, if we aim at processing tweets from Twitter, we can see tweets, users, hashtags, etc, as model elements that are processed as they are generated by the Twitter users. This model is indeed potentially infinite, and cannot be queried, matched or transformed at once. Nevertheless, a streaming transformation is not only useful for those cases in which the input model is inherently streamed and infinite, but it is also a way to deal with large models by feeding a transformation process incrementally, for instance to distribute a transformation, pipeline a transformation chain, or to avoid overflowing the memory of a machine.

K. Duddy and G. Kappel (Eds.): ICMT 2013, LNCS 7909, pp. 1–16, 2013.

In this paper we report our findings on the elements and challenges involved in streaming model transformations. We have looked into which features make streaming transformations different from other types of transformations, and we have identifed several challenges that must be tackled. Then we have explored several strategies that can be used to deal with such challenges, and we have implemented a concrete proposal into the Eclectic transformation tool [12]. The paper is motivated and illustrated by means of a selected example that showcases most of the elements of streaming transformations.

Organization. In Section 2, we analyse applicability scenarios for streaming transformations. Section 3 introduces a running example, identifying challenges to be tackled by streaming transformation engines. Section 4 deals with model element streams, Section 5 with transformation scheduling, and Section 6 with arbitrarily large models and collections. Section 7 evaluates the proposal. Section 8 reviews related research and Section 9 concludes.

2   Motivating Scenarios

The problems involved in data stream processing have been investigated in the context of databases [1,20], XML [15] and the semantic web [2,24], where the main applications are directed to querying, filtering and aggregating streamed (sometimes unstructured) data. In contrast, model transformation techniques unfold their potential when applied to scenarios in which there is a transformation problem involved, either to convert already structured data or to give a model structure to unstructured data.

This difference in the applicability field implies that there is currently a lack of concrete examples and usage scenarios for streaming model transformation, which are needed to assess the potential of this new technique. For this reason we begin by introducing some possible scenarios and concrete examples.

Processing natural streams. Some systems naturally generate data continously, which might need to be transformed, e.g., for analysis or visualization. We distinguish two kinds of systems: (1) those which natively generate stream models (data conforming to a meta-model) and (2) when the data does not conform to a meta-model, but must be first converted to a model-based representation.

An example of (1) is the monitoring of a running system by generating model-based traces of its execution. This will be used as our running example.

An example of (2) is applying streaming transformations to *semantic sensor web technologies* [26]. This may include transforming native sensor data (e.g., temperature, precipitation) to the RDF format relating elements by Linked Data URIs, then further manipulating it, for instance to add information coming from other sources (e.g., amount of cars in a road segment) and to transform it to some other formalism to perform predictions (e.g., traffic jams depending on the weather conditions for certain road segments). As suggested in [25], data from physical sensors can be enriched with data from *social sensors*, like tweets, taking advantage of their attached spatial and temporal information and some defined microsyntax (like #hashtags, @usernames, subtags, or relations from predefined vocabularies, like e.g., for weather or emergency conditions).

The usefulness of model transformations in this scenario is to facilitate the implementation of stream-based applications in which there are an explicit or implicit transformation task involved. The next scenarios apply the notion of streaming data to solve problems in the model transformation domain.

Dealing with large models. An scalable solution to transform large models, is to incrementally feed the transformation process with model fragments. As suggested by [19], instead of loading a large model in memory and then transform it all at once, the model is first split into meaningful parts, which are sent to a stream. The transformation process deals with the elements of the stream incrementally, releasing resources as parts of the source model are transformed. In some way, this imitates lazy transformations [27], but using a push approach.

As a concrete example, let us assume we are reverse engineering a Java model into a KDM model [22]. The Java model would be available in some model repository, and the abstract syntax model of each Java class could be streamed separately (using lazy loading techniques [14]) to the transformation engine. The engine would transform each class individually, discarding all source elements and trace links no longer needed for transforming other classes (e.g., once a Java expression has been transformed to KDM it can be discarded).

Distributed transformations. The idea of streaming transformation can be used as a foundation to build distributed transformations. This is especially important to integrate MDE services in the Cloud [6,7] since a large transformation could use different physical resources depending on their availability. The underlying idea is to replicate the same transformation in several execution nodes. Load balancing techniques would then be used to stream disjoint parts of the input model to such nodes. A shared repository could be used to store trace links and the output models, although other advanced techniques of distributed systems needs to be studied to improve scalability. Although this scenario is not addressed in this paper, we believe that the techniques explained here are complementary for developing distributed model transformations in practice.

Pipelining transformations. This scenario exploits the possibility of starting a transformation (within a transformation chain) as soon as target elements are generated by the previous transformation, in a similar way as Unix pipes. This permits taking advantage of multi-core architectures, by scheduling the first transformation in one core, and the subsequent transformations in different cores.

As an example, consider a parser that generates a concrete syntax model of a Java system (i.e., a low-level Java model), which is then transformed into an abstract syntax model (e.g., references between type definitions and type uses are resolved), and then into KDM. Using streams, each transformation can begin as soon as the previous one has finished processing a single Java class.

3   Running Example and Challenges

Assume we are interested in the reverse engineering of sequence diagrams from the execution traces of a running object-oriented program. The example is an adaptation of the one in [5], in which the actual transformation used to process the execution traces and create the sequence diagrams is done off-line, after having generated all the traces in a text file. In our case, the transformation is on-line, that is, the sequence diagram is built as the execution traces are generated, by means of a streaming transformation. This enables the run-time monitoring of the system, and dealing with non-terminating systems.

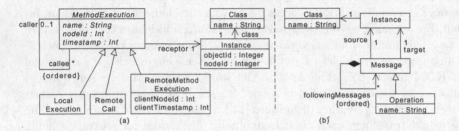

Fig. 1. (a) Trace meta-model (b) Sequence diagram meta-model (simplified)

The meta-models involved in the example are shown in Fig. 1. The *trace meta-model* represents the execution of methods (MethodExecution), including the information of which method performed the invocation, and the sequence of future method executions performed by itself (caller and callee references). Also, a method execution has a reference to the receptor instance. The meta-model is directed to distributed applications (e.g., Java RMI applications), hence there are three kinds of method executions: LocalExecution, normal method executions; RemoteCall, for invocations in the client side (e.g., over a proxy obtained using RMI); and RemoteExecution for the remote executions. Executions are identifed by the nodeId and timestamp attributes. A remote execution records the clientNodeId and clientTimestamp in order to identify the caller.

The *sequence diagram meta-model* represents messages from a source instance to a target instance (note that the source and target are explicitly represented by references, instead of by ids), and the sequence of messages that follows each Message (reference followingMsgs).

Our aim is to specify streaming transformations using regular constructs of rule-based model transformation languages. To illustrate the paper we have used the Eclectic transformation tool [12]. In particular, we use the mapping language which also allows attaching methods to metaclasses (helpers). The language can be seen as a simplified version of ATL [17]. Fig. 2 shows the corresponding transformation. Each LocalExecution is mapped to an Operation (lines 4-10). The source and target instances of the message are obtained from the local_context of the call (i.e., the object in which the call is performed, a helper in lines 29–31)

```
1   mapping trace2seqdiagram(trc) −> (seq)        23
2   trc : 'platform:/resource/example/trc.stream'  24   from src : trc!Class to seq!Class
3                                                   25     tgt.class <− src.class
4   from exec : trc!LocalExecution                  26   end
5     to msg : seq!Operation                        27
6                                                   28   // Start of helper methods
7     msg.source <− exec.local_context             29   def trc!MethodExecution.local_context
8     msg.target <− exec.receptor                  30     self.caller.receptor
9     msg.followingMsgs <− exec.next_executions    31   end
10  end                                             32
11                                                  33   def trc!MethodExecution.remote_context
12  from exec : trc!RemoteMethodExecution           34     self.caller.caller.receptor
13    to msg : seq!Operation                        35   end
14                                                  36
15    msg.source <− exec.remote_context            37   // Find those executions that happen in the context
16    msg.target <− exec.receptor                  38   // of the current execution, but not before (excerpt)
17    msg.followingMsgs <− exec.next_executions    39   def trc!MethodExecution.next_executions
18  end                                             40     trc!LocalExecution.allInstances.select { |me|
19                                                  41       me.caller == self &&
20  from src : trc!Instance to tgt : seq!Instance   42       me.timestamp > self.timestamp
21    tgt.class <− src.class                        43     }.union(...)
22  end                                             44   end
```

Fig. 2. Transforming traces to simplified sequence diagrams

and the receptor object. These bindings require rules that resolve the source instance to target instances, which is done in lines 20-22. Classes are also mapped (lines 24-26). Finally, the followingMsgs reference is filled by resolving those messages that correspond to the method executions calculated by the next_executions helper (lines 39–44), which basically retrieves all executions performed as part of the execution of the current method (for simplicity only local executions are considered here). A RemoteMethodExecution is mapped similarly (lines 12–18), except that the source is obtained from remote_context which access the actual receptor object in the server side, and thus the client stub, which corresponds to the first caller, must be skipped.

3.1 Challenges

From the transformation engine point of view, this is a simple transformation, when applied in batch mode. However, it poses several challenges when the source model is processed in streaming. We next review these challenges, using the execution example shown in Fig. 3. The events are numbered in the order in which they are received by the streaming transformation.

- **Infinite model.** The input model is potentially infinite, as a program may be in execution indefinitely. The notion of infinite model has been studied in [10]. Similarly, the trace model that keeps the correspondences between source and target elements could also be infinite.
  In the example, each time a method is invoked over a local instance, MethodExecution, Instance and Class elements are created. They need to be transformed as they arrive from the stream, generating the corresponding trace links to allow bindings to be resolved (e.g., msg.target ← exec.receptor). As the program generating the execution traces may be in execution for a long

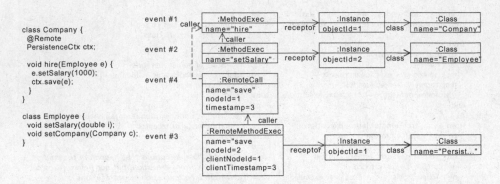

Fig. 3. Execution example

time, strategies to reduce the amount of model elements and trace links are needed to avoid overflowing the memory of the machine.

- **Model element identity.** Transformation engines rely on the object identities, e.g. to compare two objects for equality. In our case, fragments of models can be streamed, and two or more fragments may contain the same element, but with different in-memory object identity.

  In the example, the processes generating the stream may create different Class elements to represent the same class in the program being analysed (i.e., in a distributed enviroment the same code is running in different machines). This implies that object identity may be lost. Additionally, in a distributed setting, a mechanism to serialize and deserialize fragments is needed.

- **Dealing with references.** A model fragment that is streamed may refer to other fragments that have already been streamed or that may be streamed in the future. Both cases are shown in the figure by the dashed arrows. Fragment event #2 refers to fragment event #1 through the caller reference (same for events #3 and #4). However, we do not want to emit all the elements of the referenced fragment again, but just to refer to a particular element. Hence, a mechanism to refer to elements in other fragments is needed.

- **Transformation scheduling.** In the example, obtaining the remote context (through expression self.caller.caller.receptor, line 34), may be a blocking operation since the caller may not be available when the rule is being processed (see reference from event #3 to #4). Some mechanism is needed to avoid stopping the execution of the whole transformation, and to resume the rule execution when the expected element arrives.

  In addition, rules must be executed as elements arrive, but the order is unknown. Thus, a flexible rule scheduling mechanism is needed.

- **Features with different semantics.** Some features normally available in model transformation languages are no longer adequate or their semantics has to be changed. An example is "all instances of", whose usual semantics is not valid in this context. This is so as all objects of a certain class cannot be generally available at a certain moment, either because they still need to arrive, or perhaps they have been discarded. Other features such as iterators on collections like select also need to be adapted, as proposed in [10].

In the example, to obtain the executions that follows the current one (lines 40–43), the allInstances construct must be used. In both cases, a mechanism to process the elements as they appear are needed. In the case of allInstances an strategy to avoid dealing with a possibly infinite collection is also necessary.

As can be observed, streaming model transformations are an essentially different problem from other scenarios, such as live/change-driven [4] and incremental transformations [18,16], in which the aim is to change the model (source model for in-place transformations, or target model for model-to-model transformations) as a response to changes in the source model. In our case the only change is the generation of new elements, but the source model can be infinite.

4   Specifiying Model Streams

A streaming transformation deals with model fragments that are continously made available. Hence, it is necessary to describe their characteristics so that the transformation engine can deal with them transparently.

In our approach, the streaming unit is the *model fragment*, made of one or more model elements which may have intra-fragment references (both containment and non-containment) and inter-fragment references (only non-containment, because the ultimate goal of them is to refer to an element not defined in this fragment).

Model fragments may need to be serialized if they are to be sent to the machine where the transformation is being executed. Thus, when creating and receiving a fragment, there are two main elements to take into account: model element identity and references. We have defined a small DSL to specify these features, among others. The stream description for the running example is shown in the following listing.

```
1   stream "dynamic_trace.ecore"          7   // inter−references
2   // Defining keys: simple, multiple, custom   8   ref(MethodExecution.caller)
3   key(Class) = name                      9   // Sliding windows
4   key(Instance) = objectId, nodeId      10   sliding for MethodExecution = 200 secs
5   key(MethodExecution) = { self.name + "_" +   11   sliding for Instance = 1000 elements
6   self.nodeId + "_" + self.timestamp }
```

Model element identity. In the general case we cannot rely on plain object identity to compare model elements, as the elements of the stream may have been generated by a machine different from where the transformation is executed, as it is the case of the running example. This requires using the properties of the model elements to identify the objects (i.e., rely on value identity), similar to *keys* in the case of QVT-Relations [23]

Hence, we allow the key of an element to be specified in the stream description. Keys can be either simple, or composed of several attributes, or generated by an expression (lines 4, 5 and 6-7 respectively). Each time two elements of the same type are compared, the key value is used if a key has been specified. If the whole stream is generated in a single machine, the object identifier in this machine can be attached to each object prior to serialization.

Inter-fragment references. Our approach for inter-fragment references is based on creating a proxy per each referenced element. We do not rely on any particular technology, but we just create a new element (the proxy), of the same type as the referenced element, setting its key attributes (or attaching a "MemoryId" annotation). The advantage is that, from the serialization point of view, inter-fragment references are not cross-references but just an annotation indicating that an element is a proxy, making it straightforward to implement and meta-modeling framework agnostic.

Upon arrival, our transformation engine replaces the proxy with the actual element if it was streamed before. To this end, the engine internally uses an associative table to keep the relationship between keys and actual elements. The case in which the actual element arrives after a proxy needs a special treatment, as discussed in Section 5.3.

In the DSL we allow specifying which references may hold a proxy (line 8). While this is not compulsory, we use this information to optimize the lookup and the replacement of proxies for the actual elements.

5   Transformation Scheduling

Our approach to schedule streaming transformations builds on our previous work using continuations to schedule batch model transformations [11,12], extended to consider the streaming setting, that is, rules fed incrementally by stream events and partial execution of navigation expressions. Our Eclectic transformation tool relies on an intermediate language, called IDC (Intermediate Dependency Code), to which high-level languages are compiled to.

IDC is a simple, low-level language composed of a few instructions, some of them specialized for model manipulation and transformation scheduling. IDC is compiled to the Java Virtual Machine (JVM). Fig. 4(a) shows an excerpt of its meta-model. Every instruction inherits from the Instruction abstract metaclass. Since most instructions produce a result, they also inherit from Variable (via InstructionWithResult) so that the produced result can be referenced as a variable.

The IDC language provides instructions to create closures, invoke methods, create model elements and set and get properties (Set and Get in Figure 4), among others. In IDC, there is no notion of rule, but the language provides a more general mechanism based on queues. Compilers for high-level languages are in charge of mapping actual rules to queues. A Queue holds objects of some type, typically source model elements and trace links. The ForAllIterator receives notifications of new elements in a queue, and executes the corresponding instructions. There are two special instructions to deal with queues: Emit puts a new object into a queue, while Match retrieves an element of a queue that satisfies a given predicate. If such an element is not readily available, the execution of this piece of code is suspended into a *continuation* [9] until another part of the transformation provides the required value via an Emit.

In the following we discuss, in the context of IDC, the elements involved to schedule a streaming model transformation.

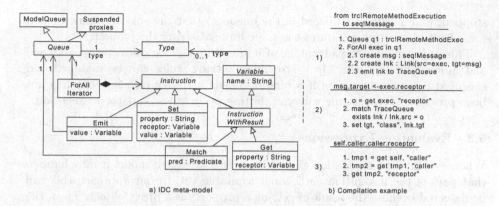

Fig. 4. (a) Excerpt of the IDC meta-model, (b) Compilation example between the Eclectic mapping language and IDC

5.1   Feeding Transformation Rules

Each time a new model fragment arrives, the source pattern of the transformation rules must be evaluated to trigger a rule if there is a match. Figure 4(b.1) shows how the rule to transform RemoteMethodExecutions is compiled to IDC. We create one queue per each type in the source pattern, and a ForAllIterator instruction which acts as a closure that is invoked each time a new element in the queue appears. In the example, a new Message element is created, as well as the corresponding trace link which is sent (via the emit instruction) to a default queue which is in charge of processing trace links (TraceQueue).

This mechanism permits the execution of rules on demand, as queues are filled. ForAllIterator instructions can be nested allowing complex patterns to be detected, and, as we will see in Section 6.1, our queues have "memory" (they have a sliding window), which is needed to allow the nesting of iterators.

In contrast to batch transformations, we needed to check that the rule has not been applied before for the current element, since an element with the same key may have arrived before. To this end we have an index with the received model elements, which is checked before feeding a queue. As explained in Section 3.1 this is the case with Class elements.

5.2   Resolving Source-Target Relationships

A common operation in model-to-model transformations is to retrieve a target element from a source one already transformed by some rule. In the example this is achieved using a binding construct, such as msg.target ← exec.receptor.

We compile a binding as shown in Figure 4(b.2). (1) The expression to the right is compiled using regular model manipulation instructions, a Get in this case. Then, (2) the source element resulting from evaluating the expression, o, is used to match a trace link in the TraceQueue whose source is precisely o. If such trace already exists (i.e., it has been previously added with an Emit, as in Figure 4(b.1)), it is immediately retrieved. If not, the execution of the rule is stopped, and a request is placed in the queue so that the rule is resumed when some Emit instruction generates the trace link satisfying the request.

This approach has the advantage of its flexibility, since rules can be matched and applied in any order. In a streaming setting, rules can be matched and executed as elements arrive: if a binding needs a source element that has not been processed yet, the rule will wait, letting other rules start their execution.

5.3 Evaluating Expressions

When evaluating a navigation expression over a streamed model it may happen that part of the navigation path is not available yet. In our approach this can be detected because the result of getting a property is a proxy object. Thus, the evaluation of the expression must be suspended until the real object arrives. This may in turn suspend the rule that depends on the evaluation of the expression.

We use a similar approach as for resolving trace links, applied to change the semantics of the Get instruction to deal with incomplete models. It is worth noting that this design is transparent to the high-level language, which see property access as a regular Get, as illustrated in the compilation example of Figure 4(b.3).

The process is as follows. Given an instruction such as get self, "caller" we check whether the receptor object or the result of the instruction is a proxy, and we try to resolve the proxy with one of the already streamed elements. If not, the evaluation of the expression is suspended into a continuation, placing a request in a queue (*Suspended proxies*). Later, as new objects arrive they are passed to this queue, to check if some of them satisfies one or more of the enqueued requests, in order to resume the suspended Get instruction.

6   Infinite Models

Streaming model transformations deal with possibly very large models, whose size is unknown. This requires strategies to reduce the memory footprint of the transformation process. Besides, the fact that the whole model is unknown from the beginning implies that some collection operations must be adapted to the new setting. In this section we present our approach to both issues.

6.1 Reducing Memory Footprint

Model transformation engines typically keep the source model, the target model and the traceability links in main memory. In many practical scenarios this is the best alternative, but when the source model is expected to be very large, alternative strategies to reduce the memory footprint are needed. So far, we have considered two approaches: sliding windows and using secondary storage.

Sliding windows. A direct mechanism to deal with an infinite data stream is to use a sliding window. In our setting, both source elements and trace links outside the window will be discarded. As noted in [1], this is an approximation mechanism that may produce an incomplete target model, although in some scenarios it is acceptable to assume this limitation.

In our approach sliding windows are specified with the DSL (see lines 10–11 in the example). There are two types: windows based on time (e.g., 200 seconds) and on a number of elements of a given type (e.g., 1000 elements). A sliding window works in a "first-in, first-out fashion", so that the first element that arrived is the first element to be discarded when the window must be "moved". When a source element is discarded, any other data structure that refers to it must be discarded as well. In our case, they are the trace links, the continuations created with a Match that expects a trace link with such source element, and the index keeping the already streamed objects by key.

Please note that, when defining the windows, it is important to consider the expected amount of data for each type. In the example we decided never discard Class objects, as the number of classes in a system is limited.

Using secondary storage. If we want to guarantee that all bindings and proxies are resolved (provided the corresponding elements are eventually streamed), a solution would be to resort on a model repository, such as Morsa [14], to store all or part of them. The main problem is that accessing the repository may slowdown the transformation execution. Hence, this strategy may be practical depending on the pace of stream, and therefore it will be best suited for a distributed scenario in which load balancing is possible (see Section 2).

As an optimization we would like to use asynchronous I/O for accessing secondary storage. This approach fits naturally in our continuation-based scheduling algorithm, since the access to the repository can be scheduled in a different thread, storing the rule execution into a continuation, and so other elements in the stream can be processed. When the repository provides the result, the rule is seamlessly resumed.

6.2   Collection Operations

The implementation of collection operations such as select, collect, or allInstances need to be adapted to take into account that the source model is not completely available from the beginning. In our setting, this problem can be seen as a simplification of the incremental evaluation of OCL expressions, in which there are only addition events (elements are not deleted).

There are several approaches proposed in the literature [18,16,4], but we have adapted and implemented the *active collection operations* proposed in [3] into our transformation engine. For space reasons we just outline some of its elements. Fig. 5 shows the API of our implementation.

We have added two extensions to the original ImmutableList type of IDC: ActiveGenerator and ActiveOperation. The former is a collection in which elements are initially injected from the stream. The ActiveAllInstances is connected to a model queue that provides elements of the corresponding types as they arrive (e.g., MethodExecution.allInstances), whereas ActiveGet is used to retrieve elements from a multiple-valued feature (e.g., self.callee).

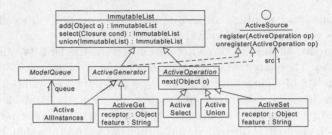

Fig. 5. Excerpt of the API of our active collection operations implementation

The second extension reifies collection operations as classes (ActiveOperation and operation subclasses such as ActiveSelect and ActiveCollect), so that an operation is kept active as an object that receives events through a source. A source is represented by the ActiveSource interface, which permits registering and deregistering an ActiveOperation. Given an expression such as the one in lines 39–44 in Fig. 2, a tree of active operations is constructed. When an element arrives, it is propagated from an active generator to the root.

Currently, we do not permit operations such as size or indexOf, as their semantics cannot be naturally aligned to a streaming setting. Finding out an apropppriate semantics for these operations is left for future work.

7   First Results and Evaluation

We have implemented a proof of concept streaming model transformation engine on top of the Eclectic transformation tool[1] [12], using the techniques presented in the previous sections. To evaluate our approach we carried out three initial experiments [2], which stress different elements of our approach (corresponding to three scenarios explained in Section 2).

Natural streaming. We used the running example to test the first versions of our implementation. Then, we built a simulator to generate execution traces indefinitely, to feed the transformation. The mechanisms proposed in the paper allowed us to keep the simulator running for some time, using different sizes of sliding windows and available memory (from 24 MB to 256 GB, generating between 10.000 and 100.000 execution traces).

Dealing with large models. We injected into the Morsa repository [14] the models provided in the Grabats 2009 contest [3]. They represent Java projects (conforming to the Eclipse JDT meta-model) ranging from 70,000 to 500,000 elements (only injecting the largest model requires a setting with 3 GB RAM). To test the

---

[1] Source code and examples are at http://sanchezcuadrado.es/projects/eclectic
[2] We have run the tests in an Intel i7 Quad Core, with 8 GB RAM, configuring the JVM with different heap sizes (up to 2GB).
[3] http://www.emn.fr/z-info/atlanmod/index.php/GraBaTs_2009_Case_Study

possibility of dealing with such large models, we implemented a transformation from JDT models to KDM. It transforms classes, methods, fields and resolve types, and therefore only parts of the source model needs to be in memory at a given time. We used the load-on-demand facility of Morsa to incrementally feed the transformation, which allowed us to transform even the largest model (requiring 2 GB RAM, taking 16 minutes).

Pipelining transformations. We implemented a simple pipeline with two processes. The first process was in charge of parsing individual Java files into an AST (using the JDK's parser). The AST representing each class was then transformed into the MoDisco Java meta-model. In this case we have considered compilation units, classes and methods, and the inheritance reference between classes. We compared the execution time of performing the transformation in batch mode (parsing all models at once and then transforming) against scheduling the transformation two threads: parsing and transforming. Our streaming approach premits that, as soon as the parsing thread generates the AST of a file, it is passed to the transformation thread. We have tested with projects between 2,000 and 15,000 Java files (roughly 30,000 and 300,000 objects), and our results showed an speedup between 10% and 15% for the threaded approach. Even more, if we manually release resources not needed for subsequent executions (compilation units and method declarations in this case), speedup increases upto 10%, and memory footprint decreases 25%. As future work we aim at automatically identifying in which case resources can be safely released.

All in all, this initial evaluation shows the feasability of the approach, but more work is still required. For instance, this experience taught us that we had a few memory leaks which become very relevant in this setting, and that a mechanism to discard parts of the target model or to incrementally store it in a model repository is needed if the target model grows too large. Another future line of work is to evaluate how Event Stream Processing engines, such as Esper[4], could be used as a backend for the transformation engine.

8   Related Work

Data stream processing has been investigated in the database community, proposing extensions for SQL and mechanisms for sliding windows, sampling and summarization [1]. Adapting query language designs and sliding windows implementation techniques is particularly interesting for our case [20,21].

Works dealing with the processing of XML are also focussed on providing query facilities [15] or in the case of XLST, simple transformations (in-place substitution). Notably, STX is a variant of XSLT intended for streaming transformations of XML documents, based on SAX events instead of DOM [8]. These approaches could be used to complement our work, in the pattern matching phase, which we have currently implemented just by nesting *forall iterators*.

---

[4] http://esper.codehaus.org/

Proposals such as the *semantic sensor web technologies* [26] requires processing streamed semantic data, typically in the form of RDF triples, which can be queried with SPARQL extensions [13]. As noted in Section 2 our approach could be applicable to this context to data format transformations and to integrate data from heterogenous sources.

In [10] the authors provide a formal foundation for infinite models, as well as a redefinition of some OCL operators to tackle infinite collections using coalgebra. They identify transformations of such infinite models as a challenge. Lazy model transformations [27] somehow deal with the converse scenario we tackle here: on-demand generation of the target model. This scenario is useful if only some part of the generated model is needed, which is produced on-demand. That is, target elements are only produced when they are accessed. Change-driven transformations [4], incorporate the notion of *change* (in the source model) as a first-class concept in transformation languages. While this approach can be used to implement, e.g., incremental transformations, our approach enables the uniform specification of transformations, as if they were designed for a batch scenario, but are applicable for streaming data.

Techniques for incremental transformations are closely related [16,18], but taking into account that in our case just additions need to be considered. Thus, we have used continuations to schedule the transformation execution [11,12] and *active collection operations* [3] to implement infinite collections.

9 Conclusions and Future Work

In this paper we have presented our approach to streaming model transformations. We have motivated the problem by presenting four applicability scenarios, and providing a complete example. From the example we have derived the set of challenges that has driven our proposal, which includes mechanisms for specifying model fragments, transformation scheduling and dealing with infinite models. Our first experiments show promising results, not only to deal with natural streams, but also to deal with large models and to take advantage of multi-core architectures. Additionally, we contribute a prototype implementation for the Eclectic transformation tool. To the best of our knowledge, this is the first model transformation engine with this capability.

As future work, we plan to perform further experiments, and to improve our implementation, for instance to allow the incremental store of the target model in a model repository and to take advantage of asynchronous I/O. Finally, we aim at using streaming transformations to implement distributed transformations.

Acknowledgements. This work was funded by the Spanish Ministry of Economy and Competitivity (project "Go Lite" TIN2011-24139) and the R&D programme of the Madrid Region (project "e-Madrid" S2009/TIC-1650).

References

1. Babcock, B., Babu, S., Datar, M., Motwani, R., Widom, J.: Models and issues in data stream systems. In: PODS, pp. 1–16. ACM (2002)
2. Barbieri, D.F., Braga, D., Ceri, S., Valle, E.D., Grossniklaus, M.: Querying rdf streams with c-sparql. SIGMOD Record 39(1), 20–26 (2010)
3. Beaudoux, O., Blouin, A., Barais, O., Jézéquel, J.-M.: Active operations on collections. In: Petriu, D.C., Rouquette, N., Haugen, Ø. (eds.) MODELS 2010, Part I. LNCS, vol. 6394, pp. 91–105. Springer, Heidelberg (2010)
4. Bergmann, G., Ráth, I., Varró, G., Varró, D.: Change-driven model transformations - change (in) the rule to rule the change. SoSyM 11(3), 431–461 (2012)
5. Briand, L., Labiche, Y., Leduc, J.: Toward the reverse engineering of uml sequence diagrams for distributed java software. IEEE TSE 32(9), 642–663 (2006)
6. Brunelière, H., Cabot, J., Jouault, F.: Combining Model-Driven Engineering and Cloud Computing. In: MDA4ServiceCloud 2010 Workshop at ECMFA 2010 (2010)
7. Cauê Clasen, M.T.: Marcos Didonet Del Fabro. Transforming very large models in the cloud: a research roadmap. In: Workshop on MDE on and for the Cloud (2012)
8. Cimprich, P.: Streaming transformations for xml (stx) version 1.0 working draft (2004), http://stx.sourceforge.net/documents/spec-stx-2004070.html
9. Clinger, W.D., Hartheimer, A., Ost, E.: Implementation strategies for first-class continuations. Higher-Order and Symbolic Computation 12(1), 7–45 (1999)
10. Combemale, B., Thirioux, X., Baudry, B.: Formally defining and iterating infinite models. In: France, R.B., Kazmeier, J., Breu, R., Atkinson, C. (eds.) MODELS 2012. LNCS, vol. 7590, pp. 119–133. Springer, Heidelberg (2012)
11. Cuadrado, J.S.: Compiling ATL with Continuations. In: Proc. of 3rd Int. Workshop on Model Transformation with ATL, pp. 10–19. CEUR-WS (2011)
12. Sánchez Cuadrado, J.: Towards a family of model transformation languages. In: Hu, Z., de Lara, J. (eds.) ICMT 2012. LNCS, vol. 7307, pp. 176–191. Springer, Heidelberg (2012)
13. Della Valle, E., Ceri, S., van Harmelen, F., Fensel, D.: It's a streaming world! reasoning upon rapidly changing information. IEEE Int. Sys. 24(6), 83–89 (2009)
14. Espinazo Pagán, J., Sánchez Cuadrado, J., García Molina, J.: Morsa: A scalable approach for persisting and accessing large models. In: Whittle, J., Clark, T., Kühne, T. (eds.) MODELS 2011. LNCS, vol. 6981, pp. 77–92. Springer, Heidelberg (2011)
15. Green, T.J., Gupta, A., Miklau, G., Onizuka, M., Suciu, D.: Processing XML streams with deterministic automata and stream indexes. ACM Trans. Database Syst. 29(4), 752–788 (2004)
16. Hearnden, D., Lawley, M., Raymond, K.: Incremental model transformation for the evolution of model-driven systems. In: Wang, J., Whittle, J., Harel, D., Reggio, G. (eds.) MoDELS 2006. LNCS, vol. 4199, pp. 321–335. Springer, Heidelberg (2006)
17. Jouault, F., Allilaire, F., Bézivin, J., Kurtev, I.: Atl: A model transformation tool. Science of Computer Programming 72(1), 31–39 (2008)
18. Jouault, F., Tisi, M.: Towards incremental execution of atl transformations. In: Tratt, L., Gogolla, M. (eds.) ICMT 2010. LNCS, vol. 6142, pp. 123–137. Springer, Heidelberg (2010)
19. Kolovos, D.S., Paige, R.F., Polack, F.: The grand challenge of scalability for model driven engineering. In: Chaudron, M.R.V. (ed.) MODELS 2008. LNCS, vol. 5421, pp. 48–53. Springer, Heidelberg (2009)

20. Krämer, J., Seeger, B.: Semantics and implementation of continuous sliding window queries over data streams. ACM Trans. Database Syst. 34(1) (2009)
21. Law, Y.-N., Wang, H., Zaniolo, C.: Relational languages and data models for continuous queries on sequences and data streams. ACM Trans. Database Syst. 36(2), 8 (2011)
22. KDM, v1.0, http://omg.org/spec/KDM/1.0
23. OMG. QVT, v1.1 (2011), http://www.omg.org/spec/QVT/1.1/
24. Le-Phuoc, D., Xavier Parreira, J., Hauswirth, M.: Linked stream data processing. In: Eiter, T., Krennwallner, T. (eds.) Reasoning Web 2012. LNCS, vol. 7487, pp. 245–289. Springer, Heidelberg (2012)
25. Sakaki, T., Okazaki, M., Matsuo, Y.: Earthquake shakes twitter users: real-time event detection by social sensors. In: WWW, pp. 851–860. ACM (2010)
26. Sheth, A.P., Henson, C.A., Sahoo, S.S.: Semantic sensor web. IEEE Internet Computing 12(4), 78–83 (2008)
27. Tisi, M., Martínez, S., Jouault, F., Cabot, J.: Lazy execution of model-to-model transformations. In: Whittle, J., Clark, T., Kühne, T. (eds.) MODELS 2011. LNCS, vol. 6981, pp. 32–46. Springer, Heidelberg (2011)

Genetic-Programming Approach to Learn Model Transformation Rules from Examples

Martin Faunes[1], Houari Sahraoui[1], and Mounir Boukadoum[2]

[1] DIRO, Université de Montréal, Canada
[2] Université du Québec à Montréal, Canada

Abstract. We propose a genetic programming-based approach to automatically learn model transformation rules from prior transformation pairs of source-target models used as examples. Unlike current approaches, ours does not need fine-grained transformation traces to produce many-to-many rules. This makes it applicable to a wider spectrum of transformation problems. Since the learned rules are produced directly in an actual transformation language, they can be easily tested, improved and reused. The proposed approach was successfully evaluated on well-known transformation problems that highlight three modeling aspects: structure, time constraints, and nesting.

1 Introduction

The adoption of new technologies generally follows a recurrent cycle described by Moore in [16]. In this cycle, user categories adopt a technology at different moments depending on their profiles and the technology's maturity. Moore identified the move from the *early adopters* category to the *early majority* category as the gap that is the most difficult to cross and in which many technologies spend a long time or just fail. Model Driven Engineering (MDE), as a new technology that changes considerably the way we develop software, does not escape this observation. MDE received much attention in recent years due to its promise to reduce the complexity of the development and maintenance of software applications. However, and notwithstanding the success stories reported in the past decade, MDE is still at the early-adopters stage [15]. As mentioned by Selic[1], in addition to the economic and cultural factors, the technical factors, particularly the difficulty of automation, represent major obstacles for MDE's adoption.

Automation is a keystone and a founding principle of the MDE paradigm. According to Schmidt, MDE technologies combine domain-specific modeling languages with transformation engines and generators to produce various software artifacts [21]. By automating model-to-model and model-to-code transformations, MDE fills the conceptual gap between source code and models, and ensures that models are up to date with regards to the code and other models. In recent years, considerable advances have been made in modeling environments

---

[1] Bran Selic, "The Embarrassing Truth About Software and Automation and What Should be Done About It", Keynote talk, ASE 2007.

K. Duddy and G. Kappel (Eds.): ICMT 2013, LNCS 7909, pp. 17–32, 2013.
© Springer-Verlag Berlin Heidelberg 2013

and tools. However, in practice, automated model transformation and code generation has been restricted to niche areas such as database mapping and data-intensive-application generation [15]. To address this limitation, a large effort has been made to define languages for expressing transformation rules (e.g., ATL [9]) to make the writing of transformation programs easier.

Having a good transformation language is only one part of the solution; the most important part is to define/gather knowledge about how to transform any model conforming to a particular metamodel into a model conforming to another metamodel. For many problems, this knowledge is incomplete or not available. The difficulty of writing transformation rules is the main motivation behind the research on learning transformation rules from examples. Although the idea goes back to the early nineties, the first concrete work on Model Transformation by Example (MTBE) was proposed by Varro in 2006 [24]. MTBE's objective was to derive transformation programs by generalizing concrete transformations found in a set of prototypical examples of source and target models. Since then, many approaches have been proposed to derive the transformation rules (e.g., [22,1,6,4,12,20]) or to transform a model by analogy with transformed examples [10].

Still, the existing MTBE approaches only solve the problem of rule derivation partially. Most of them require detailed mappings (transformation traces) between the source and target model examples [1], which are difficult to provide in some situations; others cannot derive rules that test many constructs in the source model and/or produce many construct in the target model, many-to-many rules [22], a requirement in complex transformation problems. A third limitation is the inability of some approaches to automatically produce complex rule conditions to define precise patterns to search for in the source model [20]. Finally, some approaches produce abstract, non-executable rules that have to be completed and mapped manually to an executable language [4].

In a previous work [5], we proposed a preliminary approach for the derivation of complex and executable rules from examples without the need of transformation traces. The approach was inspired from genetic programming (GP) and exploits GP's ability to evolve programs in order to improve their capacity to approximate a behavior defined by a set of valid pairs of inputs/outputs. The approach was quantitatively evaluated on the transformation of class diagrams to relational schemas. Although 75% of the model constructs were correctly transformed, many key transformation rules were not derived or only derived partially. In this paper, we propose an improved version of the algorithm with new ways of solution initialization, new program derivation from existing ones, and program evaluation. This new version is evaluated on two transformation problems that cover three important software modeling characteristics: structure, time constraints, and nesting. In the first problem, the transformation of class diagrams to relational schemas, we test the ability of our approach to handle the transformation of structural models. Time-constrained-model transformation is considered in the second case study through the problem of sequence diagrams to state charts. In this problem, the derived transformation should preserve the time constraints between the constructs. Our second case study also handles the complex problem of nested-sequence-diagrams to state-charts transformation. In this case, the transformation control is non trivial as the rules should transform the nested elements before those that contain them. The obtained quantitative and qualitative results show that our approach allows the derivation the correct transformation rules for both problems.

2 Learning Rules from Examples

Our goal is to define a transformation-rule derivation process that may apply to a wide range of transformation problems. To this end, our approach should work even if fine-grained transformation traces are not available. Additionally, constraints on the shape or size of the rules should be as limited as possible. This includes the numbers of source and target-construct types and the nature of rule conditions. Finally, the produced rule sets must be executable without a manual refinement step.

2.1 Rule Derivation as an Evolutionary Process

Transformation rules are programs that analyze certain aspects of source models given as input and synthesize the corresponding target models as output [21]. Learning complex and dynamic structures such as programs is not an easy task [2]. Of the possible tools that can be used for automatic programs generation, Genetic Programming (GP) [13] is a strong contender for supremacy as it was originally created for the purpose. This motivated our investigation of GP to automatically derive rule sets, *i.e.*, declarative programs, using examples of models transformations, *i.e.*, complex inputs/outputs. GP draws inspiration from Darwinian evolution and aims to automatically derive a program to solve a given problem, starting from some indications about how the problem should be solved. These usually take the form of input and output examples, and the derivation process is done by iteratively improving an initial population of randomly-created programs, *i.e.*, by keeping the fittest programs for reproduction at each step, the reproduction being made by means of *genetic operators* similar to those observed in nature. The typical GP cycle is sketched in Figure 1.

Before, starting the evolution process, the user must have a set of example pairs describing the expected program behavior in the form of <input, output>. The user must also define a way to encode and create the initial population of random programs. Finally, a mechanism is needed to run the programs on the provided inputs and compare the execution results with the expected outputs. This is typically done by defining a fitness function that evaluates the closeness between the produced and expected outputs.

To apply GP to the MTBE problem, we have to consider two issues. First, transformation rules are not imperative programs and cannot be encoded as trees as usually done in GP [13]; second, the outputs of transformations are models (usually graphs) that are not easy to compare for evaluating the correctness of

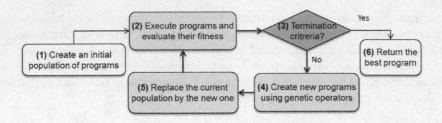

Fig. 1. A typical GP cycle

a program. In the following subsections, we detail our adaptation of the GP algorithm to the specific problem of MTBE. Note that, for our investigation, we decided to use a simple metamodeling language to describe the metamodels and a generic rule language/engine JESS [8] for the writing and execution of transformation rules. This decision was made to separate, in a first phase of this research project, the intrinsic complexity of MTBE from the accidental complexity of conformance to standards and interoperability concerns. The mapping between JESS and a transformation language such as ATL is pretty easy to perform since both languages offer similar features such as declarative and imperative structures as well as control mechanisms.

2.2 Encoding Rule Sets

Typical transformation problems require a set of transformation rules to cover all the patterns in the source models. A program p is accordingly encoded as a set of transformation rules, $p = \{r_1, r_2, ..., r_n\}$. Each transformation rule r_i is in turn encoded as a pair $r_i = (SP, TP)$, where SP is the pattern to search for in the source model and TP is the pattern to instantiate when producing the target model.

Source Pattern. A source pattern SP is a pair $SP = (SGC, G)$, in which SGC is a set of generic source constructs and G is a guard. A generic source construct is the specification of an instance of a construct type that has to be matched with concrete constructs in the source model. For example, in the rule of Listing 1.1, $SGC = \{C, A, S\}$, where C, A and S represent respectively a class, an attribute, and an association. SGC could include more than one generic construct from the same construct type, *e.g.*, two classes and an association. Each generic construct has the properties of its construct type in the source metamodel. When matched with a concrete construct from the source model, these properties take the values of the latter. For instance, an attribute A has its name (descriptive property) and the name of the class it belongs to (join property) as properties. During execution, the value of a property can be accessed as shown in Listing 1.1, *e.g.*, $A.name$ and $A.class$.

The guard G contains two types of conditions: join conditions and state conditions. Join properties are used to define the set of join conditions, which allow to specify a source pattern as a model fragment, *i.e.*, a set of interrelated constructs according to the metamodel. For example, in the rule of Listing 1.1, the join condition $A.class = C.name$ states that A should be an attribute of class C whereas $S.classFrom = C.name$ restricts the pattern to only classes that are at the origin of associations.

Listing 1.1. Rule encoding example

```
Source pattern:
//   Generic source element
     Class C, Attribute A, Association S
//   Guard: Join condition
     (and (A.class = C.name) (S.classFrom = C.name))
//   Guard: State condition
     (and (S.maxCardFrom < 1) (S.maxCardTo   > 1))
Target pattern:
//   Generic target element
     Table T, Column O
//   Bindings
     T.name  := C.name
     O.name  := A.name
//   Join-statement
     O.table = T.name
```

State conditions involve the properties of the generic source constructs (both join and descriptive ones). They are encoded as a binary tree containing elements from terminal (T) and primitive (I) sets. T is the union of the properties of the constructs in SGC and a set of constants C. For the rule of Listing 1.1, the properties are $C.name$, $A.name$, $A.class$, $S.classFrom$, $S.classTo$, $S.MaxCardFr$, $S.MaxCardTo$, etc. As the properties are numbers and strings, numeric and string constants such as $\{0, 1, Empty, ...\}$ are added to the terminals. As conditions are manipulated, the Boolean constants $true$ and $false$ are also added. The set of primitives I is composed minimally of logical operators and comparators $(I = \{and, or, not, =, >, <, ...\})$. Other operators, such as arithmetic or string operators, could be added to test values derived from the basic properties. Since this work uses the concrete rule language JESS [8], the conceptual distinction between join and state conditions is not reflected in the actual code. Both types of conditions form the condition tree with terminals as leaf nodes and primitives as the other nodes. A rule without any condition will be represented by a tree with the single node "true". A rule is fired for any combination of instances for which the condition tree is true.

Target Pattern. The target pattern TP is a triple $TP = (TGC, B, TJ)$, where TGC, B and TJ represent respectively a set of generic target constructs, a set of binding statements, and a set of join statements. A generic target construct specifies a concrete construct to create in the target model when the rule is fired. In the example of Listing 1.1, two constructs are created: a table T and a column O. The set of bindings B determines how to set the property values of the created constructs with the property values of the constructs that match the source pattern. In Listing 1.1, the created table and column will respectively have the same names as the selected class and attribute. Finally, the join statements TJ allow to connect the created constructs to form a fragment in the target model.

In the example provided, column O is assigned to table T. The join statements must conform to the target metamodel.

2.3   Creating Rule Sets

As stated in Section 2.1, deriving transformation rules using genetic programming requires the creation of an initial population of random rule sets. Each rule set has to be syntactically correct with respect to the rule language (JESS in this work). Moreover, a rule set should be consistent with the source and target metamodels. In this respect, rules should describe valid source and target patterns. For the initial population, a number of rule sets nrs is created (nrs is a parameter of the approach). The number of rules to create for each rule set is selected randomly from a given interval. For each rule, we use a random combination of elementary model fragments (building blocks) to create the source and target patterns. The random combination of building blocks is intended to reduce the size of the search space by considering connected model fragments rather than arbitrary subsets of constructs. For each rule, two combinations are performed respectively over the graphs of the source and target metamodels to create the source and target patterns of the rule, SP and TP.

A building block is a minimal model fragment which is self-contained, *i.e.*, its existence does not depend upon the existence of other constructs. For example, in a UML class diagram, a single class could form a building block. However, an attribute should be associated to its class to form a block. Similarly, an inheritance relationship forms with two classes (superclass and subclass) a building block. The determination of the building block for a given metamodel depends only on this latter and not on the transformation of its models.

To create random patterns (source or target), a maximal number of generic constructs nc is first determined randomly. Then, a first building block is randomly selected and included within the pattern. If nc is not reached yet, another building block is selected among those that could be connected to the blocks in the current fragment. Two blocks could be connected if they share at least one generic construct. The connection is made by considering both constructs to connect as the same generic construct. The procedure is repeated until nc is reached. To illustrate the pattern creation procedure, consider the following example. Imagine that the maximum number of constructs is set to four. A first random selection could add to the pattern the block ($ClassC_1, AttributA_1, A_1.class = C_1.name$) containing two connected generic constructs C_1 and A_1. As the size of the pattern is less than four, another random selection could add an inheritance block with constructs $InheritanceI_1$, $ClassC_3$, and $ClassC_4$, and links $I_1.class = C_3.name$ and $I_1.super = C_4.name$. One of the two possibilities of connections ((C_1, C_3) or (C_1, C_4)) is selected, let us say (C_1, C_4). C_4 is then replaced by C_1 in the pattern including the links.

The last step toward the pattern creation is the random generation of the state conditions (for a source pattern) or the binding statements (for a target pattern). For a source pattern, a tree is created by randomly mixing elements from the terminal set T, *i.e.*, properties of the selected constructs and constants consistent with their types, and elements from the primitive set P of operators. The creation of the tree is done using a variation of the "grow" method defined in [13]. In the case of a target pattern, the binding statements are generated by randomly assigning elements in the terminal set T of the source pattern to the properties of the generic constructs of the target pattern that were not set by the join statements (links). The random property-value assignments are done according to the property types.

2.4   Deriving New Rule Sets

In GP, a population of programs is evolved and improved by applying genetic operators (mutation and crossover). These operators are specific to the problem to solve. As with the initial-population creation, the genetic operators should guarantee that the derived programs are syntactically and semantically valid. Before applying the genetic operators to produce new programs, programs from the current generation are selected for reproduction depending on their fitness values. For the derivation of transformation rule sets, *roulette-wheel* selection is used. This technique assigns to each rule set a probability of being selected that is proportional to its fitness. This selection strategy favors the fittest rule sets while still giving a chance of being selected to the others. Note that some program could be included directly into the new population, *i.e.*, elitist strategy.

Crossover. The crossover operation consists of producing new rule sets by combining the existing genetic material. It is applied with a given probability to each pair of selected rule sets. After selecting two-parent rule sets for reproduction, two new rule sets are created by exchanging parts of the parents, *i.e.*, subsets of rules. For instance, consider the two rule sets $p_1 = \{r_{11}, r_{12}, r_{13}, r_{14}\}$ having four rules and $p_2 = \{r_{21}, r_{22}, r_{23}, r_{24}, r_{25}\}$ with five rules. If two cut-points are randomly set to 2 for p_1 and 3 for p_2, the offspring obtained are rule sets $o_1 = \{r_{11}, r_{12}, r_{24}, r_{25}\}$ and $o_2 = \{r_{21}, r_{22}, r_{23}, r_{13}, r_{14}\}$. Because each rule is syntactically and semantically correct before the crossover, this correctness is not altered for the offspring.

Mutation. After the crossover, the obtained offspring could be mutated with a given probability. Mutation allows the introduction of new genetic material while the population evolves. This is done by randomly altering existing rules or adding newly-generated ones. Mutation could occur at the rule set level or at the single rule level. Each time, a rule set is randomly selected for mutation, a mutation strategy is also randomly selected. Two mutation strategies are defined at the rule-set level: (1) *adding a randomly-created rule* to the rule set and (2) *deleting a randomly-selected rule*. To avoid empty rule sets, deletion could not be performed if the rule set has only one rule.

At the rule level, many strategies are possible. For a randomly-selected rule, one could *replace the target pattern* by a new one, randomly created. One could also *rebind one or more target pattern properties* by picking a random number of properties in the target pattern and randomly bind them to properties in the source pattern and constants. These modifications, when done as in Section 2.2, preserve the rule's validity, both syntactically and semantically. For the source pattern, it is also possible to introduce random modifications as for the target pattern. However, the target pattern has to be modified accordingly to avoid semantical and syntactical errors.

2.5 Evaluating Rule Sets

For the initial population and during the evolution, each generated rule set is evaluated to assess its ability to perform correct transformations. This evaluation is performed in two steps: (1) rule set execution on the examples and (2) comparison of produced vs. expected target models. Rule sets are translated into the JESS, and executed on the examples using the JESS rule engine. Metamodels are represented as sets of fact templates and models as fact sets. The rule translation is straightforward with the particularities that generic-target-construct declaration, join statements and bindings are merged into fact-assertion clauses. Listing 1.2 shows the JESS translation of the rule in Listing 1.1.

Listing 1.2. An example of a JESS Rule

```
(defrule RuleListing1
 (class (name ?C1))
 (attribute (name ?A1)(class ?A2))
 (association (maxCardFrom ?S1) (maxCardTo ?S2)(classFrom ?S3))
 (test (and (and (eq ?A2 ?C1)(eq ?S3 ?C1))
             (and (< ?S1 1)(> ?S2 1))))
=>
 (assert (table(name ?C1)))
 (assert (column(name ?A1)(table ?C1))))
```

Our fitness function measures the similarity between the target models produced by a rule set and the expected ones as given in the example model pairs. Consider E the set of examples e_i composed each of a pair of a source and a target model (ms_i, mt_i). The fitness $F(E, p)$ of a rule set p is defined as the average of the transformation correctness $f(mt_i, p(ms_i))$ of all examples e_i. The transformation correctness $f(mt_i, p(ms_i))$ measures to which extent the target model $p(ms_i)$, obtained by executing p on the source model ms_i, is similar to the expected target model mt_i of e_i.

Comparing two models, *i.e.*, two graphs with typed nodes, is a difficult problem (graph isomorphism). Considering that in the proposed GP-based rule derivation, the fitness function is evaluated for each rule set, on each example, and at each iteration, this cannot afford exhaustive graph comparisons. Instead, a quick an efficient graph kernel f is used. f, which is a model similarity measure, calculates the weighted average of the transformation correctness per construct type $t \in T_{mt_i}$ in the expected model mt_i. This is done to give the same importance to all construct types regardless of their frequencies. Formally:

$$f(mt_i, p(ms_i)) = \sum_{t \in T_{mt_i}} \frac{f_t(mt_i, p(ms_i))}{|T_{mt_i}|} \tag{1}$$

f_t is defined as the weighted sum of percentages of the constructs of type t that are respectively fully (fm_t), partially (pm_t), or non(nm_t) matched:

$$ft(mt_i, p(ms_i)) = \alpha fm_t + \beta pm_t + \gamma nm_t, \ \alpha + \beta + \gamma = 1 \qquad (2)$$

For each construct of type t in the expected model, we first determine if it is fully matched by a construct in the produced model, *i.e.*, it exists in the produced model a construct of the same type that have the same property values. For the constructs in the expected model that are not matched yet, we determine, in a second step, if they can be partially matched. A construct is partially matched if it exists in the produced model a construct of the same type that was not matched in the first step. Finally, the last step is to classify all the remaining constructs as not matched.

Coefficients α, β, and γ have each a different impact on the derivation process during the evolution. α, which should be set to a high value (typically 0.6), is used to favor rules that correctly produce the expected constructs. As mentioned earlier, β, with an average value (≈ 0.3), allows to give more chances to rules producing the right types of the expected constructs and helps converging towards the optimal solution. Finally, γ has to be set to a small value (≈ 0.1). The idea of giving a small weight to the not-matched constructs seems counterintuitive. However, our experience shows that this promotes diversity, particularly during the early generations, and this helps avoid local solution optima.

The calculation of the transformation correctness assesses whether the constructs of the expected model are present in the produced model. As a consequence, a good solution could include the correct rules that generate the right constructs, but it could also contain redundant rules or rules that generate unnecessary constructs. To handle this situation, we consider the size of the rule set when selecting the best solution. Consequently, even if an optimal solution is found in terms of correctness, the evolution process continues to search for equally-optimal solutions, but with fewer rules.

3   Evaluation

We evaluate our approach from two perspectives. First, a quantitative evaluation allows to answer the question: To which extent our approach generates rules that correctly transform the set of provided examples? In a second phase, a qualitative evaluation will help answering the question: If the examples are correctly transformed, are the produced rules those that are expected? In this context, we constructed a semi-real environment where the transformation solutions are known and where the examples models are simulated by creating prototypical source models and by deriving the corresponding target models using the known transformations. We were aware of the limitations of this setting, but it helps investigate more problems and it clearly defines the reference rule sets that the approach should derive. Additionally, it reasonably simulates situations where the examples have been manually created over a long period of time by experts.

The preliminary version of our approach was evaluated on the transformation of class diagrams to relational schemas [5]. This transformation, call it case A, illustrates well the problem of transforming structural models. Its complexity resides, among others, in the multiple possibilities of transforming the same construct according to the values of its properties. In the evaluation of the improved version presented in this paper, we also studied the transformation of UML2 sequence diagrams to state machines (Case $B1$ for basic sequence diagrams and Case $B2$ for advanced ones). Such a transformation is difficult because, in addition to considering the transformation of single model fragments and ensuring the structural coherence, it introduces two important modelling characteristics: time constraints and nesting. In this transformation, the coherence in terms of time constraints and weak sequencing should be guaranteed. On the other hand, nesting is tested because this transformation have to deal with combined fragments (alternatives, loops, and sequences) that can be nested at different levels, and thus, this transformation has to manage the recursive compositions in addition to handling the structural and time coherence. For case A, we used the transformation described in [3], whereas for cases $B1$ and $B2$, we rewrote, as rules, the graph-based transformations given in [7]. As GP-based algorithms are probabilistic in nature, five runs were performed in parallel for each case. For each run, we set the number of iterations to 3000, the population size to 200 and elitism to 20 programs. Crossover probability was set to 0.9 and mutation probability to 0.9. Unlike classical genetic algorithms, having a high mutation probability is not unusual for GP algorithms (e.g. [18]). The weighs (α, β, γ) of the fitness function were set to $(0.6, 0.3, 0.1)$, as explained in Section 2.5.

3.1   Quantitative Results

For each case, an optimal solution was found in at least one of the five runs. This is an indication that the search process has a good probability of convergence. The charts with sampled data that are shown in figures 2 and 3 illustrate the evolution of a successful run for cases A and $B2$[2]. Three curves are displayed in each plot: the fitness function value (F) and the proportion of full matches (FM) (vertical axis on the left), and the rule set size (PS) (vertical axis on the right). The curves correspond to the fittest rule set at each generation (iteration) identified in the horizontal axis.

The solution evolutions for both cases follow the same pattern and differ only in the number of generations needed to converge toward a solution and to reach a minimal rule-set size. As expected, case A, with structural constraints only, is the one with the fastest convergence. At the initial generation, which is considered as a random transformation generation, half of the constructs are correctly transformed $(FM = 0.5)$. These are simple one-to-one transformations (class-to-table or attribute-to-column) that have high chances of being generated randomly. The optimal solution in terms of FM is found at the 59th generation

---

[2] The complete data can be downloaded at
http://geodes.iro.umontreal.ca/en/projects/MOTOE/ICMT13

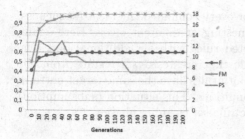

Fig. 2. Search evolution for case A

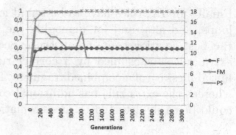

Fig. 3. Search evolution for case $B2$

with 10 rules. Once a solution with $FM = 1$ is found, the search process continues so that the current solution is replaced if another one with fewer rules is found. This happened three times for case A, with the last occurrence at the 129th generation where the number of rules dropped to 7. No further improvement was observed during the rest of the evolution in terms of number of rules. Compared to the results obtained on this case with our previous work [5], a significant improvement was observed (100% *vs.* 75% for FM).

Case $B2$, for which structural, time and nesting constraints are involved, took many more generations (991) to converge to 100% of full match, with minimal rules achieved at generation 2280. The complexity of the transformation and the increase in the size of the search space also reduced the proportion of correct transformations obtained randomly in the initial population ($FM = 0.4$ for the initial generation compared to $FM = 0.5$ in case A). Case $B1$ has similar results as $B2$, but with a faster convergence curve. From the computational perspective, the parallel five runs took collectively between one hour for case A and three hours for case $B2$ on a standard workstation (CPU @ 3.40GHz with 16 Go of RAM). Although this time could be reduced by optimizing the code, it is not considered excessive knowing that the process of learning new transformations is not intended to be executed frequently.

3.2 Qualitative Results

Obtaining 100% correct transformations of examples does not necessarily mean that we have derived the expected rules. In theory, for a limited sample of test cases, the same output values could be produced by different programs. Thus, to assess our results qualitatively, we need to compare the produced rules with those used to generate the examples (expected ones).

For cases A, we were searching for rules to transform classes, associations with various cardinalities and inheritance relationships. The expected rule set was found with a slight difference in one rule. Indeed, as all the classes in our examples contain at least one attribute, the rule that creates a table from a class has an unnecessary condition on the presence of an attribute. This kind of situations cannot be detected automatically because there is no counterexample. In the case of $B1$, the expected rules to create a state machine for every object in the sequence diagram, considering messages as events, were perfectly recovered.

Finally for $B2$, rules have to be found for every combined fragment (sequences, loops, and alts) and for managing the nesting at different levels. Here again, the best solution contains all the expected rules with an additional one. The extra rule is subsumed by a correct rule that creates a *start* state from the initial message of a combined fragment. Both rules have the same target pattern, whereas the extra rule has additional conditions. This situation (subsumption) could be easily detected by an automatic rule-set cleaning phase.

3.3 Discussion

During the development and evaluation of our approach, we faced several challenges to address or circumvent. This section discusses the most important ones.

Rule Execution Control. In the existing MTBE approaches, including ours, rules are defined to search for model fragments in the source model following a source pattern, and instantiate corresponding model fragments in the target model according to a target pattern. The target model fragments are usually not independent and have to be properly connected to form a coherent target model. Connecting target model fragments is difficult because, in most transformation languages, rules cannot check if a construct is present in the target model to connect to the produced fragment. In most MTBE approaches, the connection is achieved implicitly by using the same naming space both for source and target models. In our work, we circumvent partially the connection problem by recreating the target constructs. This technique was sufficient to handle the studied transformation cases, but it may be of limited use for other complex transformation problems. A good solution to handle the connection problem may be an explicit approach that uses global variables and meta-rules (execution control) as explained in [17]. In such an approach, the derivation process would learn the control separately or along with the transformation rules. We plan to explore this idea in a future work.

Complex Value Derivation. In our experimental setting, rule conditions and binding statements consider property values as data elements that cannot be combined to create new data elements. For example, for a construct C_1 in the source model with two numeric properties p_1 and p_2 and a string property p_3, a condition like $C_1.p_1 + C_1.p_2 \leq 2$ could not be created. Similarly, for a construct C_2 to create in the target model with a string property p_4, we cannot derive the binding statement $C_2.p4 = "Der - " + C_1.p3$. In our approach, such conditions and binding statements could be recovered by adding value-derivation operators such as arithmetic and string operators in the primitive set I (see Section 2.2). However, this can be done only at the cost of increasing the search-space size, with an impact on convergence. We plan to consider these new operators in the future after a code optimization phase to handle the extra computational cost.

Transformation Examples. In the evaluation of our initial approach [5], we used examples collected from the literature, whereas in the evaluation of the improved version, we used prototypical examples. Using prototypical examples helped to find the correct solution faster, because a reduced number of examples was necessary to cover the modeling space. However, these could be difficult to define in real situations. The choice of using prototypical or existing examples depend on the context: availability of expertise *vs.* availability of examples.

Model Comparison. The search for a solution is guided by the transformation correctness (fitness function). As mentioned in Section 2.5, an exhaustive comparison between the produced and expected models is costly. A trade-off is necessary between the comparison precision and the computational constraints. From our experience, sophisticated comparisons such as the one described in [5] do not impact the search much, when contrasted against the simple comparison described in this paper. We plan to conduct a rigorous cost benefit study to compare different alternatives of model-comparison functions.

4   Related Work

Learning transformations from examples takes inspiration from other domains such as programming by example [19]. Existing work could be grouped into two categories model transformation by example and model transformation by demonstration. In the first categories, the majority of approaches takes as input a set of pairs of source and target models. Models in each pair are generally manually aligned through fine-grained mapping between constructs of the two models [22]. Rule derivation is performed using *Ad hoc* algorithms [6,22], machine learning such as inductive logic programming in [1], or association rule mining with formal concept analysis [4]. In our approach, we use a different category of derivation algorithm, *i.e.*, genetic programming. In this algorithm, candidate transformation programs are evolved with the objective of better matching the provided transformation examples. The derivation does not require the user alignment/mapping of models that could be difficult to formalize in many cases. Indeed, once a candidate program is derived, it is executed on the example source models and its output is compared to the example target models. One positive side effect of our approach is that the obtained rules are executed and tested during the derivation process, which helps assessing each rule individually and the rule set globally. In some of the above-mentioned approached, the rules are not executable or are mapped in a subsequent step to an executable language. For example, the work in [4] is extended by mapping the derived association rules into executable ones in JESS [20]. In the same category of contributions, the work by Kessentini et al. [11] brings a different perspective to the MTBE problem. Rather than deriving a reusable transformation program, it defines a technique that automatically transforms a source model by analogy with existing transformation examples. Although this could be useful for some situations, the inability to derive transformation rules/knowledge could be seen as a limitation.

The second category of contributions in transformation rule learning is the model transformation by demonstration (MTBD). The goal here is to derive transformation patterns starting from step by step recorded actions on past transformations. In [23], Sun et al. propose an approach to generalize model editing actions (e.g., add, delete, update) that a user performs to refactor a model. The user editing actions are recorded and serve as patterns that can be later applied on a similar model by performing a pattern-matching process. This approach is intended to perform endogenous transformations (refactoring) and its generalization to exogenous transformation is not trivial. in [14], Langer et al. proposes an MTBD approach, very similar to the previous one, with the improvement of handling exogenous transformations. MTBD solves many problems of MTBE, as complex transformation could be abstracted. However, transformation patterns are derived individually and there is no guarantee that patterns could be applied together to derive consistent target models. In our case, the fact that rule sets are evaluated by executing them on the example source models, helps assessing the consistency of the produced models.

In addition to the differences highlighted in the previous paragraphs, our approach allows generating many-to-many rules that search for non trivial patterns in the source models and instantiate non trivial patterns in the target models. In contrast with the state-of-the-art approaches, we do not try to derive patterns by explicitly generalizing situations found among the examples. We instead use an evolutionary approach that evolves transformation programs, guided by their ability to correctly transform the example at hand. Finally, it is difficult to compare quantitatively and qualitatively with the other approaches. The validations of most of these are not or only partially reported.

5   Conclusion

Prior work has demonstrated that model transformation rules could be derived from examples. However, these contributions require fine-grained examples of model mapping or need a manual refinement phase to produce operational rules. In this paper, we propose a novel approach based on genetic programming to learn operational rules from pairs of unrelated models, given as examples. This approach was evaluated on structural and time-constrained model transformations. We found that in virtually all the cases, the produced rule sets are operational and correct. Our approach is a new stone in the resolution of the MTBE problem, and our evaluation provides a compelling evidence that MTBE could be an efficient solution to many transformation problems. However, some limitations are worth noting. Although the approach worked well for the addressed problem, the evaluation showed that convergence is difficult to reach for complex transformations. Future work should therefore include the explicit reasoning on rule execution control to simplify the transformation rules. It should also better consider transformations with complex conditions and bindings. In particular, we consider dealing with source and target models that do not share the same naming space using natural-language processing techniques.

References

1. Balogh, Z., Varrò, D.: Model transformation by example using inductive logic programming. Soft. and Syst. Modeling 8 (2009)
2. Banzhaf, W.: Genetic Programming: An Introduction on the Automatic Evolution of Computer Programs and Its Applications. Morgan Kaufmann Publishers (1998)
3. Czarnecki, K., Helsen, S.: Feature-based survey of model transformation approaches. IBM Systems Journal 45(3) (2006)
4. Dolques, X., Huchard, M., Nebut, C., Reitz, P.: Learning transformation rules from transformation examples: An approach based on relational concept analysis. In: Int. Enterprise Distributed Object Computing Workshops (2010)
5. Faunes, M., Sahraoui, H., Boukadoum, M.: Generating model transformation rules from examples using an evolutionary algorithm. In: Aut. Soft. Engineering (ASE) (2012)
6. García-Magariño, I., Gómez-Sanz, J.J., Fuentes-Fernández, R.: Model transformation by-example: An algorithm for generating many-to-many transformation rules in several model transformation languages. In: Paige, R.F. (ed.) ICMT 2009. LNCS, vol. 5563, pp. 52–66. Springer, Heidelberg (2009)
7. Grønmo, R., Møller-Pedersen, B.: From UML 2 sequence diagrams to state machines by graph transformation. Journal of Object Technology 10 (2011)
8. Hill, E.F.: Jess in Action: Java Rule-Based Systems (2003)
9. Jouault, F., Kurtev, I.: Transforming models with ATL. In: Bruel, J.-M. (ed.) MoDELS 2005. LNCS, vol. 3844, pp. 128–138. Springer, Heidelberg (2006)
10. Kessentini, M., Sahraoui, H.A., Boukadoum, M.: Model transformation as an optimization problem. In: Czarnecki, K., Ober, I., Bruel, J.-M., Uhl, A., Völter, M. (eds.) MODELS 2008. LNCS, vol. 5301, pp. 159–173. Springer, Heidelberg (2008)
11. Kessentini, M., Sahraoui, H.A., Boukadoum, M., Omar, O.B.: Search-based model transformation by example. Soft. and Syst. Modeling 11(2) (2012)
12. Kessentini, M., Wimmer, M., Sahraoui, H., Boukadoum, M.: Generating transformation rules from examples for behavioral models. In: Proc. of the 2nd Int. WS on Behaviour Modelling: Foundation and Applications (2010)
13. Koza, J., Poli, R.: Genetic programming. In: Search Methodologies (2005)
14. Langer, P., Wimmer, M., Kappel, G.: Model-to-model transformations by demonstration. In: Tratt, L., Gogolla, M. (eds.) ICMT 2010. LNCS, vol. 6142, pp. 153–167. Springer, Heidelberg (2010)
15. Mohagheghi, P., Gilani, W., Stefanescu, A., Fernandez, M.: An empirical study of the state of the practice and acceptance of model-driven engineering in four industrial cases. In: Empirical Software Engineering
16. Moore, G.: Crossing the Chasm: Marketing and Selling Disruptive Products to Mainstream Customers. HarperCollins (2002)
17. Pachet, F., Perrot, J.: Rule firing with metarules. In: SEKE (1994)
18. Ratcliff, S., White, D.R., Clark, J.A.: Searching for invariants using genetic programming and mutation testing. In: GECCO (2011)
19. Repenning, A., Perrone, C.: Programming by example: programming by analogous examples. Commun. ACM 43(3) (2000)
20. Saada, H., Dolques, X., Huchard, M., Nebut, C., Sahraoui, H.: Generation of operational transformation rules from examples of model transformations. In: France, R.B., Kazmeier, J., Breu, R., Atkinson, C. (eds.) MODELS 2012. LNCS, vol. 7590, pp. 546–561. Springer, Heidelberg (2012)

21. Schmidt, D.C.: Model-driven engineering. IEEE Computer 39(2) (2006)
22. Strommer, M., Wimmer, M.: A framework for model transformation by-example: Concepts and tool support. In: Paige, R.F., Meyer, B. (eds.) TOOLS EUROPE 2008. LNBIP, vol. 11, pp. 372–391. Springer, Heidelberg (2008)
23. Sun, Y., White, J., Gray, J.: Model transformation by demonstration. In: Schürr, A., Selic, B. (eds.) MODELS 2009. LNCS, vol. 5795, pp. 712–726. Springer, Heidelberg (2009)
24. Varró, D.: Model transformation by example. In: Wang, J., Whittle, J., Harel, D., Reggio, G. (eds.) MoDELS 2006. LNCS, vol. 4199, pp. 410–424. Springer, Heidelberg (2006)

Walk Your Tree Any Way You Want

Anya Helene Bagge[1] and Ralf Lämmel[2]

[1] Bergen Language Design Laboratory
Dept. of Informatics, University of Bergen, Norway
[2] Software Languages Team
University of Koblenz-Landau, Germany

Abstract. Software transformations in the NUTHATCH style are described as walks over trees (possibly graphs) that proceed in programmer-defined steps which may observe join points of the walk, may observe and affect state associated with the walk, may rewrite the walked tree, may contribute to a built tree, and must walk somewhere, typically along one branch or another. The approach blends well with OO programming. We have implemented the approach in the NUTHATCH/J library for Java.

1 Introduction

Software transformations rely fundamentally on traversing tree or graph structures, applying rules or computations to individual scopes, and composing intermediate results. This is equally true for model transformation (in the narrow sense), e.g., based on ATL [9] and for program transformation (including program generation and analysis), e.g., based on Rascal [13], Stratego [4], Tom [2], and TXL [6] as well as for less domain-specific programming models such as adaptive (OO) programming [19], generic (functional) programming [15], or OO programming with visitor combinators [30].

Transformation languages and programming models differ in how traversal is specified and controlled. For instance, in plain term rewriting with a hardwired normalization strategy such as innermost, traversal must be encoded in rewrite rules tangled up with the more interesting rules for primitive steps of transformation. By contrast, in Stratego-style programming [29,30,18] and some forms of generic functional programming [18,15], schemes of traversal are programmer-definable abstractions that are parameterized in the rules or computations to be applied along the traversal, possibly tailored to specific nodes. For instance, consider this Stratego fragment for simplifying arithmetic expressions:

```
strategies
  simplify = bottomup(try(UnitLawAdd <+ ZeroLawMult))
rules
  UnitLawAdd : Add(x,0) -> x
  ZeroLawMult : Mult(x,0) -> 0
```

The library-defined traversal scheme *bottomup* is applied to rewrite rules for some laws of addition and multiplication. The programmer can reuse traversal schemes or define problem-specific ones, if needed.

K. Duddy and G. Kappel (Eds.): ICMT 2013, LNCS 7909, pp. 33–49, 2013.

In this paper, we describe a new transformation approach and a corresponding transformation language NUTHATCH,[1] which focuses programmer attention on the step-wise, possible state-accessing progression of a traversal, in fact, a *walk*, as opposed to the commitment to a traversal scheme and its application to rules. As an illustration, consider the following NUTHATCH fragment which matches the earlier Stratego example:

```
1 walk simplify {
2   if up then {
3     if ?Add(x, 0) then !x;
4     if ?Mult(x, 0) then !0;
5   }
6   walk to next;
7 }
```

The defined `walk` abstraction defines a complete walk over a tree. A walk starts at the root of the input term and (usually) ends there as well. In each step of the walk, a conditional statement is considered (line 2); it constrains rewrite rules (lines 3–4) to be applied when the walk goes up to the parent of the current node. Each rewrite rule consists of a match condition (see '?') and a replacement action (see '!'). The step is completed with a `walk to` statement (line 6) which defines the continuation of the walk. That is, the walk continues to the `next` node according to a default path for a comprehensive traversal.

Contributions

– We describe a notion of walks that proceed in programmer-defined steps which may observe join points of the walk, may access state associated with the walk, may rewrite the walked tree, may contribute to building a tree, and must walk somewhere, typically along one branch or another.

– We describe the realization of walks in the transformation language NUTHATCH. Conceptually, NUTHATCH draws insights from the concepts of tree automata [5], tree walking automata [1], continuations [24], and zippers [8]. Importantly, NUTHATCH incorporates state and supports OO-like reuse.

– We sketch NUTHATCH/J, an open-source library for walks in Java.[2]

The paper and accompanying material are available online.[3]

Road-map

§2 develops the basic notion of walks. §3 describes the NUTHATCH transformation language. §4 sketches the library-based implementation of NUTHATCH in Java. §5 discusses related work. §6 concludes the paper.

---

[1] Named after the nuthatch (*Sitta* spp.), a small passerine bird known for its ability to walk head-first towards the root of a tree, and on the underside of branches.
[2] http://nuthatchery.org/
[3] http://nuthatchery.org/icmt13/

2   The Notion of Walks

Walks walk along trees. Walks select branches. Walks complete paths. The default path is the starting point for all paths. Tree mutation may happen along the way.

2.1   Trees

In this paper, we mainly walk *trees*; graphs can also be walked as long as some distinguished entry node can replace the role of a root to reach all other nodes, also subject to precautions discussed in §3.10. In fact, we commit to *ordered trees*, i.e., trees with an ordering specified for the children. Ordered trees may be defined in two common ways, i.e., recursively (like terms of a term algebra) and graph-theoretically (with a designated root node and further constraints on nodes and edges for ordered trees as opposed to more general graphs). The graph-theoretical view is more helpful for intuitive understanding of walks.

We assume 'rich' trees in that nodes may be annotated with constructors and types (as needed for common term representations); leaves may carry some data (as needed for literals); edges (or '*branches*', as we will call them) may be annotated with labels (as needed for records, for example).

Thus, any node n of a tree t can be observed as follows:

- n.arity: The *arity* ≥ 0 of t's subtree rooted by n.
- n.root: Test for n being the root of t.
- n.leaf: Test for n being a leaf of t, i.e., n.arity $= 0$.
- n.name: The constructor name, if any, of n.
- n.type: The type, if any, of n.
- n.data: The data, if any, of n.
- n.parent: The parent node of n for n.root $=$ false.
- n.child[i]: The i-th child of n for $1 \leq i \leq n$.arity.
- n.label[i]: The label, if any, of the i-th child of n for $1 \leq i \leq n$.arity.

2.2   Branches

We limit ourselves to walks along the branches of trees as opposed to 'jumps', which would be possible in principle. This limitation seems to imply a more 'structured' programming technique. No need for jumps has arisen from our applications so far.

It is convenient to use natural numbers for referring to branches because 1, ..., n.arity readily refer to the children of n, leaving 0 for the parent. Hence, it makes sense to use branch numbers to say that we walk to the parent or to a specific child. We may also use branches to track where we came from by referring to the 'previous node' with the corresponding branch number.

2.3   Paths

If we assume immutable trees for a moment, then the walk over a tree may be described as a *path*, i.e., sequence of nodes as they are encountered by the walk.

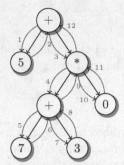

The edge labels denote the order of walking along branches. The default walk combines pre-, in-, and post-order in that we walk down from the parent in a depth-first manner, and *we return to the parent after each subtree.*

Fig. 1. Illustration of the default path for an arithmetic expression

Paths always start at the root of a tree. In the regular case, paths also end at the root. Paths for walks along branches can be effectively represented as sequences of natural numbers.

We refer to the *default path* as the path which goes along each edge in the tree in both directions (i.e., along each branch) to achieve depth-first, left-to-right visiting order. Notably, a parent is visited before and after each child; see Fig. 1 for an illustration. The visiting order of the default path can be described by defining uniformly the `next` node (in fact, branch) relative to the `current` node and one of its branches, `from`:

$$\texttt{next} \mapsto \begin{cases} \texttt{from} + 1, \text{if } \texttt{current.arity} > \texttt{from} \\ 0, \text{otherwise} \end{cases}$$

We think of `from` as referring back to the node *from* which we walked to the `current` node. This is the information that needs to be tracked by a walk. That is, if we entered the `current` node from its parent (i.e., branch 0), then we walk to the first child; if we (re-) entered the `current` node from its i-th child, then we walk to the $i + 1$-th child, if there is a next child, and to the parent otherwise.

The definition of `next` is powerful in so far as it is also usefully describes continuation in 'default order', even for walks that diverted from the default path. This follows from the fact that the definition only looks at the branch to the immediately preceding node in the walk.

2.4   Join points

Walks (according to the default path or otherwise) expose 'join points' for transformations, i.e., the join points corresponding to the encounter of nodes along certain branches. Two important join points are described by these conditions on `current` and `from`:

- `down` $\equiv$ `from` $= 0$
- `up` $\equiv$ `current.leaf` $\|$ `from` $=$ `current.arity`

The `down` join point captures whether `current` was just entered from its parent. The `up` join point captures whether the walk is about to return to the parent of current. In §3 (see §3.6 specifically), we will see additional join points at work. Programmers quantify join points combined with other conditions on the tree and custom state to control the walk and to select stateful behavior.

2.5   Mutation

Let us consider walks on *mutable trees*. Thus, the steps of a walk may add and remove nodes and edges before they pick any branch. While a walk on an immutable tree is simply characterized by a sequence of contiguous branches, a walk on a mutable tree is characterized by a sequence of states. A *state* s has the following components:

- s.tree: The tree as seen in state s.
- s.current: The walk's current node in s.tree.
- s.from: The branch referring back to the node prior to s.current.

We assume that state transition breaks down into two components: the mutation of the tree and the actual step to advance current. Clearly, if we were to allow arbitrary mutation, the semantics of walking becomes totally operational and properties such as termination are no longer attainable.

We are specifically interested in the case that mutation replaces current and its subtree, as in the application of a rewrite rule. When replacing current, though, the associated from may no longer be meaningful. Consider these cases:

- If from = 0, prior to mutation, then the first child, if any, of current was set up to be next. In this case, from shall be retained so that the first child, if any, of current is also set up to be next past mutation.
- If current.arity > 0 ∧ from = current.arity, prior to mutation, then the parent of current was set up to be next. Thus, from shall be assigned current.arity, as seen past mutation, so that again the parent of current is set up to be next.

These two cases cover rewrite rules on the down and up join points; for now, we take the view that current should not be replaced otherwise.

3   A Language for Walks

The NUTHATCH transformation language supports walks, as described in the previous section, on the grounds of an abstraction form for organizing walks in steps along branches. NUTHATCH can be mapped to an OO language such as Java, as discussed briefly in §4.

At runtime, a walk encapsulates basic state, as described in §2.5, extra state to be declared, and it provides a step action to be invoked repeatedly. (We assume that walks are under the control of a main program which can start walks on trees, observe results after a walk is complete, and possibly restart suspended walks.)

3.1 Syntax Summary

A walk abstraction has a name (an id), an optional declaration part for extra state associated with the walk and a statements part describing a step in terms of observing, matching, and rewriting the tree, accessing the walk's state and identifying the branch to follow. Walks may be parameterized, as discussed in §3.8. Thus:[4]

```
walk : 'walk' closure ;
closure : id paras? '{' ('state' declaration)* statement+ '}' ;
paras : '(' id (',' id)* ')' ;
```

There are Java-like variable declarations, but with an optional type and a required initializer:

```
declaration : type? id '=' expression ';' ;
```

These are the available statement forms:

```
statement : '{' statement+ '}'
  | 'if' expression 'then' statement ('else' statement)?
  | declaration | id '=' expression ';' | expression ';'
  | 'return' expression ';'
  | 'walk' 'to' expression ';' | 'stop' ';' | 'suspend' ';'
  | '!' term ';'
  ;
```

Statement grouping, if-then-else with dangling else, (local) variable declarations, assignments, and expressions are Java-like. 'returns' are needed for functions; see below. There are special statement forms to specify what branch to walk to, to stop or suspend a walk. There is another special statement form to replace the current term (see '!').

In addition to Java-like expression forms, there are these special forms:

```
expression : ... | '?' term | getter | '~' id paras? ;
```

That is, there is a special expression form for matching the current term (see '?') in a condition that also binds variables. Further, there are 'getters' for trees (arity, root, etc.), the basic walk state (tree, current, from), join points (down, up), and next, as we set them up in §2. Tree observers are applied to the current term if not specified otherwise. The last expression form (see '~') deals with nested walks, as discussed in §3.9.

NUTHATCH also offers a simple abstraction form for *actions* which do not walk anywhere. Other than that, they can maintain state and observe the basic state of a walk in which they participate, if any. Likewise, there are *functions* for expression abstraction. Thus:

```
action : 'action' closure ;
function : 'function' closure ;
```

Actions and functions are illustrated in §3.8.

---

[4] We use ANTLR (http://antlr.org/) grammar notation.

3.2   The Default Walk

The following NUTHATCH walk captures the default path of §2.3:

```
walk default {
  walk to next;
}
```

Each control-flow path of a NUTHATCH action must end in a walk-to statement which identifies the branch to walk to. The obvious options are next, parent (overloaded to refer to branch 0), child[i] (overloaded to refer to branch i), first (assumed to represent the branch 1 for the first child), and last (assumed to represent the branch for the last child).

3.3   Diversion from the Default Path

The following example shows how a walk can be diverted depending on the current node; in this case, to avoid traversing Expr subtrees. To this end, we observe the type of the current node; we assume that Expr is one of the types of terms that are walked:

```
walk skipExpr {
  walk to (if type==Expr then parent else next);
}
```

(We use expression-level if-then-else.)

3.4   Derived Walks

New walks can be derived from existing walks. To this end, walk abstractions are referred to in statements. The underlying semantics is that the referenced walk's step action is inlined. For instance:

```
walk skipExpr {
  if type==Expr then walk to parent;
  default;
}
```

If the referenced walk includes extra state (which is not the case in the above example), then such state would be included into the referring walk automatically.

Because the default path is so prevailing, we assume that any walk abstraction derives implicitly from default such that default's action is appended at the end of the step action. Accordingly, we shorten skipExpr:

```
walk skipExpr {
  if type==Expr then walk to parent;
}
```

We note that this implicit derivation occurs only at the top level, not when a walk is used to create a derived walk.

3.5   Stateful Walks

A walk may carry state. Actions may hence read and write such state. For instance, the following walk abstraction counts nodes; it takes advantage of the implicit derivation from `default`, as just explained above:

```
walk countNodes {
  state count = 0;
  if down then count++;
}
```

That is, we declare a variable `count` to maintain the node count, which we initialize to 0 and increment for each node, but only along the `down` join point—so that we do not count nodes multiple times. (We could also use `up` as a condition here.)

3.6   Flexible Point-Cuts

We have started to invoke the AOP-like terminology of join points. Accordingly, walks may quantify the join points of interest; in AOP speak: walks need to express point-cuts. Consider the following walk abstraction which converts a tree into a string, using a term-like representation with prefix operators and comma-separated arguments as in "add(add(x,y),0)":

```
walk toString {
  state s = "";
  if leaf
    then s += data;
  else {
      if down then s += name + "(";
      if up then s += ")";
      if from>=first && from<last then s += ", ";
  }
}
```

In the code, we carefully observe the position along the walk to correctly parenthesize and place commas where appropriate. For instance, "(" belongs before the first child; thus the condition `down`, i.e., `from==parent`. This simple example clearly demonstrates how NUTHATCH style does not explicitly recurse / traverse into compound structures, as is the case with functional programming or Stratego-like traversal schemes. Instead, NUTHATCH style entails observation of the branch on which the current node was entered and possibly other data.

3.7   Walks with 'In Place' Rewriting

Rewriting is straightforward; it relies on a special condition form for use in an if-then-else statement to match ('?') a term pattern with the current term and to bind variables for use in the replace ('!') statement within the then-branch. We also say 'in place' rewriting to emphasize the fact that the tree is modified.

Let us revisit the example from the introduction (§1). The example follows the default path. When applied to the sample tree of Fig. 1, the result is '5'.

For what it matters, we mention that simplification would not be complete, if we were using the down instead of the up join point in the example. (The unit law of addition would not be applicable in the example on the way down.)

'In place' rewriting is suitable for endogenous transformations [20] and specifically transformations that are meant to preserve many nodes and edges, as in the case of 'refining models' according to [26], but see §3.11 for a discussion of exogenous transformations [20].

3.8   Parameterized Walks

Common Stratego-like traversal schemes can be easily expressed by parameterizing walk abstractions, e.g.:

```
walk bottomup(s) { if up then s; }
```

The parameter s may abstract over actions such as rewrite rules. Let us revisit the example from the introduction (§1); we capture these actions (as of §3.1):

```
action UnitLawAdd { if ?Add(x, 0) then !x; }
action ZeroLawMult { if ?Mult(x, 0) then !0; }
action BothLaws { UnitLawAdd; ZeroLawMult; }
```

Thus, bottom-up traversal for simplification can be recomposed as follows:

```
bottomup(BothLaws)
```

Here is a more problem-specific, still language-parametric example of a parameterized walk which deals with state-based scope-tracking as opposed to Stratego-like traversal; such tracking is needed in various transformations, e.g., for the purpose of hosting new abstractions in the same context as the current scope or be it just for generating error messages.

```
walk scopeTracker(isDeclaration) {
  state scopes = new Stack[Node]();
  if down && isDeclaration then scopes.push(current);
  if up && current==scopes.top() then scopes.pop();
}
```

In the context of a transformation for Java, isDeclaration may be a condition (a function as of §3.1) that tests for a Java class declaration:

```
function isClassDec { return ?ClassDec(ClassDecHead(_,name,_,_,_),_); }
```

3.9   Nested Walks

Consider again the definition of bottomup, as given above. Now imagine that the argument s is not a plain action, such as rewrite rule, but it is meant to be a walk in itself. The existing definition would inline that walk according to the derivation semantics of §3.4, thereby disrupting the bottomup traversal. Instead, the argument walk should be performed atomically, as part of the referring step's action, as opposed to participating in the enclosing walk. References to arguments (which may be walks) can be accordingly marked as nested walks by '~':

```
walk topdown(s) { if down then ~s; }
walk bottomup(s) { if up then ~s; }
walk downup(s,t) { topdown(s); bottomup(t); }
```

('~' is a no-op on non-walks such as actions.) We note that each nested walk views the current node of the enclosing walk as the root. Note that no nested walk designation happens for downup because derivation semantics (as of §3.4) is appropriate here, if we want s to be applied on the way down and t on the way up. For comparison, consider these definitions:

```
walk badDownup1(s,t) { ~topdown(s); ~bottomup(t); }
action badDownup2(s,t) { ~topdown(s); ~bottomup(t); }
```

badDownup1 performs a top-down walk followed by a bottom-up walk for each node in the tree. badDownup2 performs a top-down walk followed by a bottom-up walk for a given tree; both walks start from the root.

3.10   Termination of Walks

A walk terminates regularly, if the walk encounters the root of a tree through the parent branch. A walk terminates irregularly if an unhandled exception is thrown by the step action. A walk may also be terminated explicitly or suspended via designated actions stop and suspend.

Accidentally, one may describe walks that do not terminate. This is implied by the expressiveness and flexibility of the abstraction form for walks. For instance, a transformation may continuously expand some redex for the down join point. Other programming techniques for traversals are also susceptible to this problem [16].

Another major challenge for termination is when graphs are walked. That is, walks may be cyclic. In adaptive programming [19], strategic programming on graphs [11], and OO programming with visitor combinator [30], this problem can arise as well. The problem can be solved, if we can make sure that no object is visited more than once. In NUTHATCH, we can use an 'enter once' walk as the starting point for any walk on a graph. Thus:

```
walk enteronce {
  state seen = new WeakHashSet();
  if down then
    if seen.contains(current)
      then walk to parent;
      else seen.add(current);
}
```

Thus, the walk keeps track of all nodes that were encountered. This scheme is not just useful for avoiding cyclic walks; it generally prevents walks from entering nodes more than once, even in directed acyclic graphs. The problem of non-termination or repeated walks into the same nodes can also be addressed if additional metamodel information is available to distinguish composition versus reference relationships, as in the case of walking EMF models, for example. That is, edges for reference relationships shall not be followed by walks.

3.11 Walks Building Terms

When facing exogenous transformations [20] (i.e., transformations with a target metamodel that is different from the source metamodel), then 'in place' rewriting (see §3.7) may not be appropriate, unless it is acceptable to operate on trees that use a 'union' metamodel for source and target models.

Suitable *tree builders* can be used to describe exogenous transformations or even endogenous transformations, when the source of the transformation is to be preserved. Consider the following walk that uses a tree builder to copy the walked tree, which is a good starting point for an endogenous transformation which preserves the walked tree:

```
walk copyall {
  state result = new TreeBuilder();
  if down then { result.add(current); result.moveDown(); }
  if up then result.moveUp();
}
```

The idea is that a tree builder provides an interface to (building) a tree; there are operations for adding nodes and edges. Further, the builder uses a *cursor* to maintain the current focus for addition. The cursor is a pointer to the children list of some node. Upon construction, the cursor points to the degenerated children list that will hold the root of the built tree. In the 'copy all' walk, we use the following operations:

- *add*: A given node (current in the example) is added to the children list pointed to by the cursor, where information such name, type, and data as well as label (for the edge to the parent) is copied over.
- *moveDown*: The cursor is set to point to the children list of the last node in the children list currently pointed to by the cursor.
- *moveUp*: The cursor is set to point to the children list of the parent node of the last node in the children list currently pointed to by the cursor.

When implementing exogenous transformations, tree builders are invoked to add 'terms' specific to the target model.

4 Walking in Java

In the following, we sketch the NUTHATCH/J library for walking in Java. NUTHATCH transformations can be mapped to Java code that uses the NUTHATCH/J library.

4.1 Basic Interfaces

NUTHATCH/J is designed as a generic tree walking library for Java which is independent of the underlying data representation. Thus, the library can be adapted by parameterization and subclassing for use with different kinds of trees, including those of existing transformation systems; see §4.4.

Walks are specified by implementing the Walk interface:

```
public interface Walk<W extends Walker<?, ?>> {
    int step(W walker);
}
```

The step method performs a single step of the walk, can observe and manipulate state, and returns the next branch to walk to. The Walker type of the library encapsulates the tree-walking functionality and maintains the current node and state as described in §2.5, and provides the tree observers of §2.1.

The Walk interface is parameterized by the walker type, thereby making the extended features of a walker accessible in a type-safe manner. For example, the following code (also available online) implements the example from §1:

```
public int step(ExprWalker w) {
    if (down(w)) {
        if (w.match(Add(var("x"), Int(0)))) w.replace(w.getEnv().get("x"));
        if (w.match(Mul(var("x"), Int(0)))) w.replace(Int(0));
    }
    return NEXT;
}
```

ExprWalker is a subtype of Walker which fixes the generics parameters for the expression terms of the example.

4.2   Extra State

Walk state is handled either by using variables in a closure or field variables in the class which implements Walk. The following Java code uses the former technique to replicate the example from §3.6:

```
final StringBuffer s = new StringBuffer(); // Accumulate result here.
Walk<ExprWalker> toTerm = new BaseWalk<ExprWalker>() {
    public int step(ExprWalker w) {
        if (leaf(w)) // We are at a leaf; print data value.
            s.append(w.getData().toString());
        else if (down(w)) // First time we see this node; print constructor name.
            s.append(w.getName() + "(");
        else if (up(w)) // Just finished with children; close parenthesis.
            s.append(")");
        else // Coming up from a child (not the last); insert a comma.
            s.append(", ");
        return NEXT;
    }
};
```

4.3   Combinator Style

A library of common parameterized walk or action combinators (in the sense of §3.8) is available for various join points. In a combinator style, the simplifier of §1 can be expressed as follows:

```
Walk<ExprWalker> w =
  walk(up(sequence(match(Add(var("x"), Int(0)), replace(var("x"))),
                   match(Mul(var("x"), Int(0)), replace(Int(0))))));
```

The walk is built up using static methods calls, where 'walk' represents the default walk, 'up' builds a conditional action for the up join point, 'sequence' executes all its arguments in the given order, 'match' executes its argument, if the pattern matches, and 'replace' performs a replace action.

4.4 Tool Integration

NUTHATCH/J integrates with Spoofax/Stratego/XT [4] and Rascal [13] so that these systems can be used in NUTHATCH/J applications. This is well in line with other transformation systems that support diverse access methods. For instance, Tom [21] can be applied to parse trees and object graphs of a domain model; POM adapters [12] allow Stratego to transform an Eclipse JDT AST.

The NUTHATCH/J+Stratego library supports untyped trees using the same term implementation as the Java version of Stratego. It also provides an interface to the JSGLR parser, including a pattern generator which generates pattern builders from an abstract syntax specification. Syntax definitions and minimal tooling for working on Java programs is also available, through the JavaFront package for Stratego.

The NUTHATCH/J+Rascal library wraps the Rascal data types into NUTHATCH trees, and can work on both concrete and abstract syntax trees (though without support for making concrete syntax patterns, at the time of writing).

4.5 Performance

As of writing, NUTHATCH/J has not yet been optimized for performance. Nevertheless, we have done some measurements of traversal and rewriting performance on Java programs, comparing against Stratego. All NUTHATCH/J measurements were done using Stratego terms as the underlying data structure, so that we could use the exact same data for both NUTHATCH/J and Stratego, and check that both implementations gave the exact same results.[5]

For reference, we also measured hand-written Java versions of some of the transformations, in order to get an idea of the top performance possible using the Stratego term library.

A few selected experiments are summarized in Table 1.[6] The experiments show that performance of NUTHATCH/J is similar to that of the Stratego interpreter for trivial traversals (*topdown*, *downup*), but slower than compiled Stratego code.

---

[5] Stratego measurements were done using both interpreted and compiled code, both using version 1.1 of the Spoofax language workbench. For interpretation, we used the *hybrid interpreter*, which uses compiled-to-Java versions of the standard libraries, but interprets user code on the fly. Measurements are an average of 5000 iterations, run on an otherwise idle AMD FX-8350 computer, running OpenJDK 7u15.

[6] See http://nuthatchery.org/icmt13/benchmarks.html for more details.

Table 1. Some performance measurements of NUTHATCH/J vs. Stratego, with execution times in milliseconds (average over 5000 runs) for NUTHATCH/J, interpreted Stratego, compiled Stratego (STRJ), and hand-written Java

	Nuthatch/J	Stratego	STRJ	Java
Collect Strings	3.0	5.0	4.2	—
Commute	4.6	29.8	0.9	0.8
Bottomup Build	5.6	3.2	1.2	—
Topdown	1.5	1.0	0.5	0.5
Downup	1.5	1.7	0.6	0.5

Simple transformations (*commute*) are a lot faster in NUTHATCH/J than with interpreted Stratego code, but again, compiled Stratego is faster. NUTHATCH/J has an advantage when using plain Java to accumulate state, and outperforms compiled Stratego on collecting strings from a tree.

5   Related Work

Walks à la NUTHATCH combine generic traversal, stateful behavior, OO-like derivation, and parameterization. Accordingly, walks relate to Stratego-like programming, visitor programming including visitor combinators, adaptive programming, generic functional programming, and model transformation.

Stratego et al. Walks are inspired by the seminal work on strategies à la Stratego [29,4]—the combination of term rewriting and programmable strategies, also for traversal purposes. Walks depart from strategies in that the basic traversal expressiveness is about continuous walking along branches as opposed to recursive one-layer traversal. Further, walks are designed around state, whereas strategies only uses state in the special sense of dynamic rewrite rules [3]. Also, walks are designed to be derivable (and parameterized), whereas strategies leverage parameterization only. §3.8 shows how walks represent Stratego-like traversal schemes. The AspectStratego [10] variation on Stratego was proposed to leverage some means of aspect orientation in the context of term rewriting. In this work, join points of rewriting or the strategic program can be intercepted. By contrast, walks à la NUTHATCH interact with join points for walks along trees.

Visitor programming. In the OO programming context, traversal problems can be addressed by means of visitors [22]. Specifically, advanced approaches use visitor combinators [30,21] inspired by Stratego. The cited approaches transpose Stratego style to an OO language context; they make limited use of OO-like derivation and imperative state. When compared to walks, 'visits' are controlled strategically (as above), as opposed to exposing join points of the walks to the problem-specific functionality.

Adaptive programming. The notion of processing object graphs in a structure-shy fashion has been realized in seminal work on adaptive programming [19], where traversal specifications of objects to be visited are separated from actions to be actually applied to the objects on the path. Stratego-like strategic programming and adaptive programming are known to be related in a non-trivial manner [17]. Walks differ from adaptive programs in that they do not leverage any special language constructs for traversal specifications. Also, each step of a walk may affect the remaining path.

Generic functional programming. The parameterization- or combinator-based approach of traversal programming has been pushed particularly far in a generic functional programming context; see, e.g., the 'mother of traversal' [14,23]. Indeed, such approaches offer highly parameterized abstractions for different traversal instantiations. By contrast, walks à la NUTHATCH additionally offer i) OO-like derivation, ii) imperative OO-like stateful behavior, and iii) exposure of join points of walks (traversals) for customized traversal behavior.

Model transformation. Because of the large amount MT languages in existence, it is hard to compile a useful comparison. Overall, NUTHATCH style is closer to term rewriting approaches. We have in mind ATL [9] as a representative in what follows. Thus, model transformations match source model elements and map them to target model elements. Endogenous transformations, specifically, may rely on some degree of implicit behavior (refinement) to copy or retain model elements when not said otherwise [26]. MT rules are essentially declarative, with some built-in scheme of applying rules to the source model. Escapes to imperative features are needed in practice and thus supported. Join points of walks à la NUTHATCH are not established for MT languages.

6   Concluding Remarks

We have described a new approach to traversal programming with walks as the central abstraction form. The development of the walk notion and all of our related experiments were based on the NUTHATCH/J library for walks in Java. The NUTHATCH transformation language should be viewed as an ongoing effort to extract a transformation DSL from the NUTHATCH/J library. NUTHATCH can express traversal schemes à la Stratego and thus, it provides 'proven expressiveness'. Importantly, OO idioms (such as state, encapsulation, closures, and type derivation) are also part of the NUTHATCH programming model. The NUTHATCH/J library leverages adapters for tree formats of other transformation tools in the interest of tool integration.

Proper DSL notation enables conciseness (when compared to Java), type checking, static analyses for other properties of walks, and compile-time optimizations. However, an external DSL approach makes it harder to provide all language services. Therefore, we continue research on the NUTHATCH/J's combinator style of §4.3 to perhaps settle on an internal DSL (in fact, DSL embedding) which is a popular approach for transformation languages with functional host languages [18,25,7]. NUTHATCH/J's combinator style would also permit on-the-fly optimization, as it has been used elsewhere for embedded DSL implementation [27,28].

Acknowledgments. This research is funded in part by the Research Council of Norway.

References

1. Aho, A.V., Ullman, J.D.: Translations on a Context-Free Grammar. Information and Control 19(5), 439–475 (1971)
2. Balland, E., Brauner, P., Kopetz, R., Moreau, P.E., Reilles, A.: Tom: Piggybacking Rewriting on Java. In: Baader, F. (ed.) RTA 2007. LNCS, vol. 4533, pp. 36–47. Springer, Heidelberg (2007)
3. Bravenboer, M., van Dam, A., Olmos, K., Visser, E.: Program Transformation with Scoped Dynamic Rewrite Rules. Fundamenta Informaticae 69(1-2), 123–178 (2006)
4. Bravenboer, M., Kalleberg, K.T., Vermaas, R., Visser, E.: Stratego/XT 0.17. A language and toolset for program transformation. Sci. Comput. Program. 72(1-2), 52–70 (2008)
5. Comon, H., Dauchet, M., Gilleron, R., Löding, C., Jacquemard, F., Lugiez, D., Tison, S., Tommasi, M.: Tree Automata Techniques and Applications (2007), http://www.grappa.univ-lille3.fr/tata (release October 12, 2007)
6. Cordy, J.R.: The TXL source transformation language. Sci. Comput. Program. 61(3), 190–210 (2006)
7. George, L., Wider, A., Scheidgen, M.: Type-Safe Model Transformation Languages as Internal DSLs in Scala. In: Hu, Z., de Lara, J. (eds.) ICMT 2012. LNCS, vol. 7307, pp. 160–175. Springer, Heidelberg (2012)
8. Huet, G.: The Zipper. J. Funct. Program. 7(5), 549–554 (1997)
9. Jouault, F., Allilaire, F., Bézivin, J., Kurtev, I.: ATL: A model transformation tool. Sci. Comput. Program. 72(1-2), 31–39 (2008)
10. Kalleberg, K.T., Visser, E.: Combining Aspect-Oriented and Strategic Programming. In: Workshop on Rule-Based Programming (RULE 2005). ENTCS, vol. 147, pp. 5–30 (2006)
11. Kalleberg, K.T., Visser, E.: Strategic Graph Rewriting: Transforming and Traversing Terms with References. In: 6th Intl. Workshop on Reduction Strategies in Rewriting and Programming (WRS 2006) (2006), online publication
12. Kalleberg, K.T., Visser, E.: Fusing a Transformation Language with an Open Compiler. In: 7th Workshop on Language Descriptions, Tools and Applications (LDTA 2007). ENTCS, pp. 18–31. Elsevier (2007)
13. Klint, P., van der Storm, T., Vinju, J.J.: Rascal: A Domain Specific Language for Source Code Analysis and Manipulation. In: 9th IEEE Intl. Working Conf. on Source Code Analysis and Manipulation (SCAM 2009), pp. 168–177. IEEE CS (2009)
14. Lämmel, R.: The Sketch of a Polymorphic Symphony. In: Reduction Strategies in Rewriting and Programming (WRS 2002). ENTCS, vol. 70, pp. 135–155 (2002)
15. Lämmel, R., Peyton Jones, S.L.: Scrap your boilerplate: a practical design pattern for generic programming. In: ACM SIGPLAN Intl. Workshop on Types in Languages Design and Implementation (TLDI 2003), pp. 26–37. ACM (2003)
16. Lämmel, R., Thompson, S., Kaiser, M.: Programming errors in traversal programs over structured data. Sci. Comput. Program (2012) (in press), doi:10.1016/j.scico.2011.11.006
17. Lämmel, R., Visser, E., Visser, J.: Strategic programming meets adaptive programming. In: 2nd Intl. Conf. on Aspect-Oriented Software Development (AOSD 2003), pp. 168–177 (2003)
18. Lämmel, R., Visser, J.: A *Strafunski* Application Letter. In: Dahl, V. (ed.) PADL 2003. LNCS, vol. 2562, pp. 357–375. Springer, Heidelberg (2002)

19. Lieberherr, K.J., Patt-Shamir, B., Orleans, D.: Traversals of object structures: Specification and Efficient Implementation. ACM Transactions on Programming Languages and Systems 26(2), 370–412 (2004)
20. Mens, T., Van Gorp, P.: A taxonomy of model transformation. ENTCS, vol. 152, pp. 125–142 (2006)
21. Moreau, P.E., Reilles, A.: Rules and Strategies in Java. In: Reduction Strategies in Rewriting and Programming (WRS 2007). ENTCS, vol. 204, pp. 71–82 (2008)
22. Palsberg, J., Jay, C.B.: The Essence of the Visitor Pattern. In: 22nd Intl. Computer Software and Applications Conf (COMPSAC 1998), pp. 9–15. IEEE Computer Society (1998)
23. Ren, D., Erwig, M.: A generic recursion toolbox for Haskell or: scrap your boilerplate systematically. In: Proceedings of the ACM SIGPLAN Workshop on Haskell, pp. 13–24. ACM (2006)
24. Reynolds, J.C.: The Discoveries of Continuations. Lisp and Symbolic Computation 6(3-4), 233–248 (1993)
25. Sloane, A.M.: Lightweight Language Processing in Kiama. In: Fernandes, J.M., Lämmel, R., Visser, J., Saraiva, J. (eds.) GTTSE 2009. LNCS, vol. 6491, pp. 408–425. Springer, Heidelberg (2011)
26. Tisi, M., Martínez, S., Jouault, F., Cabot, J.: Refining Models with Rule-based Model Transformations. Tech. Rep. 7582, INRIA (2011)
27. Veldhuizen, T.L.: Expression templates. C++ Report 7(5), 26–31 (1995), reprinted in C++ Gems, ed. Stanley Lippman
28. Viera, M., Swierstra, S.D., Lempsink, E.: Haskell, do you read me?: constructing and composing efficient top-down parsers at runtime. In: 1st ACM SIGPLAN Symposium on Haskell (Haskell 2008), pp. 63–74. ACM (2008)
29. Visser, E., Benaissa, Z., Tolmach, A.: Building program optimizers with rewriting strategies. In: 3rd ACM SIGPLAN Intl. Conf. on Functional Programming, ICFP 1998, pp. 13–26. ACM Press (1998)
30. Visser, J.: Visitor combination and traversal control. In: 16th ACM SIGPLAN Conf. on Object Oriented Programming, OOPSLA 2001, pp. 270–282. ACM (2001)

On an Automated Translation of Satellite Procedures Using Triple Graph Grammars

Frank Hermann[1], Susann Gottmann[1,*], Nico Nachtigall[1,*], Benjamin Braatz[1], Gianluigi Morelli[2], Alain Pierre[2], and Thomas Engel[1]

[1] Interdisciplinary Centre for Security, Reliability and Trust,
Université du Luxembourg, Luxembourg
firstname.lastname@uni.lu
http://www.uni.lu/snt/
[2] SES, Luxembourg
firstname.lastname@ses.com
http://www.ses.com/

Model transformation based on triple graph grammars (TGGs) is a general, intuitive and formally well defined technique for the translation of models [5,6,2]. While previous concepts and case studies were focused mainly on visual models of software and systems, this article describes an industrial application of model transformations based on TGGs as a powerful technique for software translation using the tool Henshin [1]. The general problem in this scenario is to translate source code that is currently in use into corresponding source code that shall run on a new system. Up to now, this problem was addressed based on manually written converters, parser generators, compiler-compilers or meta-programming environments using term rewriting or similar techniques (see e.g. [4]).

Within the joint research project PIL2SPELL[1] with the industrial partner SES (Société Européenne des Satellites), we applied TGGs for the translation of satellite control software. SES is currently operating a fleet of 52 satellites, which are manufactured by different vendors, who often use their own proprietary languages for operational procedures. In order to reduce the high complexity during operation caused by this heterogeneity, SES decided to develop and use the satellite control language SPELL [7] (Satellite Procedure Execution Language & Library), which is nowadays used by more and more operators and may become a standard in this domain. For this reason, SES is faced with the need to convert satellite control procedures delivered by the manufacturers into SPELL procedures. The main aim of this project was to provide a fully automated translation of existing satellite control procedures written in the programming language PIL (Procedure Intermediate Language) of the manufacturer ASTRIUM into SPELL procedures. Since the procedures in PIL are already validated, several requirements are important: automation of the execution, maintainability of the translation patterns, readability of the output, and, most importantly, reliability in terms of fidelity, precision and correctness of the translation. For SES, the listed requirements are of very high importance to minimise the efforts for revalidation.

* Supported by the Fonds National de la Recherche, Luxembourg (3968135, 4895603).
[1] This project is part of the Efficient Automation of Satellite Operations (EASO) project supported by the European Space Agency (ESA).

K. Duddy and G. Kappel (Eds.): ICMT 2013, LNCS 7909, pp. 50–51, 2013.
© Springer-Verlag Berlin Heidelberg 2013

The general idea of TGGs is to specify languages of integrated models, where each integrated model contains a source model and a corresponding target model together with explicit correspondence structures. In the present case, models are given by abstract syntax trees of the source code of the source and target domains. The operational rules for executing the translation are generated from the specified TGG. The translation preserves the given source model and creates explicit traceability links between corresponding fragments of the input and output. These correspondence links are used in the validation phase for assuring quality concerning precision and fidelity of the translation.

In the present scenario, the bidirectional features of TGGs were not of interest, such that it would have been possible to use another unidirectional transformation approach, like ATL (ATLAS Transformation Language) [3]. Still, TGGs showed benefits that were important for SES. The initial mapping document provided by SES engineers contained translation patterns for example code fragments. These patterns were loaded in the GUI of Henshin and generalised to rules of the TGG, such that the resulting translator met the industrial requirement of ensuring theses patterns in the translation. Since TGGs do not need recursion and do not cause side effects, we were able to handle the occurring intermediate modifications of the mapping document by the domain experts during the development of the TGG. The evaluation by SES and ASTRIUM domain experts delivered remarkable results concerning the listed requirements and as an effective result, the communication satellite Astra 2F is operational in space and controlled by the generated procedures that are running in ground control.

In future work, we will apply TGGs for the synchronisation between the source code of satellite procedures and corresponding visualisations.

References

1. The Eclipse Foundation: EMF Henshin – Version 0.9.4 (2013), http://www.eclipse.org/modeling/emft/henshin/
2. Hermann, F., Ehrig, H., Golas, U., Orejas, F.: Efficient analysis and execution of correct and complete model transformations based on triple graph grammars. In: Model Driven Interoperability (MDI 2010), pp. 22–31. ACM (2010)
3. Jouault, F., Allilaire, F., Bézivin, J., Kurtev, I.: ATL: A model transformation tool. Science of Computer Programming 72, 31–39 (2008)
4. Klint, P., van der Storm, T., Vinju, J.: EASY meta-programming with Rascal. In: Fernandes, J.M., Lämmel, R., Visser, J., Saraiva, J. (eds.) GTTSE 2009. LNCS, vol. 6491, pp. 222–289. Springer, Heidelberg (2011)
5. Schürr, A.: Specification of graph translators with triple graph grammars. In: Mayr, E.W., Schmidt, G., Tinhofer, G. (eds.) WG 1994. LNCS, vol. 903, pp. 151–163. Springer, Heidelberg (1995)
6. Schürr, A., Klar, F.: 15 years of triple graph grammars. In: Ehrig, H., Heckel, R., Rozenberg, G., Taentzer, G. (eds.) ICGT 2008. LNCS, vol. 5214, pp. 411–425. Springer, Heidelberg (2008)
7. SES Engineering: SPELL - Satellite Procedure Execution Language & Library – Version 2.3.13 (2013), http://code.google.com/p/spell-sat/

The Graph Grammar Library - A Generic Framework for Chemical Graph Rewrite Systems

Martin Mann[1], Heinz Ekker[2], and Christoph Flamm[2]

[1] Bioinformatics, Institut for Computer Science, University of Freiburg,
Georges-Köhler-Allee 106, 79106 Freiburg, Germany,
mmann@informatik.uni-freiburg.de
[2] Institute for Theoretical Chemistry, University of Vienna, Währingerstrasse 17,
1090 Vienna, Austria,
xtof@tbi.univie.ac.at

Graph rewrite systems are powerful tools to model and study complex problems in various fields of research [7]. Their successful application to chemical reaction modelling on a molecular level was shown [1,2,6] but no appropriate and simple system is available at the moment [8]. The Graph Grammar Library (GGL), presented in this contribution and more extensively in [4], fills this gap and provides feature-rich functionality especially for chemical transformation.

The GGL implements a simple generic Double Push Out approach for general graph rewrite systems [7] on labeled undirected graphs. The object oriented C++ framework focuses on a high level of modularity as well as high performance, using state-of-the-art algorithms and data structures, and comes with extensive end user and API documentation. Central modules (e.g. graph matching, match handling, graph storage) are combined via simple interfaces, which enables an easy combining to tackle the problem at hand.

The large GGL chemistry module enables extensive and detailed studies of chemical systems. It well meets the requirements and abilities envisioned by Yadav et al. [8] for such chemical rewrite systems. Here, molecules are represented as vertex and edge labeled undirected graphs while chemical reactions are described by according graph grammar rules, see Fig. 1. Such a graph grammar is a generating system for the explicit construction of an entire chemical space,

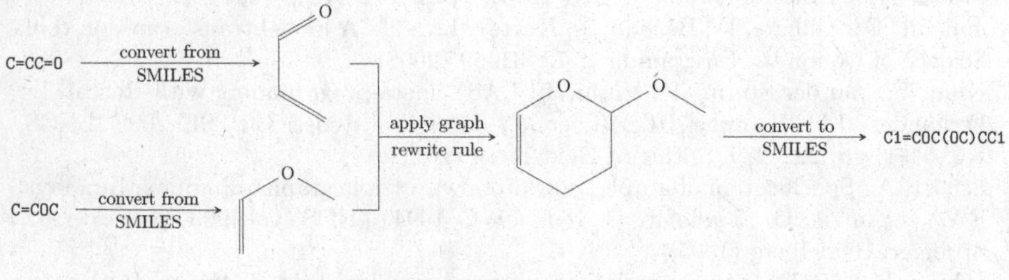

Fig. 1. Illustration of the basic steps to convert the educt molecules acolein and methyl vinyl ether via a Diels-Alder reaction [4] to the cyclic product molecule. Physicochemical properties for the molecules, such as free energies (ΔG), or for the reaction, e.g. reaction rates, can be estimated either by using GGL built-in functionality or via calls to the OpenBabel chemistry toolkit [5].

K. Duddy and G. Kappel (Eds.): ICMT 2013, LNCS 7909, pp. 52–53, 2013.
© Springer-Verlag Berlin Heidelberg 2013

i.e. all molecules reachable from the initial molecules by iterative reaction applications. An extensive system of wildcards, degree and adjacency constraints, and negative application conditions (NAC), such as the non-existence of edges, makes it easy to formulate very specific graph transformation rules by modulating their context dependent matching behaviour. Rules are encoded using the Graph Modelling Language (GML) easily understood and used by non-expert users. The molecule graphs produced by the graph grammar encoded chemical reactions have to pass extensive sanity checks and e.g. arromaticity correction to ensure the production of proper molecules only.

Besides the efficient handling of chemical transformation the GGL offers advanced cheminformatics algorithms. Among them are methods for the estimation of reaction rates or the free energies of molecules, the generation of canonical SMILES (a popular line notation for molecules) or chemical ring or aromaticity perception. Furthermore the entire functionality of the popular chemical toolbox Open Babel [5] can be harnessed from within the GGL via the implementation of a bi-directional interface for the exchange of chemical graphs. All these features are used within the GGL-based toyChem tool part of the library that enables the expansion and visualization of reaction networks given some initial molecules and a set of chemical reaction rewrite rules.

The graph grammar based simulation of chemical reactions offered by the GGL is a powerful tool for extensive cheminformatics studies on a molecular level and it already provides rewrite rules for all enzymes listed in the KEGG LIGAND database [3]. The GGL is freely available at

http://www.tbi.univie.ac.at/software/GGL

For a full description of all GGL features please refer to [4] available at
http://arxiv.org/abs/1304.1356

References

1. Benkö, G., Flamm, C., Stadler, P.F.: A graph-based toy model of chemistry. J Chem. Inf. and Comp. Sci. 43(4), 1085–1093 (2003)
2. Flamm, C., Ullrich, A., Ekker, H., Mann, M., Hoegerl, D., Rohrschneider, M., Sauer, S., Scheuermann, G., Klemm, K., Hofacker, I.L., Stadler, P.F.: Evolution of metabolic networks: A computational framework. J. Syst. Chem. 1(1), 4 (2010)
3. Kanehisa, M., Goto, S., Sato, Y., Furumichi, M., Tanabe, M.: KEGG for integration and interpretation of large-scale molecular data sets. Nuc. Acids Res. (2011)
4. Mann, M., Ekker, H., Flamm, C.: The graph grammar library - a generic framework for chemical graph rewrite systems. arXiv (2013), http://arxiv.org/abs/1304.1356
5. O'Boyle, N.M., Banck, M., James, C.A., Morley, C., Vandermeersch, T., Hutchison, G.R.: Open Babel: An open chemical toolbox. J. Cheminf. 3(1), 33+ (2011)
6. Rosselló, F., Valiente, G.: Chemical graphs, chemical reaction graphs, and chemical graph transformation. Electron. Notes Theor. Comput. Sci. 127, 157–166 (2005)
7. Rozenberg, G. (ed.): Handbook of Graph Grammars and Computing by Graph Transformation: Volume I. Foundations. World Scientific Publishing Co., Inc. (1997)
8. Yadav, M.K., Kelley, B.P., Silverman, S.M.: The potential of a chemical graph transformation system. In: Ehrig, H., Engels, G., Parisi-Presicce, F., Rozenberg, G. (eds.) ICGT 2004. LNCS, vol. 3256, pp. 83–95. Springer, Heidelberg (2004)

Fragmented Validation:
A Simple and Efficient Contribution
to XSLT Checking

(Extended Abstract)

Markus Lepper[1] and Baltasar Trancón y Widemann[1,2]

[1] <semantics/> GmbH, Berlin, DE
[2] Ilmenau University of Technology, Ilmenau, DE
post@markuslepper.eu, Baltasar.Trancon@tu-ilmenau.de

Debugging and verifying XSLT programs is a tedious but important task, and automated support is urgently requested by practice. Type checking of XSLT is untractable in general. Very different theoretical and practical work exists in this field, either restricting the involved languages, or aiming at approximations.

In contrast to these ambitious and expensive approaches, *fragmented validation* is light-weight. It does not consider the input document and the questions of control flow, in XSLT especially complicated due to the dynamic pattern matching, but restricts itself to the fragments of target language elements which are statically embedded in an XSLT script, and which are the stencils for many (in most cases: for *all*) elements of the result documents.

Fragmented Validation finds places in an XSLT program where output is produced which is certainly illegal w.r.t. the document type of the intended result. It does so by a kind of abstract interpretation. This can be performed in linear time on the fly, when parsing an XSLT program. The usual deterministic parsing alternates with a non-deterministic mode, the defining automata for which are created *dynamically* on demand by two simple operations on relations.

The intended document type of the result must be given by a regular tree grammar. This is a map from the set of all labels allowed for nodes of the document tree to regular expressions over these labels, called *content models* in the context of XML. This defines the allowed sequences of child elements, when lifted from labels to elements. A W3C DTD is an example for such a regular tree grammar. It can also be constructed for the XSLT language itself.

The structure of an XSLT program and the corresponding parsing process divide into different *zones*, which fall in one of four categories:

1. **Pure XSLT**. The top of the document tree is an element defined by XSLT (namely `stylesheet`), and contains further XSLT elements.
2. **Embedded result sequences**. As contents of selected XSLT elements, sequences of result elements may appear.
3. **Result elements' contents**. The contents of result elements in most cases consist again of result elements only.
4. **XSLT elements in result elements' contents**. The contents of result elements may be interspered with further XSLT elements.

K. Duddy and G. Kappel (Eds.): ICMT 2013, LNCS 7909, pp. 54–55, 2013.
© Springer-Verlag Berlin Heidelberg 2013

The execution of an XSLT program will result in a document which is constructed by concatenating the contained result elements sequences, and by replacing the XSLT elements embedded therein by further evaluation results recursively. This motivates the basic idea of fragmented validation.

The two "pure" zones of the input document, XSLT or result elements only, can be parsed as usual, in a deterministic way: The content models of all elements of both languages are translated into one *deterministic finite automaton, DFA* each. Each DFA has, as usual, one start state, a set of accepting states, and transitions labeled with the tags of consumed child elements. By representing these DFAs as *relations between states*, our method becomes most easy to understand and to implement. Parsing is realized by applying this relation to a *set of states*, which is a singleton set in the two cases of deterministic parsing.

Whenever the zone "2" is entered and as soon as the first result element embedded as child of an XSLT element is consumed, *all those* states from *all* content models are put into the set of current states which are reachable by a transition labelled with that element's tag. So a non-deterministic parsing process starts, which realizes a kind of "reading at more than one grammar position simultanuously", because we do not know at which position of the result grammar this particular fragment will end up later, on execution. Nevertheless, *at least one such point* must exist for the program to be sensible. So parsing in this non-deterministic way must always be able to proceed for the whole XSLT element's contents, and an error is detected as soon as the set of current states becomes empty. (To reach an accepting state is *not* required, since the contents of the future result element may be completed correctly by some other XSLT rule. This context information is beyond the scope of fragmented validation!)

When the contents of a particular result element are parsed, this starts in a deterministic way, with the set of current states containing only the start state of the DFA, as usual. But as soon as an embedded, content generating XSLT element appears, the *transitive and reflexive closure* of the transition relation (ignoring all transition labels) is applied to this set. This is an abstract interpretation of the later execution, since we do not know *how many* of the following allowed result elements the later expansion of the inserted XSLT element will contribute. Parsing continues as usual. When parsing the closing tag of the containing result element, at least one accepting state of its content model must be contained in the set, otherwise again an error is detected.

This abstract interpretation is also applied in the previous case, so that both kinds of non-determinism combine naturally, whenever necessary.

This is the whole idea, and it turned out that it is capable of finding from fifty to hundred percent of the errors found by much more sophisticated validation techniques, when applied to acknowledged real-world test material.

Model Querying with FunnyQT
(Extended Abstract)

Tassilo Horn

Institute for Software Technology
University Koblenz-Landau, Germany
horn@uni-koblenz.de

FunnyQT is a new model querying and transformation approach. It is designed as an extensible API in the functional, JVM-based Lisp dialect Clojure. FunnyQT targets the modeling frameworks JGraLab and EMF, and it is extensible to other frameworks as well. Its querying parts are already stable while its transformation parts are still in early stages of development, so this paper focuses on the former.

Clojure API. FunnyQT is not a separate language with its own concrete syntax and semantics, but a Clojure API, i.e., FunnyQT queries are essentially Clojure expressions. Clojure's JVM-basing guarantees efficient and wrapper-free interoperability with existing Java libraries including almost all modeling frameworks. Clojure provides a large set of features including higher-order functions and control structures that can be used directly. Clojure programs also tend to be much more concise than equivalent programs in imperative languages. A first case study involving complex, parallelized FunnyQT queries on large models has been released as a whitepaper [2].

Modeling frameworks. FunnyQT is applicable to any modeling framework in principle, and support for EMF [5] and JGraLab [3] are already built-in. FunnyQT uses the framework-specific model representations, and there is no adaption layer unifying access to models and model elements. Instead, for any modeling framework, FunnyQT has a framework-specific core namespace providing functions for accessing models and model elements. These functions are named according to the terminology of the corresponding framework, and they expose all its characteristics. Built on top of these framework-specific APIs, there are generic APIs applicable to any supported modeling framework which provide various features discussed in the following.

Basic querying & model management. The basic querying API contains functions for sequencing the elements contained in a model, functions for accessing the attributes and referenced elements of a given model element, comprehensions, quantified expressions, and polymorphic functions dispatching on metamodel types. Combined with Clojure's standard functions and control structures, these parts of the FunnyQT API enable model querying similar to OCL. FunnyQT's model management facilities enable loading and storing of models and metamodels, creation and deletion of model elements, setting of property values, and visualization of models or extracts thereof. Combined with the basic querying API, these facilities enable typical model management tasks and algorithmic transformations similar to the Epsilon Object Language [4].

K. Duddy and G. Kappel (Eds.): ICMT 2013, LNCS 7909, pp. 56–57, 2013.

Regular path expressions. Regular path expressions (RPEs) are a very powerful querying concept borrowed from GReQL [1]. An RPE can be used to calculate the set of elements reachable from a given element by traversing a path specified by role names and typed edge symbols combined with regular path operators such as sequence, option, alternative, or transitive (reflexive) closure.

Pattern matching. FunnyQT also supports pattern matching using an internal DSL implemented with Clojure's metaprogramming facilities. A pattern is specified using a special FunnyQT macro and contains named and typed node and edge symbols specifying the structure of the subgraph to be matched. Furthermore, negative application conditions are supported, arbitrary constraints may be specified, and patterns may be composed of other patterns. At compile-time, the macro transforms such a pattern definition to an ordinary function. When being called, the function results in a lazy sequence of all matches in the queried model. The lazyness of the sequence means that the matches are not calculated until they are retrieved from the sequence one at a time. Thus, finding the first few matches is much cheaper than computing all matches.

Concludingly, FunnyQT at the current point in time provides a comprehensive approach to model querying and model management. Its core characteristics are its support for multiple modeling frameworks, its functional alignment as Clojure API, its extensibility, and the ability to exploit existing Clojure and Java libraries like demonstrated in [2], where Java's new *ForkJoin* library has been used to parallelize complex queries.

FunnyQT's basic querying API including the features inherited by its host language Clojure already enable an expressivity comparable to OCL or EOL, and its support for regular path expressions and pattern matching provide even more powerful querying capabilities.

In future work, FunnyQT will be extended to a comprehensive querying and transformation approach. A first preview on FunnyQT transformations can be experienced at this year's Transformation Tool Contest[1], where FunnyQT solutions have been submitted for all three case studies.

References

1. Ebert, J., Bildhauer, D.: Reverse Engineering Using Graph Queries. In: Engels, G., Lewerentz, C., Schäfer, W., Schürr, A., Westfechtel, B. (eds.) Nagl Festschrift. LNCS, vol. 5765, pp. 335–362. Springer, Heidelberg (2010)
2. Horn, T.: FunQL: A Functional Graph Query Language. Whitepaper (January 2012), http://www.uni-koblenz.de/~horn/funql-whitepaper.pdf
3. JGraLab Hompage (March 2013), http://jgralab.uni-koblenz.de
4. Kolovos, D., Rose, L., Paige, R.: The Epsilon Book (March 2013), http://www.eclipse.org/epsilon/doc/book/
5. Steinberg, D., Budinsky, F., Paternostro, M., Merks, E.: EMF: Eclipse Modeling Framework, 2nd edn. Addison-Wesley Professional (2008)

Yet Another Three QVT Languages

Edward Willink[1], Horaçio Hoyos[2], and Dimitris Kolovos[2]

[1] Willink Transformations Ltd., Reading, UK
ed@willinktransformations.co.uk
[2] The University of York, York, UK,
horacio.hoyos.rodriguez@ieee.org, dimitris.kolovos@york.ac.uk

The early enthusiasm, in 2002, for model to model transformation languages led to eight submissions for an OMG standard[1] comprising three languages, yet no commercial products. The QVT Core language was intended as the foundation for QVT Relations but the available implementations have ignored the core language. Rather than ignoring the core language, we take the opposite approach and introduce three more core languages. Progressive program-to-program transformation through these core languages terminates in an easily implemented imperative language that supports declarative transformations.

There are currently only two freely available but discouragingly stable implementations of QVTr. There are no implementations for QVTc. The Eclipse QVT Declarative project provides only models, editors and parsers for both QVTr and QVTc. We outline progress to remedy the execution deficiency.

The original work for Eclipse QVTd execution considered only QVTr and confirmed that direct tooling of a complex declarative language such as QVTr is rather hard. Three years ago, the direct approach was abandoned and the progressive approach shown in the Figure was first posted on the web. Work on this approach has at last started.

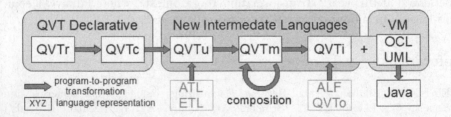

At the left we have the two QVT Declarative languages, with QVTr realized by a QVTr to QVTc program-to-program transformation. Our three new languages, QVTu, QVTm and QVTi are syntactic and semantic simplifications of QVTc. QVTi is realized by extending the OCL support of Eclipse OCL. This enables the Xtext editing, OCL and UML model support and the OCL to Java code generator to be exploited.

The utility of the new languages and the program to program transformations are summarized below.

K. Duddy and G. Kappel (Eds.): ICMT 2013, LNCS 7909, pp. 58–59, 2013.

QVTc to QVTu (Unidirectional). The QVTc transformation is aligned to the user's invocation context to extract a uni-directional declarative representation.

- the redundant multi-directionality and enforcement modes are eliminated.

QVTu to QVTm (Minimal). The QVTu transformation is normalized to give as simple and as uniform a declarative representation as possible.

- syntactic sugar is removed
- representation alternatives are normalized

QVTm to QVTi (Imperative). A practical multi-pass implementation is synthesized that can be easily executed on a model-friendly Virtual Machine.

- a reconciler is synthesized if an update transformation is required
- a pattern matching schedule serializes declarative input matches
- a pattern generation schedule serializes declarative output updates

QVTc differs from other transformation languages in requiring traceability to be made explicit in an additional middle metamodel. QVTi exploits the middle model to provide a convenient buffer between the reconciliation, input matching and output update passes. The reconciliation for an update transformation populates the middle model with the pre-existing matches. An in-place transformation ensures that all input context is cached in the middle model before any potentially conflicting output updates are made. A solution to these complexities is prepared at compile time, and expressed in QVTi, so that the run-time execution is naive and efficient.

These new languages are not just a convenience for realizing QVTc, they also offer important interchange points for other transformation technologies to exploit and so share the tool chain.

- QVTu provides a high level interchange point for other uni-directional declarative transformation languages such as ATL or ETL.
- QVTm provides a normalized representation at which declarative transformation composition and optimisation can be applied.
- QVTi provides a low level interchange point that imperative transformation languages such as QVTo, ALF or EOL may exploit.

The extension of Eclipse OCL VM[2] to support execution of QVTi proved to be surprisingly easy. Some simple transformations have confirmed how simple QVTi can be. It is now only necessary to develop the QVTr to QVTc to QVTu to QVTm to QVTi program transformation chain.

References

1. OMG: Meta Object Facility (MOF) 2.0 Query/View/Transformation Specification. version 1.1 (January 2011), http://www.omg.org/spec/QVT/1.1/
2. Willink, E.D.: An extensible ocl virtual machine and code generator. In: Proceedings of the 12th Workshop on OCL and Textual Modelling, OCL 2012, pp. 13–18. ACM (2012)

A Methodological Approach for the Coupled Evolution of Metamodels and ATL Transformations

Davide Di Ruscio, Ludovico Iovino, and Alfonso Pierantonio

Department of Information Engineering,
Computer Science and Mathematics University of L'Aquila
{davide.diruscio,ludovico.iovino,alfonso.pierantonio}@univaq.it

Abstract. Model-Driven Engineering is a software discipline that relies on (meta) models as first class entities and that aims to develop, maintain and evolve software by exploiting model transformations. Analogously to software, metamodels are subject to evolutionary pressures which might compromise a wide range of artefacts including transformations. In contrast with the problem of metamodel/model co-evolution, the problem of adapting model transformations according to the changes operated on the corresponding metamodels is to a great extent unexplored. This is largely due to its intricacy but also to the difficulty in having a mature process which on one hand is able to evaluate the cost and benefits of adaptations, and on the other hand ensures that consistent methods are used to maintain quality and design integrity during the adaptation. This paper proposes a methodological approach to the coupled evolution of ATL transformations aiming at evaluating its sustainability prior to any adaptation step based on the assessment of change impact significance.

1 Introduction

Model-driven engineering (MDE) is a software discipline that employs models for describing problems in an application domain by means of metamodels. Different abstraction levels are bridged together by automated transformations which permit source models to be mapped to target models. These artifacts and the interrelationships among them constitute an ecosystem at whose core there are metamodels [4]. Since evolution in software is anything but a rare occurrence [12], it can affect metamodels as well [19] causing a ripple effect over the rest of the ecosystem. However, whenever a metamodel undergoes modifications, it is of vital relevance that the impact of such changes is fully understood prior initiating their propagation: regardless how urgent the motivations for changing a metamodel are, underestimating the difficulties in restoring the consistency in the ecosystem can lead to an impasse, in which no progress can be made [6].

The problem of metamodel/model coupled evolution[1] has been already extensively investigated (e.g., see [6,2,16,8,10]). The existing approaches provide tools and techniques to define and apply migration strategies able to take models conforming to the original metamodel and to produce models conforming to the evolved metamodel. On the contrary, despite its relevance the metamodel/transformation co-evolution problem

---

[1] Throughout this paper we will use the terms *coupled evolution*, *co-evolution* and *co-adaptation* as synonyms whenever it does not give place to misinterpretations.

K. Duddy and G. Kappel (Eds.): ICMT 2013, LNCS 7909, pp. 60–75, 2013.
© Springer-Verlag Berlin Heidelberg 2013

is still open and requires further investigations. In fact, adapting transformations does not only take into account the *domain conformance* [14] between the definition of a transformation and its metamodels but must consider also the intelligence used by the transformation for generating the target model elements. Very few attempts have been made so far and generally they tend to re-apply the same techniques used for the metamodel/model co-evolution, as in [13] where higher-order transformations (HOTs) are used to migrate, whenever possible, existing transformations according to occurred metamodel changes. Thus, only the most obvious cases, such as renamings and deletions, are covered leaving the responsibility of managing the most complex ones to the modeler who typically face the problem with individual and spontaneous skills. This is largely due to the intricacies of the problem but also to the lack of a mature process which on one hand is able to evaluate the cost and benefits of adaptations, and on the other hand ensures that consistent methods are used to maintain quality and design integrity during the adaptation.

This paper proposes a comprehensive and methodological approach to the coupled evolution of ATL transformations. As with many engineering activity, measurement is crucial in order to assess at early stages of a process the sustainability of the costs versus the benefits. Therefore, a process is proposed for the systematic co-evolution of artifacts and which includes the following activities: *i)* establishing the dependencies between a transformation and its (source) metamodel; *ii)* evaluating the cost of the adaptation; *iii)* deciding whether it is sustainable or not by eventually reconsidering certain decisions; and finally *iv)* if the assessment has a positive outcome the impacted transformation is adapted. The main contribution of the paper is to define a methodology in which an early assessment of the impact cost and significance is conducted and which can provide the modeler with the right tools and techniques for addressing a complex problem in a more disciplined way.

The structure of the paper is as follows: In Section 2, we discuss an example which motivates the metamodel/transformation coupled evolution problem. In Section 3 we discuss a classification of metamodel changes according to their impact on the existing transformations. The proposed process for the systematic co-evolution of metamodels and ATL transformations is described in Section 4. Related work is described in Section 5, and the paper is concluded in Section 6.

2   Motivating Scenario

In MDE model transformations play a key role since they are able to generate target models starting from source ones according to transformation rules, which are defined with respect to source and target metamodels. For instance, Listing 1.1 shows an ATL transformation able to transform models conforming to the PetriNet metamodel reported in Figure 1.a, and to generate Petri Net Markup Language (PNML) [1] models conforming to the metamodel in Figure 2.

According to the metamodel in Figure 1.a a `PetriNetModel` mainly consists of `Places` and `Transitions` which are contained in the `Net` element. Concerning the metamodel in Figure 2, the metaclass `PNMLDocument` represents the root element which is composed of Petri nets specified by means of `NetElement` instances. A Petri net is composed of `NetContent` elements which are distinguished into `Arc`, `Place`, and `Transition`. Net elements and net contents can have a `Name`, which is a `Labeled Element` composed of `Labels`.

Listing 1.1. Fragment of the *PetriNet2PNML* ATL transformation

```
1 helper context PetriNetMM0!Transition def: createArcsSrc(parent:PNML!NetElement):
    PNML!Arc=
2 self.src->iterate(e; res : PNML!Arc=OclUndefined| thisModule.createArcSrc(e,
    parent,self));
3 helper context PetriNetMM0!Transition def: createArcsTrs(parent:PNML!NetElement):
    PNML!Arc=
4 self.dst->iterate(e; res : PNML!Arc=OclUndefined | thisModule.createArcTrs(self,
    parent,e));
5 rule Net {
6 from s: PetriNetMM0!Net
7 to t: PNML!NetElement   (
8       name<-s.name,
9       contents <- s.places.union(s.transitions),
10      id<-s.name
11      ),
12 ...}
13 rule Place {
14 from s: PetriNetMM0!Place(s.oclIsTypeOf(PetriNetMM0!Place))
15 to t: PNML!Place(
16   name <- name,
17   id <- s.name+'_src:'+s.src.size().toString()+'_dst:'+ s.dst.size().toString()),
18 ...}
19 rule Transition {
20 from s: PetriNetMM0!Transition
21 to t: PNML!Transition(
22   name <- s.name,
23   id <- s.name+'_dst:'+s.dst.size().toString()),
24     ...
25 do{
26 s.createArcsSrc(t.net);
27 s.createArcsTrs(t.net);
28 }}...
```

The transformation shown in Listing 1.1 is a revised version of the one available in the ATL Transformation Zoo[2] and consists of the following rules:

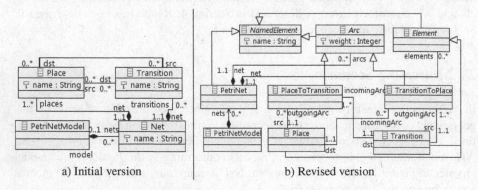

a) Initial version   b) Revised version

Fig. 1. Different versions of the source PetriNet metamodel

---

[2] http://www.eclipse.org/m2m/atl/atlTransformations/

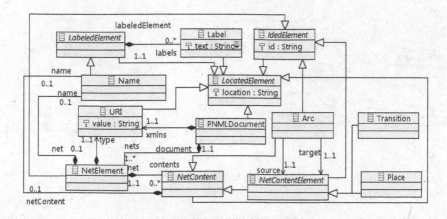

Fig. 2. Target PNML metamodel

▷ *Net* generates a target `NetElement` for each instance of the source `Net` metaclass. The name of the generated `NetElement` is the same of the source `Net`. Moreover, the content of the target `NetElement` consists of the union of the `place` and `transition` elements contained in the source Petri net model (see lines 7-11 in Listing 1.1). Figure 4 shows the PNML model (represented as an object diagram) automatically generated from the PetriNet model in Figure 3. The instance `netElement1` in Figure 4 has been generated by the *Net* rule from the source `net1` element in Figure 3. Interestingly, the content of the target `NetElement` consists of the union of the target elements corresponding to the source places and transitions;

▷ *Place* generates a target `Place` element for each place in the source model. The name of the generated element is the same as the source. Moreover, the value of the target attribute `id` is a string concatenation which considers the number of the incoming and outgoing transitions of the input `Place` (see lines 15-18 in Listing 1.1). For instance, the `id` value of the place `p2` in Figure 4 is `p2_src:1_dst:0` since the source place has only one incoming transition and no outgoing transitions;

▷ *Transition* generates a `Transition` element for each transition in the source model. The value of the `id` attribute maintains the number of destination places of the considered transition as the sample transition `t1` in Figure 4 (see lines 21-23 in Listing 1.1). The generation of target `Arc` elements is performed by means of the helpers

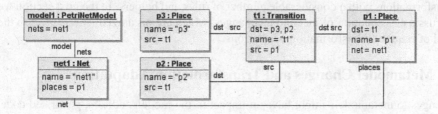

Fig. 3. Sample PetriNet model

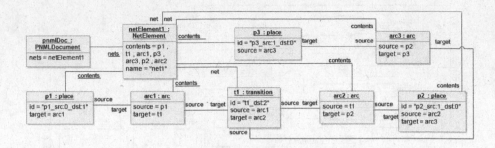

Fig. 4. Sample PNML model

createArcsSrc and createArcsTrs which are executed in the action block of the *Transition* rule (see lines 25-28 in Listing 1.1).

Let us consider the exemplar PetriNet metamodel evolution [19] by refining the metamodel in Figure 1.a to obtain the new version shown in Figure 1.b. The new version of the metamodel has been produced by operating a number of changes, such as:

1. the TransitionToPlace and PlaceToTransition metaclasses have been added;
2. the new metaclass Arc has been added as a superclass of the TransitionToPlace and PlaceToTransition metaclasses;
3. the metaclass Net has been renamed as PetriNet;
4. the old references places and transitions in the old Net metaclass have been merged in the elements reference of the new PetriNet metaclass.

Because of the operated modifications, the existing ATL transformations relying on the first version of the PetriNet metamodel can require some adaptations. For instance, in the case of the sample *PetriNet2PNML* transformation in Listing 1.1, the rule *Net* has to be adapted since the references places and transitions used in the binding of the property contents (see line 9 in Listing 1.1) do not exist in the new version of the metamodel. Also, the input pattern of the same rule has to be changed since the metaclass Net is not available because of the renaming modification operated on it to obtain the new metaclass PetriNet. In general, manually adapting ATL transformations is error-prone and can give place to inconsistencies. Moreover, it is very difficult to realize all the parts of the transformation which are potentially affected by the metamodel modifications. Such an issue becomes very relevant when dealing with complex ATL transformations with a considerable number of rules and helpers. In the next section we discuss a classification of metamodel changes, which are organized with respect to the kind of required transformation adaptations.

3   Metamodel Changes and Transformation Adaptations

Changes to metamodels might have an impact to the models, editors, generated code, and model transformations that depend on the aforementioned metamodels. Concerning model transformations, because of changes to a given metamodel, transformation inconsistencies can occur and are those elements in the transformation, which do not longer satisfy the *domain conformance* [14]. For instance, a sample domain conformance constraint might state that the source elements of every transformation rule must correspond to a metaclass in the source metamodel [15]. Consequently, when a concept is removed from a metamodel, existing transformations that use the removed concept are no longer domain conformant with the evolved metamodel. Hereafter, we say that a metamodel change *affects* a transformation when there are some transformation elements, which do not longer satisfy the domain conformance with the new metamodel.

In this section we investigate the problem by discussing some typical metamodel changes together with the corresponding co-changes of already existing ATL transformations. We depart from catalogues of metamodel changes as they are available in the literature, e.g., [19,10] and previous work of the authors [2,5]. Moreover, we take into account also the terminology proposed in [13] to classify metamodel changes. In particular, according to [13], in the case of metamodel/transformation co-evolution, metamodel changes can be classified as follows:

- *fully automated*, when they affect existing transformations which can be automatically migrated without user intervention;
- *partially automated*, when they affect existing transformations which can be adapted automatically even though some manual fine-tuning is required to complete the adaptation;
- *fully semantic*, when they affect transformations which cannot be automatically migrated, and the user has to completely define the adaptation.

To better comprehend such a classification, in the following we discuss three metamodel changes, one representative for each category in the previous classification. The interested reader can refer to [2] and to the material available on-line[3] for an extensive catalogue of metamodel changes and their effects on corresponding artifacts.

Rename metaelement. There are changes which can be automatically managed without user intervention. This is the case of metaelement renaming, where transformations can be fully adapted by simply replacing all the occurrences of the old metaelement with the new one. For instance, the input pattern of the adapted Net rule shown in Listing 1.2 has been obtained by replacing Net with PetriNet (see line 3) according to the renaming change operated on the source Net metaclass.

Listing 1.2. Fragment of the *Net* rule which has been adapted after the *rename metaelement* and *merge references* changes

```
1 rule Net {
2   from
3     s : PetriNetMM0!PetriNet --Warning: element Net has been changed !
4   to
5     t : PNML!NetElement (
6       name <- name,
7       document <- thisModule.document,
8       contents <- s.elements->select(e | e.oclIsKindOf(PetriNetMM0!Place)).union(s'
                .elements->select(e | e.oclIsKindOf(PetriNetMM0!Transition))),
9       ...
10    ),
```

---

[3] http://www.metamodelrefactoring.org/

Merge references. Given an existing metamodel, existing references can be merged by giving place to a new one. For instance, in the new version of the PetriNet metamodel shown in Figure 1.b, the references `places` and `transitions` in the metaclass `Net` have been merged in the new reference `elements` having the new metaclass `Element` as type. `Element` is also the superclass of `Place` and `Transition` metaclasses. In this case, a default migration policy can be adopted by changing the occurrences of the merged references as reported in the adapted version of the `Net` rule shown in Listing 1.2. In particular, each occurrence of the references `places` and `transitions` is replaced with a `select` statement to filter `Place` and `Transition` instances on the new `elements` reference (see line 8 in Listing 1.2).

Add metaclass. According to [13] this modification is fully semantic since it is impossible to derive new transformation rules from new metaclasses, without any information about how the added elements should be automatically manipulated. However, we believe that in these cases, some default actions can be undertaken, then the user can refine or amend them. For instance, whenever a new metaclass is added, the considered ATL transformation can be migrated by adding a new transformation rule having the added metaclass as a source input pattern. Then, the user can refine such a rule by implementing the target pattern. For example, because of the addition of the metaclasses `TransitionToPlace` in the initial PetriNet metamodel in Figure 1.a, the matched rule in Listing 1.3 can be added to the transformation shown in Listing 1.1.

Listing 1.3. New transformation rule to manage the addition of the *TransitionToPlace* metaclass

```
1 --@Rule for TransitionToPlace added subclass
2 rule TransitionToPlace {
3   from
4     s_TransitionToPlace : PetriNetMM0!TransitionToPlace ( s_TransitionToPlace.
          oclIsTypeOf(PetriNetMM0!TransitionToPlace) )
5   to
6     -- t_TransitionToPlace : PNML!"Type your matching element name"
7 }
```

According to the discussion above, the metamodel/transformation co-evolution problem is complex especially because in most of the cases transformations can be adapted in different manners and user intervention is required. Existing approaches, like [13,14] introduce techniques mainly to support fully automated changes. However, adaptations are performed by means of individual and spontaneous skills without adhering to a well-established process, which beyond the actual adaptation activities would include also an evaluation of the cost and benefits of the changes to be operated.

4   Adaptation of ATL Transformations

In this section we propose a methodology for supporting the adaptation of ATL transformations according to the changes operated on the corresponding metamodels. The methodology consists of a number of activities that encompass the specification of the metamodel changes, the evaluation of their impact on the existing artifacts, the sustainability of the induced adaptations, and the actual migrations of the affected artifacts. For each activity, supporting techniques that can be employed are mentioned, and more space is devoted to the cost evaluation of the required adaptations (Section 4.2), and to their concrete application (Section 4.3).

4.1 Overview of the Methodology Activities

The activities of the proposed methodology are shown in Figure 5 and detailed in the rest of the section.

Relation Definition. This activity is independent from the specific metamodel evolution and the affected transformations, thus it is performed once forever as long as both the transformation language and the metamodeling language do not evolve. In particular, in this activity the ATL and the ECore metamodels are considered in order to establish correspondences between them. Such correspondences are used later in the process to automatically derive the dependencies between an evolving metamodel and the existing transformations. This activity can be done by using the work in [11] that exploits weaving models and megamodels to specify and manipulate correspondences among related and evolving artifacts. The upper side of Figure 6 shows a sample weaving model (as defined in [11]), which specifies the relation between the ECore metaclass EClass and the ATL metaclass OclModelElement.

Dependencies Elicitation. Given the correspondences defined in the previous activity, it is possible to automatically derive a weaving model representing all the dependencies between the evolving metamodel, and the existing ATL transformations. The lower side of Figure 6 shows the dependencies between the metaclasses of the PetriNet metamodel and the elements of a given ATL transformation having it as source metamodel. For instance, the first rule of the transformation shown on the right-hand side of Figure 6 contains an OclModelElement named *Net*, thus it is connected with the EClass element similarly named on the left-hand side of the figure. Such a dependency link specifies that changing the name of the Net metaclass in the PetriNet metamodel implies to propagate such a change to each OclModelElement linked to it.

Metamodel Changes Specification. The changes that modeler wants to operate on a given metamodel should be properly represented in order to enable automatic manipu-

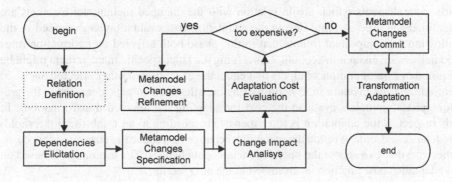

Fig. 5. Methodology activities

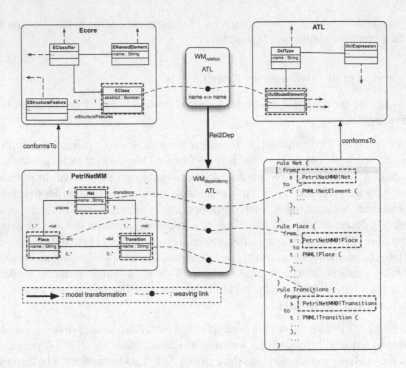

Fig. 6. Relation Definition and Dependencies Elicitation

lations and the subsequent phases of the process. For instance, in this phase it is possible to adopt the metamodel independent approach to difference representation proposed in [3] already used to deal with other coupled evolution problems (e.g., adaptation of models [2], and GMF editors [5]).

Change Impact Analysis. In general, change impact analysis can be considered as the activity of detecting which modeling artifacts within the metamodeling ecosystem are impacted by a change made in the evolving metamodel. In the specific case of ATL model transformations, according to the dependencies previously elicited, all the transformation elements which are in relation with the changed metamodel elements are identified and used as input during the adaptation cost evaluation as discussed in the following. It is important to note that in this phase both affected transformation rules and helpers are taken into account. Concerning the latter specific management might be required in case of complex helpers that entail the execution of other affected ones.

Adaptation Cost Evaluation. By considering the affected elements identified in the previous phase, modelers evaluate the cost for adapting the affected transformations. In this respect, if the adaptation is too expensive (according to an established threshold) modelers can decide to refine the metamodel changes to reduce the corresponding costs, otherwise they can accept the operated metamodel changes. The evaluation is based on an adaptation cost function as discussed in the next section.

Metamodel Changes Commit. Once the metamodel changes have been evaluated, modelers can commit them in order to concretely apply the previously evaluated transformation adaptations.

Transformation Adaptation. In this phase the existing transformations which have been affected by the committed metamodel changes are adapted. Proper tools are required to support this step. Over the last years different approaches have been proposed to support the coupled evolution of metamodels and related artifacts. In Section 4.3 we show how EMFMigrate [4] can be used as possible supporting tool in this phase.

4.2 Evaluating the Adaptation Cost of Model Transformations

Proper cost functions have to be considered to evaluate the sustainability of adapting existing transformations. The cost related to the adaptation cannot be uniquely defined since it depends on many factors, e.g., the application domain, the stage of the considered development process, and the execution environment. In this section we present a possible adaptation cost function, and show an explanatory example about how it can influence the choice of the metamodel changes to be operated.

Definition 1. *(Adaptation Cost) Let $\Delta = \{\delta_1, \delta_2, ..., \delta_n\}$ be a difference model conforming to the difference metamodel DM and consisting of metamodel changes δ_i as in the catalogue in [2]. The cost of adapting ATL transformations affected by the metamodel changes in Δ is the function $c : DM \to \mathbb{N}$ defined as*

$$c(\Delta) = c_{env} + \sum_{i=1}^{n} k_i w(\delta_i)$$

where $c_{env} \in \mathbb{N}$ is the cost for setting up the used adaptation environment, k_i is the number of transformation elements which are affected by δ_i (as discovered in the change impact analysis activity) and

$$w(\delta_i) = \begin{cases} c_a & \text{if } \delta_i \text{ is automated} \\ c_{pa} & \text{if } \delta_i \text{ is partially automated} \\ c_{fs} & \text{if } \delta_i \text{ is fully semantic} \end{cases} \tag{1}$$

where $c_a, c_{pa}, c_{fs} \in \mathbb{N}$ are the costs of automated, partially automated, and fully semantic adaptations, respectively.

To discuss a simple application of the previous adaptation cost function, let us consider the situation in Figure 7. It consists of a simple metamodel, and an endogenous ATL transformation, which creates a copy of models conforming to the shown metamodel. For some reason, let us assume that the modeler wants to refine the metamodel by renaming all the occurrences of the attributes name as id (see the left-hand side of Figure 8). Even though this is a simple modification, it has some impact on the ATL transformation. According to the previous adaptation cost function, since the modification is fully automated, the cost of the adaptation is $c_{env} + 5 \times c_a$ and corresponds to the cost for operating the changes highlighted in the right-hand side of Figure 8 (i.e., all the bindings name <- s.name have to be replaced by id <- s.id).

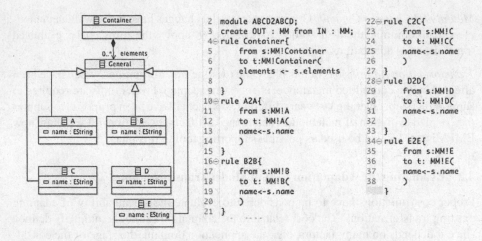

Fig. 7. Simple metamodel and endogenous ATL transformation

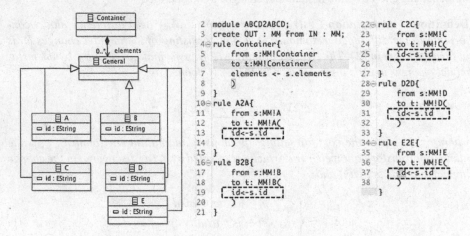

Fig. 8. First proposed metamodel refactoring and corresponding adaptation

As it is possible to notice, the metamodel in Figure 8 can be enhanced by adding a superclass for the metaclasses A, B, C, D, and E, in order to pull-up the attribute id as shown in Figure 9. Even though the resulting metamodel is more well-designed than the metamodel in Figure 8, the consequent transformation adaptation cost is higher than the previous one. In fact, by considering the cost function previously defined, adapting the transformation would cost $c_{env} + 7 \times c_a$, corresponding to the addition of an abstract rule for managing the new superclass, and the changes to be operated on the existing transformation rules (see the right-hand side of Figure 9). It is important to note that such a transformation adaptation is one of possible ones that can be selected from a library of adaptations (and in case manually refined) as discussed in Section 4.3. Even tough this is a simplified case, it permits to show how in some cases, modelers have to make a trade-off by accepting less elegant metamodel changes while reducing the

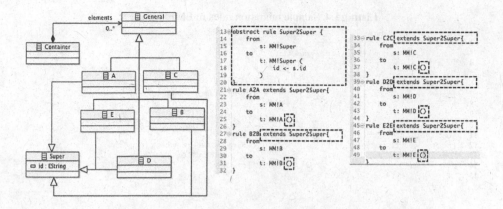

Fig. 9. Second proposed metamodel refactoring and corresponding adaptation

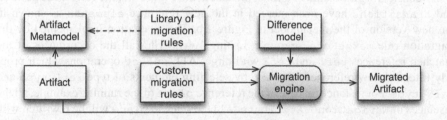

Fig. 10. Overview of EMFMigrate

impact on existing transformations. This aspect is more evident in cases of complex transformations, which have been already tested and validated. In such situations, it might have sense performing metamodel changes, which do not require a complete re-validation of the new transformations. Informally, we can say that we are talking about optimization problems whose solutions depend on a number of contrasting factors, most importantly the expressiveness of the resulting metamodels against the impact on the affected transformations.

4.3   Transformation Adaptation with EMFMigrate

In this section we propose the adoption of EMFMigrate as a possible tool supporting the last step of the methodology proposed in Section 4.1. EMFMigrate permits to specify, customize, and apply migrations of any kind of artifact, which has been affected by changes operated on the corresponding metamodel. Thus, we show how it is possible to employ EMFMigrate to adapt ATL transformations. The overall architecture of the approach is shown in Figure 10. EMFMigrate permits to specify default adaptations, and collect them in *libraries*. The idea is having one library for each kind of artifacts. Adaptations are applied with respect to the occurred metamodel changes, properly represented by means of a difference model. The default migrations can be

Listing 1.4. Sample migration rules in EMFMigrate

```
1 rule mergeReferences
2  [
3    mergeReferences(ref1,ref2,newName)
4  ]
5 {
6  <NavigationOrAttributeCallExp s>
7  [name == ref1.name]              ->   [[%{newName}->select(e |
8                                          e.oclIsKindOf(%{ref1.type}))
9                                          ]];
10
11  <NavigationOrAttributeCallExp s>
12  [name == ref2.name]              ->   [[%{newName}->select(e |
13                                          e.oclIsKindOf(%{ref2.type}))
14                                          ]];
15 ...}
```

extended or even amended by users which can specify *custom migration rules* to refine or replace default transformation adaptations.

By considering the sample PetriNet metamodel in Figure 1.a, the references `places` and `transitions` have been merged in the new reference `elements` as shown in the new version of the metamodel in Figure 1.b. The adaptation implemented by the migration rule `mergeReferences` in Listing 1.4 rewrites all the occurrences of the matched references `ref1` and `ref2` with target ATL `select` operations which properly filter the new reference `newName` by selecting elements of type `ref1.type` and `ref2.type`. For instance, in case of the reference `place` of the running example, all the instances of `NavigationOrAttributeCallExp` named `place` will be rewritten with `elements->select(e | e.oclIsKindOf(Place))` (see lines 6-14 in Listing 1.4). It is important to recall that `NavigationOrAttributeCallExp` is the metaclass of the ATL metamodel which is used to refer to structural features of a given element. For instance, on the right-hand side of Figure 11, there are two `NavigationOrAttribute CallExp` instances since the references `places`, and `transitions` of the source metaclass `Net` are used to set the value of the target `contents` reference.

To simplify the specification or rewriting rules, EMFMigrate permits to specify terms by using the concrete syntax of ATL between the symbols "`[[`" and "`]]`", instead of its abstract syntax (see the right-hand side of the rewriting rules in Listing 1.4).

As said in Section 3, there are metamodel changes that require the intervention of the users since it is not possible to fully automate the migration of the affected transformations. However, in such situations it is possible to implement default migration policies which can be refined/completed or even fully replaced by the user. Interested readers can refer to [6,4,20] for a more detailed presentation of EMFMigrate and its comparison with related approaches.

5   Related Work

The techniques and the methodology of our work are inspired by research on co-evolution in model-driven engineering [7]. Much of this work is concerned with co-transforming models in reply to metamodel changes [19,16,2,10].

In this work we deal with another kind of co-evolution problem, even though related to the previous one, which concerns the adaptation of ATL transformations that

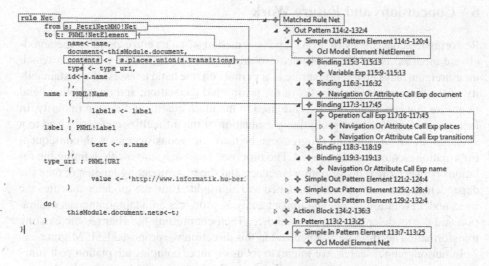

```
rule Net {
    from s: PetriNetMMO!Net
    to  t: PNML!NetElement  {
        name<-name,
        document<-thisModule.document,
        contents <-  s.places.union(s.transitions),
        type <- type_uri,
        id<-s.name
        ),
    name : PNML!Name
        (
            labels <- label
        ),
    label : PNML!Label
        (
            text <- s.name
        ),
    type_uri : PNML!URI
        (
            value <- 'http://www.informatik.hu-ber:
        )

    do{
        thisModule.document.nets<-t;
    }
}|
```

- Matched Rule Net
  - ◆ Out Pattern 114:2-132:4
    - ◆ Simple Out Pattern Element 114:5-120:4
      - ◆ Ocl Model Element NetElement
      - ◆ Binding 115:3-115:13
        - ◆ Variable Exp 115:9-115:13
      - ◆ Binding 116:3-116:32
        - ◆ Navigation Or Attribute Call Exp document
      - ◆ Binding 117:3-117:45
        - ◆ Operation Call Exp 117:16-117:45
          - ◆ Navigation Or Attribute Call Exp places
          - ◆ Navigation Or Attribute Call Exp transitions
      - ◆ Binding 118:3-118:19
      - ◆ Binding 119:3-119:13
        - ◆ Navigation Or Attribute Call Exp name
    - ◆ Simple Out Pattern Element 121:2-124:4
    - ◆ Simple Out Pattern Element 125:2-128:4
    - ◆ Simple Out Pattern Element 129:2-132:4
  - ◆ Action Block 134:2-136:3
  - ◆ In Pattern 113:2-113:25
    - ◆ Simple In Pattern Element 113:7-113:25
      - ◆ Ocl Model Element Net

Fig. 11. Sample ATL transformation rule and its abstract syntax

have been affected by metamodel changes. Only recently, the problem of metamodel evolution/transformation adaptation has gained attention and so far, only few attempts have been provided to deal with it in a dedicated way [13,9,14]. In [13] the authors propose HOTs which are able to support the adaptation of existing transformations developed in the GME/GReAT toolset. The approach is able to automate certain parts of the evolution and when automation is not possible, their algorithms automatically alert the user about the missing information, which can then be provided manually after the automatic part of the interpreter evolution. The process proposed in [9] is divided in two main stages: the detection stage, where the changes to the metamodel are detected and classified, while the required actions for each type of change are performed at the co-evolution stage. Our approach permits to specify ATL migrations by means of constructs which are easier than specifying HOTs. Moreover, a dedicated support is also provided to develop customizations in an integrated manner. In [14] the authors investigate the problem of metamodel/transformation co-evolution and introduce the *domain conformance* as the relation between occurring between metamodels and transformations. Even though the authors propose an adaptation process consisting of three phases (impact detection, impact analysis, and transformation adaptation) the cost related to the adaptations (as shown in this paper) are completely neglected.

In [17] the authors propose a change impact analysis for Object-Oriented programs. The authors provide feedback on the semantic impact of a set of program changes. This analysis is used to determine the existing test programs affected by a set of changes. Similarly to our approach, the authors consider of crucial relevance the activity of analyzing the change impact even though they do not propose a measure for the adaptation cost, which has to be considered to evaluate if the changes have to be actually performed. In [18] Vignaga presents a set of metrics which make ATL transformations measurable, and enables assessing their quality. Such metrics can be used in our approach to extend the adaptation cost function in order to take into account also quality aspects of the transformations during their adaptation.

6 Conclusions and Future Work

Restoring the consistency of an ATL transformation when its corresponding metamodels are modified is a difficult problem. In this paper, we proposed a process in which measurement plays an important role as it permits on one hand to assess the sustainability of the costs versus the benefits of the prospected adaptation; and on the other hand to ensure that consistent methods are used to maintain quality and design integrity. In fact, proceeding without a preliminary evaluation of the difficulties can easily lead to a situation, in which either no progress can be made or inconsistencies with consequent information erosion are introduced. The proposed approach starts with defining the relations between the transformation language and the metamodeling language; then the dependencies are automatically obtained and highlighted and the modeler specifies the metamodel evolution. A change impact analysis produces an adaptation costs evaluation and the modeler has to make a choice. Then committing the changes the existing transformation needs to be adapted and in this direction we proposed EMFMigrate.

In our ongoing research, we intend to focus on more complex adaptation cost functions in order to take into account all the possible aspects which are involved in the adaptation process. The function proposed in this paper, even though simplified, is a starting point to formalize the problem as a multi-objective optimization since different objective functions have to be optimized simultaneously. For instance, as shown in the paper, typically modelers want to maximize the expressive power of the evolving metamodels and minimize the cost related to the adaptation of the affected transformations.

References

1. Billington, J., Christensen, S., van Hee, K.M., Kindler, E., Kummer, O., Petrucci, L., Post, R., Stehno, C., Weber, M.: The Petri Net Markup Language: Concepts, Technology, and Tools. In: van der Aalst, W.M.P., Best, E. (eds.) ICATPN 2003. LNCS, vol. 2679, pp. 483–505. Springer, Heidelberg (2003)
2. Cicchetti, A., Di Ruscio, D., Eramo, R., Pierantonio, A.: Automating co-evolution in model-driven engineering. In: Procs. ECOC 2008, pp. 222–231. IEEE Computer Society (2008)
3. Cicchetti, A., Di Ruscio, D., Pierantonio, A.: A Metamodel Independent Approach to Difference Representation. Journal of Object Technology 6(9), 165–185 (2007)
4. Di Ruscio, D., Iovino, L., Pierantonio, A.: Evolutionary togetherness: How to manage coupled evolution in metamodeling ecosystems. In: Ehrig, H., Engels, G., Kreowski, H.-J., Rozenberg, G. (eds.) ICGT 2012. LNCS, vol. 7562, pp. 20–37. Springer, Heidelberg (2012)
5. Di Ruscio, D., Lämmel, R., Pierantonio, A.: Automated co-evolution of GMF editor models. In: Malloy, B., Staab, S., van den Brand, M. (eds.) SLE 2010. LNCS, vol. 6563, pp. 143–162. Springer, Heidelberg (2011)
6. Di Ruscio, D., Iovino, L., Pierantonio, A.: Coupled evolution in model-driven engineering. IEEE Software 29(6), 78–84 (2012)
7. Favre, J.-M.: Meta-Model and Model Co-evolution within the 3D Software Space. In: Procs. of ELISA 2003, Amsterdam (September 2003)
8. Garcés, K., Jouault, F., Cointe, P., Bézivin, J.: Managing model adaptation by precise detection of metamodel changes. In: Paige, R.F., Hartman, A., Rensink, A. (eds.) ECMDA-FA 2009. LNCS, vol. 5562, pp. 34–49. Springer, Heidelberg (2009)

9. García, J., Diaz, O., Azanza, M.: Model transformation co-evolution: A semi-automatic approach. In: Czarnecki, K., Hedin, G. (eds.) SLE 2012. LNCS, vol. 7745, pp. 144–163. Springer, Heidelberg (2013)

10. Herrmannsdoerfer, M., Benz, S., Juergens, E.: Cope - automating coupled evolution of metamodels and models, pp. 52–76 (2009)

11. Iovino, L., Pierantonio, A., Malavolta, I.: On the impact significance of metamodel evolution in mde. Journal of Object Technology 11(3), 1–33 (2012)

12. Lehman, M.M., Belady, L.A. (eds.): Program evolution: processes of software change. Academic Press Professional, Inc., San Diego (1985)

13. Levendovszky, T., Balasubramanian, D., Narayanan, A., Karsai, G.: A novel approach to semi-automated evolution of DSML model transformation. In: van den Brand, M., Gašević, D., Gray, J. (eds.) SLE 2009. LNCS, vol. 5969, pp. 23–41. Springer, Heidelberg (2010)

14. D. Méndez, A. Etien, A. Muller, and R. Casallas. Transformation migration after metamodel evolution. In *International Workshop on Models and Evolution - MODELS 2010*.

15. Rose, L., Etien, A., Méndez, D., Kolovos, D., Paige, R., Polack, F.: Comparing model-metamodel and transformation-metamodel coevolution. In: Petriu, D.C., Rouquette, N., Haugen, Ø. (eds.) MODELS 2010, Part I. LNCS, vol. 6394, Springer, Heidelberg (2010)

16. Rose, L.M., Kolovos, D.S., Paige, R.F., Polack, F.A.C.: Model migration with epsilon flock. In: Tratt, L., Gogolla, M. (eds.) ICMT 2010. LNCS, vol. 6142, pp. 184–198. Springer, Heidelberg (2010)

17. Ryder, B.G., Tip, F.: Change impact analysis for object-oriented programs. In: Proceedings of PASTE 2001, pp. 46–53. ACM, New York (2001)

18. Vignaga, A.: Metrics for measuring atl model transformations. Technical report (2009)

19. Wachsmuth, G.: Metamodel Adaptation and Model Co-adaptation. In: Ernst, E. (ed.) ECOOP 2007. LNCS, vol. 4609, pp. 600–624. Springer, Heidelberg (2007)

20. Wagelaar, D., Iovino, L., Di Ruscio, D., Pierantonio, A.: Translational semantics of a co-evolution specific language with the EMF transformation virtual machine. In: Hu, Z., de Lara, J. (eds.) ICMT 2012. LNCS, vol. 7307, pp. 192–207. Springer, Heidelberg (2012)

Metamodel-Specific Coupled Evolution Based on Dynamically Typed Graph Transformations

Christian Krause[1,*], Johannes Dyck[2], and Holger Giese[2]

[1] SAP Innovation Center Potsdam
me@ckrause.org
[2] Hasso Plattner Institute, University of Potsdam

Abstract. A key challenge in model-driven software engineering is the evolution of metamodels and the required effort in migrating their instance models. Even though there already exist both theoretical work and tool support for coupled evolution of metamodels and models, the existing approaches lack expressive power for defining metamodel-specific coupled changes or are too generic to permit assurance of metamodel conformance. In this paper, we devise a mechanism to define and execute coupled evolutions of metamodels and instance models based on graph transformations. We target the Eclipse Modeling Framework (EMF) and achieve the coupling of changes by bridging the conceptual gap between the metamodel and the instance model levels using a wrapper for EMF instance models. Coupled evolutions are then defined by means of dynamically typed graph transformation rules. This specification approach is expressive as it allows the developer to model customized migration rules, which are pivotal for metamodel-specific changes. We present static and run-time consistency checks and show how to decouple the execution of migrations. Our implementation consists of a wrapper package that is used in conjunction with the model transformation tool Henshin.

1 Introduction

Metamodels constitute central artifacts in model-driven engineering as they are used to define the abstract syntax of domain-specific modeling languages. At the same time, metamodels are subject to constant change because the requirements and the concepts of the specified languages evolve over time. Metamodel changes, however, can break the conformance of instance models. Therefore it is necessary to migrate the instance models to accommodate for the metamodel changes.

The main aspect which makes metamodel evolution and instance model migration challenging is the fact that changes on the two modeling levels have circular dependencies. To remove a concept realized by a class in a metamodel, it is first necessary to remove or migrate all instances of this class. Conversely, using a new concept on the instance level requires that the corresponding class has been added to the metamodel first. Thus, it is crucial to realize metamodel evolutions and model migrations in a coordinated way, which is referred to as *coupled evolution* [1] or *co-evolution* in the literature.

---

* Corresponding author.

K. Duddy and G. Kappel (Eds.): ICMT 2013, LNCS 7909, pp. 76–91, 2013.
© Springer-Verlag Berlin Heidelberg 2013

An empirical study on the histories of two industrial metamodels [2] indicates that different types of metamodel changes are relevant in practice. In this study, half of the metamodel changes required the migration of instance models. This class of *coupled changes* further divides into *metamodel-independent* and *metamodel-specific* changes. Metamodel-independent changes can be realized by generic evolution strategies, e.g., refactorings [3], and form the majority of these changes. However, the study also revealed that for the two industrial case studies 22% of the coupled changes were metamodel-specific, i.e., they required domain knowledge about the target language and manually specified migration strategies. A typical example of a metamodel-specific change is the refinement of a metamodel concept based on the properties of its instances. For example, a language for Petri nets that includes a class for places with a capacity attribute could be refined into one class for places with finite capacities and another class for places with unbounded capacities. The required metamodel changes alone could be easily achieved using standard refactorings. However, the migration of the instance models is non-trivial as place instances need to be mapped to different concepts depending on the specific values of their capacity attributes.

In the recent years, several approaches and tools have been developed for coupled metamodel and model evolutions (see Section 7). All of them are suitable for realizing metamodel-independent changes, such as the renaming of a class. However, metamodel-specific changes as described above are either not well supported or the approaches are too generic to statically ensure metamodel conformance. A uniform approach for modeling the coupled evolution at the metamodel and the instance model levels and ensuring its consistency is still missing.

In this paper, we present an approach for specifying coupled evolutions of metamodels and instance models based on graph transformations. The key idea is to bridge the conceptual gap between the metamodel and the instance model levels using instance model wrappers. These wrappers allow us to access and change the type information of objects using ordinary structural class features. Wrappers also provide generic access to an object's links and attribute values. We then specify coupled evolutions using dynamically typed graph transformation rules. In this approach, only the changes to the metamodels and instance models are specified. Moreover, metamodel-specific changes are directly supported. In particular, non-trivial migration strategies can be directly specified along the metamodel changes. To ensure consistency, specifically, type conformance of the migrated models, we provide static and run-time checks. The former can be used to guarantee conformance at design-time. Moreover, we show how the execution of instance model migrations can be decoupled from the metamodel evolution.

Our prototypical tool support targets metamodels defined in the Eclipse Modeling Framework [4] (EMF) and is based on the model transformation language and tool Henshin [5]. Our implementation is entirely encapsulated in the wrapper model. Thus, no intrusive changes to EMF or Henshin are required.

The rest of this paper is organized as follows. In Section 2 we recall preliminaries on EMF and Henshin. In Section 3 we introduce our wrapper model. In Section 4 we present our approach to coupled evolution. In Section 5 we define consistency checks. In Section 6 we show how to decouple the execution of migrations. Section 7 contains related work, Section 8 conclusions and future work.

2   Preliminaries

Our approach targets the Eclipse Modeling Framework [4] (EMF) and is based on graph transformations and the model transformation tool Henshin [5]. EMF is widely used in the industry for defining domain-specific languages (DSLs) as well as the basis for higher-level modeling languages such as UML.

The concepts for defining metamodels in EMF are defined in the *Ecore* metametamodel. Fig. 1 shows the for us relevant parts of Ecore and a user-defined metamodel for Petri nets. Ecore's metaclasses EClass, EReference, and EAttribute are used to define classes, associations, and attributes, respectively. Ecore also defines the metaclass EObject, which serves as the base class for all instance objects. EMF supports reflection, i.e., it is possible to find out the type of an EObject. However, the type information cannot be accessed through a structural feature, i.e., there is no reference from EObject to EClass. Instead, types must be obtained using reflection methods defined in EObject (not shown here).

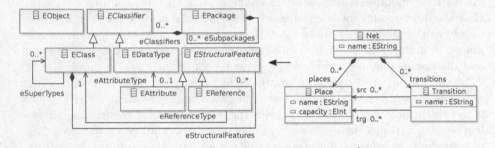

Fig. 1. Ecore metametamodel (left) and a user-defined metamodel for Petri nets (right)

Graphs and graph transformations are means for both formal and intuitive descriptions of structure and structural changes (see, e.g., [7]). A graph consists of sets of nodes and edges representing entities and relations between them. The instance-of relationship between a model and its metamodel can be captured using (instance) graphs and type graphs. Similarly to classes in a metamodel, nodes in a type graph can define a number of primitive typed attributes.

Graph transformation rules are used to specify changes to graphs, i.e., removing or adding nodes or edges or changing attribute values. Formally, a rule is given by two graphs: A left-hand side (LHS) describing the precondition and a right-hand side (RHS) specifying the changes. The application of a transformation rule to a graph amounts to finding a match of the LHS in

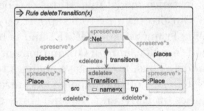

Fig. 2. Rule deleteTransition(x)

this graph and replacing it by the RHS. In this paper, we depict a rule using a single graph with node and edge stereotypes for the action to be performed. Fig. 2 shows an example rule that deletes a transition in a Petri net model including all its source and target edges.

We use the EMF model transformation tool Henshin [5] which is based on graph transformations. Transformations are executed in Henshin in-place, i.e., directly to a given model. A feature of Henshin essential to our approach of coupled evolution is rule amalgamation [5,8]. Formally, a *kernel-rule* can be embedded in one or more *multi-rules*. While a kernel-rule is matched and applied only once, a multi-rule is executed for all possible matches. In Henshin, multi-rules can be used again as kernel-rules and thus nested. In this paper, we employ amalgamation to specify the transformation of all relevant instance entities during model migration whereas we execute the evolution rule only once. Elements in multi-rules are denoted using *-stereotypes, e.g., the place nodes in Fig. 2.

3 Wrapping EMF Instance Models

Our approach for coupled metamodel and model evolution is based on the idea of making the type-instance relations for objects, attributes and links between objects available as ordinary structural features of objects. Moreover, the attribute values of an object and its links to other objects should be accessible in a generic way, i.e., without the need of knowing the type of the object resp. feature.

One approach to achieve such a functionality is to enrich Ecore itself by such reflective structural features. For instance, the EObject metaclass could be extended with a structural feature for accessing its type, i.e., with a reference to EClass. The other required features could be realized in a similar way. This approach, however, would be an intrusive change to Ecore and would require the use of a customized version of EMF.

An alternative approach which we advocate in this paper is based on the idea of *wrapping* the objects in EMF instance models, i.e., instances of EObject, by appropriate wrapper objects that provide the necessary features. The wrapper objects and their features are defined again by a metamodel.

3.1 The Wrap Metamodel

The wrap metamodel is shown in Fig. 3. An instance of the class WObject represents a wrapper for an arbitrary EObject. The wrapped EObject can be obtained using the eObject reference and its type using the eClass reference. Thereby, we bridge the conceptual gap between the instance and the metamodel level. Wrapper objects contain a set of members, which are instances of either WValue or WLink. WLinks represent links to other (wrapped) objects and can be regarded as instances of EReferences. Similarly, WValues represent specific values of an attribute of the object and can be seen as instances of EAttributes. The type of a WMember can be accessed via the eStructuralFeature reference. The data value encapsulated in a WValue can be accessed through the eValue attribute.

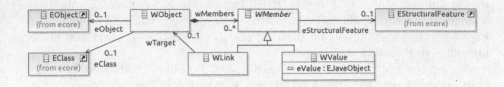

Fig. 3. The wrap metamodel and its references to Ecore

This simple wrap metamodel provides all features needed in our approach for a coupled metamodel and model evolution. In particular, it allows us to match an object together with its type, to dynamically create an instance of a type that is unknown at design-time, and also to change the type of an object at run-time. A similar functionality is available for attribute values and links to other objects. In addition to these object level operations, the wrapper concept also allows us to make changes to the type level, i.e., to the metamodels.

3.2 Usage

To illustrate the usage of wrapper models and the achieved higher expressiveness, we use a simple graph transformation rule shown in Fig. 4, and the equivalent rule using wrappers in Fig. 5. The simple rule matches an object n of type Net with a value x for the name attribute. The rule creates an object p of type Place and a link of type places between n and p. Thus, it realizes the creation of a place in a Petri net. The corresponding rule with wrappers contains in total eight objects. The four objects in the upper row represent the metamodel level and contain class and feature definitions. Specifically, two classes with the names 'Net' and 'Place' are matched together with an attribute feature called 'name' and a reference 'places'. The lower row consists of wrapper objects which represent instances of the metamodel elements. The type-instance relations manifest here as edges from the wrapper objects to the metamodel elements.

The simple and the wrapper-based rules are in fact behaviorally equivalent. Furthermore, wrapper-based rules can be automatically generated from simple rules. However, there are important differences in the usage and the expressiveness. In the classical approach, the metamodel is fixed and must be available

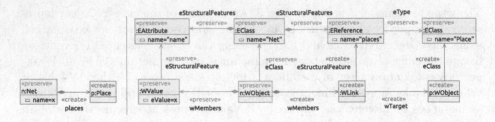

Fig. 4. A statically typed rule   **Fig. 5.** Corresponding rule with wrappers (dynamically typed)

at design-time. In contrast, the rule using wrappers matches the required meta-model elements at run-time together with their instances. The only design-time dependencies of the wrapper-based rule are to Ecore and the (generic) wrap metamodel. Due to these differences in the typing, we say that the simple rule is *statically typed* whereas the wrapper-rule is *dynamically typed*. Since there are no design-time dependencies to the targeted metamodel, the wrapper-based rule could even transform the metamodel and the instance models at the same time. For example, the rule could create a new class and directly create instances of it. Thus, the wrapper-based approach has a higher expressive power which is the basis for realizing coupled evolutions of metamodels and instance models.

Although the two rules in Fig. 4 and 5 are behaviorally equivalent, we cannot naively apply the wrapper-based rule in the same way as the simple rule. To ensure that the wrapper-based approach works in the intended way, the usage scenario with wrappers should consist of the following three steps. First, all instance models are wrapped using a provided implementation of the wrap metamodel. Specifically, for every EObject, a corresponding WObject is created. For every attribute value of an EObject, a corresponding WValue is created in its wrapper. Similarly, for every link to an EObject, a corresponding WLink is created. This functionality is provided as part of the implementation of the wrap package and can be reused. Second, the wrapper models and the meta-models are transformed using either an in-place model transformation language or a general-purpose programming language. The provided implementation of the wrap metamodel transparently performs all locally consistent changes made to the wrappers also at the wrapped EObjects (see Section 3.3). Changes are allowed to be made only to the wrappers and the metamodels, but not to the wrapped EObjects. Third, the changed metamodels are directly available and can be persisted. To obtain the migrated instance models, the changed EObjects are extracted from the wrapper objects using the eObject reference in WObject.

Thus, we first wrap all instance models, then transform the wrappers (and the metamodels), and finally extract the changed metamodels and the migrated instances. Hence, the actual coupled metamodel and model evolution is performed in step 2. An important aspect of this approach is that the provided implementation of the wrap metamodel automatically reflects all consistent changes made to the wrappers to the wrapped EObjects, thereby ensuring compliance of the models. We discuss compliance and consistency in detail in the following section.

3.3   Compliance and Consistency

A wrapper model is *compliant* with its underlying instance model if they are structurally equivalent. This notion of equivalence can be formalized by requiring that the map that associates WObjects with their wrapped EObjects forms a graph isomorphism for typed, attributed graphs which makes appropriate type conversions and translates WLink objects to edges. We omit the formal definition here. Note that step 1 in the previous section produces by construction a compliant wrapper model. Our goal is to ensure that after step 2, the wrapper model is still compliant, meaning that the transformation performed on the wrapper model is also correctly performed on the instance model. However, compliance can be ensured only if the transformation yields a *consistent* wrapper model.

Definition 1 (Consistency). *A WObject is called* locally consistent *if its eClass is set and instantiable and all its members are locally consistent. A WLink is locally consistent if its eStructuralFeature is a valid EReference of the wrapper's EClass and the wTarget is set and its eObject is a valid value for this reference. A WValue is locally consistent if its eStructuralFeature is a valid EAttribute of the wrapper's EClass and the eValue is set and a valid value for this attribute. A wrapper model is consistent if all its wrapper objects are locally consistent and all involved metamodels are consistent.*

Consistency of a metamodel is defined and can be checked using standard constraints for Ecore, e.g., the type of an EReference must be always set.

All locally consistent changes made to a wrapper model during the transformation are performed also on the underlying instance model. The execution of inconsistent changes is deferred until the local inconsistencies are resolved in the wrapper. The default implementation of WObject performs the following actions when changes are made to its features:

- **Setting the class.** If the new EClass is set and instantiable, the eObject reference is updated with a fresh instance of the new EClass. For all locally consistent WValues and WLinks, the corresponding attribute and reference values are also set in the new EObject. If the eClass reference has been unset or is not instantiable, the eObject reference is unset. All incoming WLinks are notified that their targets changed.
- **Adding or removing a member.** If the eObject reference is set and the member is locally consistent, then the feature change is also performed on the EObject.

Similarly, changes to a WMember have the following effects:

- **Setting the structural feature.** If the member was locally consistent before the change, the value is removed from the old feature of the EObject. If the member is locally consistent after the change, the value is added to the new feature of the EObject.
- **Setting the target or value.** If the member is a WLink and was locally consistent before the change, the old target is removed from the EObject's reference. If the link is locally consistent after the change, the new target is added to the EObject's reference. Analogously if the member is a WValue.

In addition to these automatic changes, the wrappers also monitor relevant metamodel elements and perform similar actions. This behavior ensures that all locally consistent changes are correctly propagated to the wrapped objects. Local inconsistencies in the wrappers, e.g., members with incompatible features, are explicitly allowed during the migration. However, if the migration follows steps 1-3 in the previous section, and all wrapper models are consistent after the transformation in step 2, then they are also compliant. Thus, it suffices to ensure that the transformation result is consistent. We discuss means to ensure consistency later in Section 5.

4 Coupled Metamodel and Model Evolution

The key problem for realizing coupled metamodel evolution and instance model migration is that the transformations have to be defined both on the type level and the object level. Moreover, as described in Section 1, there are dependencies between these two modeling levels. Our solution to this problem is to use wrappers, which provide us with a technical means to connect the metamodel and the instance model levels. Specifically, wrappers allow us to use standard model transformation languages with in-place semantics to realize coupled evolution.

4.1 Evolution Scenario

We consider an example of a metamodel evolution for a Petri net metamodel, shown in Fig 6. The evolution consists of two main parts.

In the first part, the src reference from Transition to Place is removed in favor of a new class, called ArcPT, which is used to represent an arc from a place to a transition. The new class ArcPT contains an integer attribute weight which can be used to specify the weight of an arc. Similarly, we could also introduce a class ArcTP for modeling arcs from transitions to places. We omit this for simplicity here. This part of the evolution is essentially a replacement of a reference with a class and introducing a new attribute with a default value for all instance models. Therefore, this part of the evolution can be regarded as metamodel-independent.

The second part of the evolution concerns the class Place, which is made abstract and refined into the two new classes UnboundedPlace and BoundedPlace. The capacity attribute of Place is moved to BoundedPlace. The migration of the instance models should translate instances of Place with a positive capacity to BoundedPlace, and instances with a negative capacity value to instances of UnboundedPlace. This change is metamodel-specific because the migration of Place objects non-trivially depends on the specific values of the capacity attribute.

4.2 Solution

We realize this coupled metamodel and model evolution using wrapper-based graph transformation rules in Henshin [5].

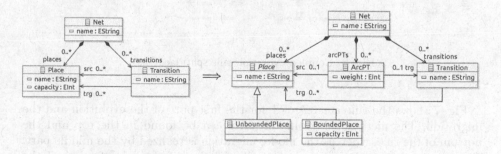

Fig. 6. Example of a Petri net metamodel evolution

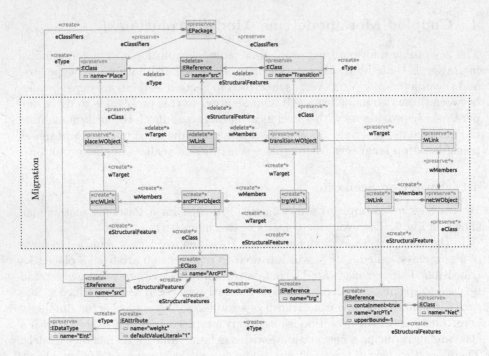

Fig. 7. Coupled evolution rule createArcPT

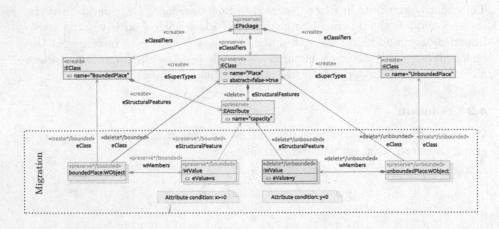

Fig. 8. Coupled evolution rule splitPlaceClass

Fig. 7 shows the rule createArcPT for the first part of the evolution and the migration. The metamodel evolution parts can be found in the top and the bottom of the rule, whereas the model migration is realized by the middle part. The metamodel evolution consists of the deletion of the src reference of the Transition-class, the creation of the new class ArcPT together with its structural features, and the creation of a new containment reference for arcs in the Net-class. The model migration part consists of replacing every wrapper object that represents a src-link from a transition to a place by a fresh instance of the new class ArcPT. Note that this migration is performed on all such links because of the star in the action stereotypes, which is Henshin's syntax for multi-rules [5,8]. This also means that the coupled evolution is realized as a transaction that performs the metamodel evolution and the migration of all instances in an atomic step.[1]

Fig. 8 shows the rule splitPlaceClass which realizes the second part of the coupled evolution. The upper part specifies the metamodel evolution where Place is made abstract, the two new classes BoundedPlace and UnboundedPlace are created, and the capacity attribute is moved to the new class BoundedPlace. The model migration is realized using two star-rules, respectively call bounded and unbounded. The star-rule bounded matches all places with a positive capacity (checked using the attribute condition $x \geq 0$) and changes their type from Place to BoundedPlace. Analogously, the star-rule unbounded matches all places with a negative capacity and changes their type from Place to UnboundedPlace. Thus, the rule expresses both the metamodel evolution as well as the non-trivial and metamodel-specific migration of instance models in a concise way. To reduce the amount of manual specification, it may be possible to generate default coupled evolution rules from metamodel evolution rules and allow for customization of the rules' migration parts to account for non-trivial conditions as seen above.

At this point we want to highlight that the in Section 1 mentioned interde-pendencies between the metamodel changes and the instance model changes are completely hidden for the designer, i.e., there is no need to define the specific order of the low-level structural operations.

5   Ensuring Consistency

As discussed in Section 3.3, the correctness of a coupled evolution mainly relies on the compliance of the transformation result, which in turn can be ensured by showing that the transformation produces a consistent wrapper model. Thus, it is important to support the developer to ensure consistency. To this end, we consider static and run-time consistency checks.

5.1   Static Consistency

Static consistency checks are performed at design-time by checking structural constraints in the transformation rules. We discuss relevant consistency condi-tions for rules which could be automatically checked or enforced by rule editors.

To ensure consistency of wrapper objects, it is important that their properties are immediately set on creation, and unset on deletion. Therefore, the following objects and edges should be created or deleted together in a rule: WObjects and their eClass edge; WValues and their eStructuralFeature edge; WLinks and

---

[1] Comparable with the notion of *coupled transactions* in [1].

their eStructuralFeature and wTarget edge. The value of a new WValue should be set on construction. In most cases, new elements should be added to an existing container object on creation, except for new root elements, such as a new package in a metamodel. When deleting a metamodel-element, all instances of this element should be also deleted. In Henshin, this can be realized, e.g., using starred action stereotypes. An example of such a scenario is the EReference "src" which is deleted together with all its instance links in the rule createArcPT. In a similar way, classes should be deleted only together with all their instances, and attributes together with all their values. If a rule does not delete the instances of a deleted type, this is a strong indicator for an incorrect migration.

Another important aspect that can be statically checked is the type conformance of links and attribute values. Specifically, the target of a link should be typed over a class that is a valid type of the links' reference. This can be ensured at design-time by using one of the rule patterns shown in Fig. 9. Similarly, type conformance of attribute values can be ensured. Together with the aforementioned constraints, these patterns allow us to automatically detect possible problems occurring during the migrations already at design-time. As one of the most crucial correctness criteria, type conformance can be ensured statically.

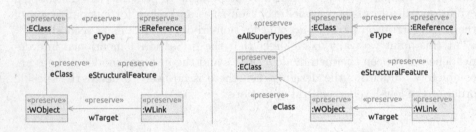

Fig. 9. Two rule patterns that statically ensure type conformance of links

5.2 Run-Time Consistency

In addition to the static analysis methods, we also employ consistency checks at run-time. The simplest way is to directly check the consistency constraints from Def. 1 on the transformation result. If this check succeeds, the transformation result is consistent and thus also compliant. Furthermore, we can also intercept possible inconsistencies already during a rule application. Specifically, by employing double-pushout graph transformations [7], a rule is applicable only if no dangling edges are produced. This ensures that a metamodel-element is deleted only if all its instances are also deleted.

Together with the static consistency checks, the automatic run-time checks are helpful tools to support the developer to safely execute the coupled evolution.

6   Decoupled Execution of Model Migrations

In practice, applying the metamodel evolution and the migrations of all instance models at the same time as suggested in the previous sections is often not a feasible solution. The typical scenario consists of two independently executed steps. First, the developer of a modeling language evolves the metamodel. Then the user is confronted with a new version of the metamodel and needs to migrate her instance models. Thus, it is important to be able to decouple the execution of the model migrations from the metamodel evolutions (cf. also [9]).

To support independently executed migrations, we propose to separate the coupled evolution rules into sets of (1) metamodel evolution rules, and (2) migration rules. These rules can be automatically generated at design-time from coupled evolution rules to execute the metamodel evolution and the model migrations separately. We describe these two steps in more detail now.

6.1   Metamodel Evolution

Metamodel evolution rules are generated from coupled evolution rules simply by deleting all instance level elements, i.e., all nodes and links that refer to types of the wrap metamodel. For the coupled evolution rules in Fig. 7 and 8 this means that the migration regions are removed.

The derived metamodel evolution rules can be directly applied to adapt the metamodels. In order to facilitate the model migrations, we assume that the new versions of the metamodels get a different namespace URI and are saved separately from the old versions. This is important to distinguish old model instance from migrated ones and to perform the migration without changing the metamodels. The user simply obtains the new version of the metamodel together with generated migration rules to migrate her instance models (see below).

6.2   Model Migration

The migration rules are also generated from the coupled evolution rules. For simplicity, we assume that only a single metamodel package was subject to changes. Let oldURI denote the namespace URI of the old version of this package and newURI be the namespace URI of the new version. For a given coupled evolution rule, we obtain the corresponding migration rule as follows:

1. Add two package declarations to the rule, one with oldURI and the other with newURI as its namespace URI.
2. Add a containment edge from the old package to all classifiers marked for deletion in the rule. Add a containment edge from the new package to all classifiers marked for creation. Change the action for all metamodel elements to preserve and remove all attribute conditions other than the name-constraints.
3. Duplicate all preserved classifiers in the rule. Add a containment edge from the old package to the original classifier and a containment edge from the new package to the duplicate.
4. For all wrapper nodes whose type is preserved, replace the preserved type edge by these two edges: one delete edge to the old type and one create edge to the corresponding new type (the duplicate created in 3). Note that the types of all other nodes are already handled by the original rule.

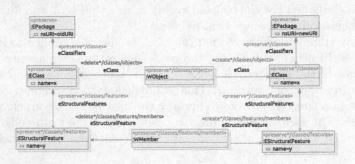

Fig. 10. Generated migration rule migrate_splitPlaceClass

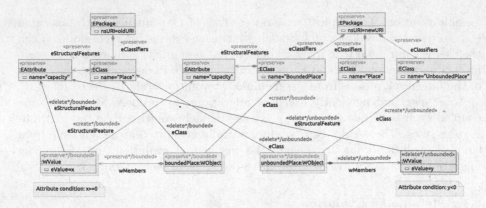

Fig. 11. Generic rule for migrating objects with unchanged types

Fig. 10 shows the migration rule generated from rule splitPlaceClass in Fig. 8. The upper left part contains the relevant elements of the old metamodel, the upper right part the relevant elements of the new metamodel, and the lower part the migration of the instance model elements. Note that the old and the new metamodels are distinguished by their namespace URIs and that no metamodel changes are performed by this rule. The effect of applying this rule is that all instance model objects targeted by this rule are properly migrated to the new metamodel. However, elements that are not handled by this rule, e.g. Transition objects, need to be migrated to the new metamodel version, too. Fortunately, we can simply change the types of these objects from the old to the corresponding new metamodel element. This can be achieved using the generic migration rule shown in Fig. 11. Thus, it suffices to first apply the generated migration rule in Fig. 10 and then the generic migration rule in Fig. 11 for the remaining objects. Thereby, the executions of model migrations can be completely decoupled from the metamodel evolution and even from migrations of other model instances.

7   Related Work

Mantz et al. present a graph transformation based approach for coupled EMF evolution which guarantees type conformance for the model migration [10]. However, migration rules are automatically generated from metamodel evolution rules and, thus, cannot be manually specified as in our approach. Similarly, Taentzer et al. present a formalization of coupled evolutions based on category theory [11] which also assumes that migration rules are automatically generated.

The COPE [1] tool (now Edapt [12]) realizes an operator-based approach for coupled evolution. Customized model migration as supported in our approach cannot be specified using operators but must be implemented in COPE using a scripting language. Moreover, COPE requires the integration of the co-evolution operators with the metamodel editing tools. The limitations of a number of approaches for automating model migrations are formalized and discussed in [13].

Epsilon Flock [9] is a domain-specific language for model migrations. Only the migration rules are specified in Flock, but not the metamodel evolution. Flock supports two types of rules: delete rules and migrate rules. Migrate rules can be applied only to a single object in the source metamodel, but not to larger structures, because Flock performs an implicit copying of all unchanged objects.

EMFMigrate [14] is a domain-specific language for defining coupled evolutions where the migration targets arbitrary dependent artifacts. Migration rules are specified separately from metamodel changes, can be assembled to reusable libraries and refined for customizations. Different to our approach, it is not possible to check the correctness of the migration rules at design-time, i.e., that the types of the migrated instance models are conform with the changed metamodel.

Hößler et al. present a graphical language for describing coupled evolutions [15] with a focus on a number of typical patterns. The syntax of the transformation language allows customizable rules but the type conformance of the migration results cannot be guaranteed. Sprinkle et al. describe a visual language for metamodel evolution [16]. The approach requires implicit copying of unchanged metamodel elements and makes no conformance guarantees.

8   Conclusions and Future Work

In this paper, we presented a new approach for specifying coupled metamodel evolutions and instance model migrations based on graph transformations. Our key idea was to enable a combined modeling approach for metamodels and instance models by introducing wrappers for EMF, thus alleviating the problem of circular dependencies between metamodel evolution and migrations. Our approach is both expressive and enables the assurance of consistency constraints.

For future work, we plan to define a more high-level syntax for coupled evolution rules that automatically ensures consistency by construction. In addition, we plan to support the generation of default coupled evolution rules from metamodel evolution rules, which then can be customized in order to refine the migration logic. In another line of research, we plan to employ critical pair analysis [17] to ensure uniqueness of migration results.

References

1. Herrmannsdoerfer, M., Benz, S., Juergens, E.: COPE - automating coupled evolution of metamodels and models. In: Drossopoulou, S. (ed.) ECOOP 2009. LNCS, vol. 5653, pp. 52–76. Springer, Heidelberg (2009), doi:10.1007/978-3-642-03013-0_4

2. Herrmannsdoerfer, M., Benz, S., Juergens, E.: Automatability of coupled evolution of metamodels and models in practice. In: Czarnecki, K., Ober, I., Bruel, J.-M., Uhl, A., Völter, M. (eds.) MODELS 2008. LNCS, vol. 5301, pp. 645–659. Springer, Heidelberg (2008), doi:10.1007/978-3-540-87875-9_45

3. Fowler, M.: Refactoring: Improving the Design of Existing Code. Addison-Wesley (1999)

4. Steinberg, D., Budinsky, F., Paternostro, M., Merks, E.: EMF: Eclipse Modeling Framework, 2nd edn. Addison-Wesley (2009)

5. Arendt, T., Biermann, E., Jurack, S., Krause, C., Taentzer, G.: Henshin: Advanced concepts and tools for in-place EMF model transformations. In: Petriu, D.C., Rouquette, N., Haugen, Ø. (eds.) MODELS 2010, Part I. LNCS, vol. 6394, pp. 121–135. Springer, Heidelberg (2010), doi:10.1007/978-3-642-16145-2_9

6. Biermann, E., Ehrig, K., Köhler, C., Kuhns, G., Taentzer, G., Weiss, E.: Graphical definition of in-place transformations in the Eclipse Modeling Framework. In: Wang, J., Whittle, J., Harel, D., Reggio, G. (eds.) MoDELS 2006. LNCS, vol. 4199, pp. 425–439. Springer, Heidelberg (2006), doi:10.1007/11880240_30

7. Rozenberg, G. (ed.): Handbook of graph grammars and computing by graph transformation. foundations, vol. I. World Scientific Publishing Co., Inc. (1997)

8. Biermann, E., Ehrig, H., Ermel, C., Golas, U., Taentzer, G.: Parallel independence of amalgamated graph transformations applied to model transformation. In: Engels, G., Lewerentz, C., Schäfer, W., Schürr, A., Westfechtel, B. (eds.) Nagl Festschrift. LNCS, vol. 5765, pp. 121–140. Springer, Heidelberg (2010), doi:10.1007/978-3-642-17322-6_7

9. Rose, L.M., Kolovos, D.S., Paige, R.F., Polack, F.A.C.: Model migration with epsilon flock. In: Tratt, L., Gogolla, M. (eds.) ICMT 2010. LNCS, vol. 6142, pp. 184–198. Springer, Heidelberg (2010), doi:10.1007/978-3-642-13688-7_13

10. Mantz, F., Jurack, S., Taentzer, G.: Graph transformation concepts for meta-model evolution guaranteeing permanent type conformance throughout model migration. In: Schürr, A., Varró, D., Varró, G. (eds.) AGTIVE 2011. LNCS, vol. 7233, pp. 3–18. Springer, Heidelberg (2012), doi:10.1007/978-3-642-34176-2_3

11. Taentzer, G., Mantz, F., Lamo, Y.: Co-transformation of graphs and type graphs with application to model co-evolution. In: Ehrig, H., Engels, G., Kreowski, H.-J., Rozenberg, G. (eds.) ICGT 2012. LNCS, vol. 7562, pp. 326–340. Springer, Heidelberg (2012), doi:10.1007/978-3-642-33654-6_22

12. Edapt: Project homepage: http://www.eclipse.org/edapt

13. Herrmannsdoerfer, M., Ratiu, D.: Limitations of automating model migration in response to metamodel adaptation. In: Ghosh, S. (ed.) MODELS 2009. LNCS, vol. 6002, pp. 205–219. Springer, Heidelberg (2010), doi:10.1007/978-3-642-12261-3_20

14. Di Ruscio, D., Iovino, L., Pierantonio, A.: What is needed for managing co-evolution in MDE? In: IWMCP 2011, pp. 30–38. ACM (2011), doi:10.1145/2000410.2000416

15. Hößler, J., Soden, M., Eichler, H.: Coevolution of models, metamodels and transformations. In: Models and Human Reasoning, pp. 129–154. Wissenschaft und Technik Verlag (2005)
16. Sprinkle, J., Karsai, G.: A domain-specific visual language for domain model evolution. Journal of Visual Languages & Computing 15(3-4), 291–307 (2004), doi:10.1016/j.jvlc.2004.01.006
17. Heckel, R., Küster, J.M., Taentzer, G.: Confluence of typed attributed graph transformation systems. In: Corradini, A., Ehrig, H., Kreowski, H.-J., Rozenberg, G. (eds.) ICGT 2002. LNCS, vol. 2505, pp. 161–176. Springer, Heidelberg (2002), doi:10.1007/3-540-45832-8_14

Robust Real-Time Synchronization between Textual and Graphical Editors

Oskar van Rest[1,2], Guido Wachsmuth[1,3], Jim R.H. Steel[2],
Jörn Guy Süß[2], and Eelco Visser[1]

[1] Delft University of Technology, The Netherlands,
o.f.vanrest@student.tudelft.nl, g.h.wachsmuth@tudelft.nl,
visser@acm.org
[2] The University of Queensland, Australia,
jsteel@uq.edu.au, jgsuess@itee.uq.edu.au
[3] Oracle Labs, Redwood Shores, CA, USA

Abstract. In modern Integrated Development Environments (IDEs),
textual editors are interactive and can handle intermediate, incomplete,
or otherwise erroneous texts while still providing editor services such
as syntax highlighting, error marking, outline views, and hover help. In
this paper, we present an approach for the robust synchronization of
interactive textual and graphical editors. The approach recovers from
errors during parsing and text-to-model synchronization, preserves textual and graphical layout in the presence of erroneous texts and models,
and provides synchronized editor services such as selection sharing and
navigation between editors. It was implemented for synchronizing textual editors generated by the Spoofax language workbench and graphical
editors generated by the Graphical Modeling Framework.

1 Introduction

Modeling languages such as Behavior Trees [3,17] or QVT Relational [18] provide
both textual and graphical concrete syntax. Textual and graphical editors for
such languages need to synchronize textual representations, graphical representations, and underlying models. During this synchronization, layout in textual
and graphical representations needs to be preserved.

Textual editors generated by textual modeling frameworks such as TEF [19]
and Xtext [8] synchronize only on user request. Embedded textual editors based
on TEF synchronize on open and close [20]. Xtext-based editors synchronize on
save [16]. This breaks the interactive nature of integrated development environments (IDEs), where editors provide a wide variety of language-specific services
such as syntax highlighting, error marking, code navigation, content completion
and outline views in real-time, while their content is edited. Furthermore, those
editors can only synchronize valid models and tend to break either textual or
graphical layout. TEF-based editors ignore textual layout by design. Xtext-based
editors typically preserve textual layout, but tend to break layout in graphical
editors once identifiers change.

Robust real-time synchronization of textual and graphical editors is mainly
prevented by current text-to-model transformation practice, where model elements are temporarily deleted and recreated during parsing, existing persisted

K. Duddy and G. Kappel (Eds.): ICMT 2013, LNCS 7909, pp. 92–107, 2013.
© Springer-Verlag Berlin Heidelberg 2013

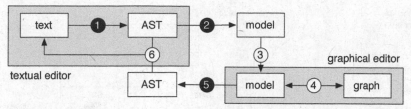

Fig. 1. Steps involved in synchronizing textual and graphical editors: ❶ Parsing, ❷ tree-to-model transformation, ③ model merge, ④ edit policy, ❺ model-to-text transformation, ⑥ pretty-printing. Steps marked black support error recovery. Steps marked white support layout preservation.

models are ignored and overwritten by new models, and error recovery is limited. In this paper, we propose a new approach which is outlined in Fig. 1. To synchronize textual changes with a model, the text is ❶ parsed into an abstract syntax tree, which is ❷ transformed into a model. The resulting model is ③ merged with the model in a graphical editor, which invokes an edit policy to ④ update its graphical representation of the model. To synchronize graphical changes with a text, the edit policy ④ changes the underlying model, which is ❺ transformed into a tree. The resulting tree is ⑥ merged with the tree in the textual editor and turned back into text. The approach was implemented for synchronizing textual editors generated by the Spoofax language workbench [13] and graphical editors generated by the Graphical Modeling Framework for the Eclipse IDE. We applied this approach to Behavior Trees. Fig. 2 shows the textual and graphical editor, which both share the same Behavior Tree model.

We proceed as follows. We first describe a mapping from grammars to metamodels and the corresponding transformations ❷❺ between trees and models. In Sect. 3, we discuss error recovery in steps ❶❷❺. In Sect. 4, we elaborate on the preservation of textual and graphical layout in steps ③④⑥. In Sect. 5, we present our case study on the development of synchronizing editors for Behavior Trees. Finally, we discuss related work in Sect. 6.

2   Tree-to-Model and Model-to-Tree Transformations

The textual syntax definition is the starting point of our approach. In this section, we present a mapping from textual syntax definitions to metamodels and a corresponding bidirectional mapping between abstract syntax trees conforming to the textual syntax definition and models conforming to the generated metamodel. We start with abstract mappings which need to be adapted for concrete formalisms. We then discuss such an adaptation using the examples of Spoofax' syntax definition formalism SDF [9,26], its name binding language NaBL [14], and EMF's metamodeling formalism Ecore [24].

2.1   Mapping Textual Syntax Definition to Metamodel

We start with minimalistic grammar and metamodeling formalisms. In these formalisms, grammars, metamodels and models are represented as terms. Fig. 3 shows

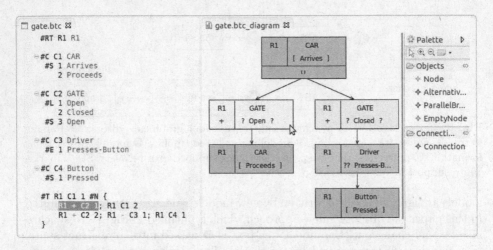

Fig. 2. Behavior Tree model in a textual editor (left) and in a graphical editor (right). Both editors edit the same model and synchronize changes with each other.

the corresponding signatures. These signatures are of the form c : T → s with c a constructor for sort s and T a declaration of the number and types of arguments of c. The mapping is specified in Fig. 4 by rewrite rules expressed in Spoofax' transformation language Stratego [1,11]. These rules are of the form r : t1 → t2 where s with r the rule name, t1 and t2 first-order terms, and s a *strategy expression*. A rule applies to a term if the term matches t1 and s succeeds, resulting in the instantiation of t2.

Grammars, metamodels, and models. A grammar consists of a lexical syntax definition, a context-free syntax definition, and a list of namespace specifications (Fig. 3, line 1). Both lexical and context-free syntax are defined by productions, which are grouped by the sorts they define (l. 2). Productions and sorts are named, and each production provides a list of symbols (l. 3). A symbol is either a character class (typically used to define lexical sorts), a string, a reference to a lexical sort, or a reference to a context-free sort (ll. 4-7). References are named (first ID), refer to a sort by name (second ID), and might come with a postfix operator for options, lists, or optional lists. References to lexical sorts can be involved in name bindings, either as definition or use sites of a name in a namespace (ll. 8-11). This integration of name binding into productions is similar to Xtext's approach. But in contrast to Xtext, we decouple namespaces from sorts and allow them to be hierarchically structured.

A metamodel consists of a list of types, which are either primitive data types, enumerated data types, abstract classes, or concrete classes (ll. 16-21). Type names are qualified, providing a simple packaging mechanism. Both kinds of classes consist of a list of qualified parent class names, defining the inheritance hierarchy, and a list of features. We distinguish attributes, references, and containments (ll. 22-24). Each feature is named, refers its type by qualified name, and defines a lower and upper bound (ll. 25-26).

```
 1  Grammar: List(Sort)*List(Sort)*List(NSpace)  → Grammar
 2  Sort   : ID*List(Prod)                       → Sort
 3  Prod   : ID*List(Symbol)                      → Prod
 4  Chars  : List(Char)                           → Symbol
 5  Literal: String                               → Symbol
 6  LSort  : ID*ID*Binding*Operator               → Symbol
 7  CfSort : ID*ID*Operator                       → Symbol
 8  None   :                                       Binding
 9  DefSite: ID                                   → Binding
10  UseSite: ID                                   → Binding
11  NSpace : ID*List(ID)                          → NSpace
12  None   : Operator
13  Option : Operator
14  List   : Operator
15  OptList: Operator
```

```
16  MM     : List(Type)                          → Metamodel
17  DType  : QID                                 → Type
18  Enum   : QID*List(Literal)                   → Type
19  AClass : List(QID)*QID*List(Feature)         → Type
20  CClass : List(QID)*QID*List(Feature)         → Type
21  Literal: ID                                  → Literal
22  Attr   : ID*QID*Bounds                       → Feature
23  Ref    : ID*QID*Bounds                       → Feature
24  Contain: ID*QID*Bounds                       → Feature
25  QID    : ID*ID                               → QID
26  Bounds : INT*UnlimitedINT                    → Bounds
```

```
27  M      : Object                       → Model
28  Obj    : Opt(URI)*QID*List(Slot)      → Object
29         : Value                        → Slot
30         : Opt(Value)                   → Slot
31         : List(Value)                  → Slot
32  Data   : String                       → Value
33  Link   : URI                          → Value
34  Contain: Object                       → Value
```

Fig. 3. Signatures for grammars (top), metamodels (center), and models (bottom)

A model is represented as a single root object (l. 27). An object consists of an optional URI, the qualified name of the class it instantiates, and a list of slots (l. 28). A slot may hold a single value or a list of values, where a value is either an instance of a data type represented as a string, a link to an object represented as the URI of this object, or a contained object (ll. 29-34). Slots do not refer to features. Instead, we assume an immutable order of the features of a class, which links slots of an object to the features of its class.

Lexical Syntax. We are not interested in the inner structure of lexical tokens and represent them as basic data at the leaves of abstract syntax trees. We can keep the same basic data in models. Thus, we map lexical sorts from a grammar to data types in a metamodel (Fig. 4, ll. 7-14). Predefined data types (enumerations and primitives) are provided by the metamodel formalism and the condition lex2qid ensures that user-defined data types are only generated when no corresponding predefined data type exists. When a lexical sort defines only a finite number of literals, an enumeration is generated (sort2enum). Only when sort2enum fails, we try to generate a primitive with sort2dtype

```
1   grammar2mm:
2     Grammar(lex*, cf*, ns*) → MM([ty1*, ty2*, ty3*])
3     where
4       <filter(sort2enum <+ sort2dtype)> lex* ⇒ ty1* ;
5       <mapconcat(sort2classes)> cf*          ⇒ ty2* ;
6       <map(ns2class)> ns*                    ⇒ ty3*
```

```
7   sort2enum:
8     Sort(name, prod*) → Enum(<lex2qid> name, <map(prod2lit)> prod*)
9
10  prod2lit: Prod(_, [Literal(name)]) → Literal(name)
11
12  sort2dtype: Sort(name, _) → DType(<lex2qid> name)
13
14  lex2qid: name → QID("lex", name) where <not(predefined)> name
```

```
15  sort2classes:
16    Sort(name, prod*) → [AClass([], QID("cf", name), [])|class*]
17    where
18      <map(prod2class(|name)))> prod* ⇒ class*
19
20  prod2class(|parent):
21    Prod(name, sym*) → CClass([parent|parent*], Q("ast", name), feat*)
22    where
23      <filter(symbol2parent)> sym*  ⇒ parent* ;
24      <filter(symbol2feature)> sym* ⇒ feat*
25
26  symbol2feature:
27    LSort(label, sort, None(), op) → Attr(label, ty, <op2bounds> op)
28    where
29      <predefined <+ user−defined> sort ⇒ ty
30
31  symbol2feature:
32    CfSort(lbl, sort, op) → Contain(lbl, QID("cf", sort), <op2bounds> op)
33
34  op2bounds: None()    → Bound(1, 1)
35  op2bounds: Option()  → Bound(0, 1)
36  op2bounds: OptList() → Bound(0, Unbound())
37  op2bounds: List()    → Bound(1, Unbound())
```

```
38  ns2class:
39    NSpace(name, ns*) → AClass(<map(ns2qid)> ns*, QID("ns", name), [])
40
41  ns2qid: name → QID("ns", name)
42
43  symbol2parent: LSort(_, _, DefSite(nspace), _) → QID("ns", nspace)
44
45  symbol2feature:
46    LSort(label, sort, DefSite(_), op) → Attr(label, ty, <op2bounds> op)
47    where
48      <predefined <+ user−defined> sort ⇒ ty
49
50  symbol2feature:
51    LSort(label, _, UseSite(ns), op) → Ref(label, QID("ns", ns), bounds)
52    where
53      <op2bounds> op ⇒ bounds
```

Fig. 4. Rewrite rules defining a grammar-to-metamodel transformation in Stratego

(in the first condition for grammar2mm, <+ encodes a deterministic choice). To avoid name conflicts, we organize generated data types in a package lex.

Context-free Syntax. Abstract syntax trees represent the structure of sentences. We can express such trees also as models. Therefore, the metamodel needs to capture the structural rules of the context-free syntax. We achieve

```
1   tree2model: t              → M(<term2obj>)
2   term2obj    : c#(t*)       → Obj(<def—uri>, QID("ast", c), <map(term2slot)> t*)
3   term2slot   : None()       → None()
4   term2slot   : Some(t)      → Some(<term2slot> t)
5   term2slot   : t*           → <map(term2slot)> t*
6   term2val    : t            → Data(t) where is—string; not(ref—uri)
7   term2val    : t            → Link(<ref—uri>)
8   term2val    : t            → Contain(<term2obj> t) where is—compound
9
10  model2tree: M(obj)                      → <obj2term> obj
11  obj2term   : Obj(_, QID("ast", c), s*)  → c#(<map(slot2term)> s*)
12  slot2term  : None()                     → None()
13  slot2term  : Some(val)                  → Some(<slot2term> val)
14  slot2term  : val*                       → <map(slot2term)> val*
15  val2term   : Data(val)                  → val
16  val2term   : Link(uri)                  → <name—of> uri
17  val2term   : Contain(obj)               → <obj2term> obj
```

Fig. 5. Rewrite rules defining corresponding tree-to-model and model-to-tree transformations in Stratego

this by generating classes from context-free sorts and productions (ll. 15-24). To avoid name conflicts, we organize them in separate packages `cf` and `ast`. For each context-free sort, we generate an abstract class (`sort2classes`). For each production of this sort, we generate a concrete class subclassing the abstract class (`prod2class`). Features are generated from the symbols of the production (ll. 26-32). We generate an attribute for each lexical sort (first rule). The type of this attribute is derived from the lexical sort. For each context-free sort, we generate a containment reference (second rule). Bounds of generated features depend on operators (ll. 34-37). Options get a lower bound of 0, while all other symbols get a lower bound of 1. Lists get an unlimited upper bound, while all other sorts get an upper bound of 1.

Name Binding. In our minimalistic grammar formalism, namespaces and sorts are separate concepts. Thus, namespaces impose their own class hierarchy on the generated metamodel. For each namespace, we generate an abstract class which subclasses its parent namespaces (ll. 38-43). When a production defines a definition site of a name, the concrete class generated from this production needs to subtype the namespace of the definition site. Therefore, `symbol2parent` collects the namespaces of definition sites. At definition sites, the generated feature is the same as for ordinary lexical sorts (ll. 45-48). At use sites, a reference to the namespace is generated instead (ll. 50-53).

2.2 Bidirectional Mapping between Trees and Models

We specify a bidirectional mapping between trees and models as a pair of unidirectional mappings `tree2model` and `model2tree` in Fig. 5.

To transform a tree into a model, we transform its term representation into an object (`tree2model`). This is done by decomposing the term into its constructor `c` and subterms `t*`. The constructor is used to identify the corresponding class in the operator and the subterms are transformed into slots. When a term is the

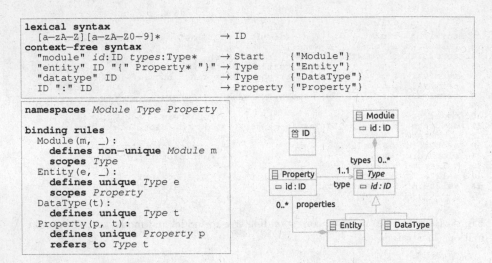

Fig. 6. Syntax definition in SDF (top), name binding rules in NaBL (left) and generated Ecore metamodel (right) for an entity language.

definition site of a name, we expect def-uri to provide a URI for it. Otherwise, it should yield None(). The first rule of term2val transforms strings (the leaves of a tree) into (one of) the slot's value(s). The rule only works if the string is not the use site of a name. The second rule covers such use sites, by generating a link with a URI. We expect ref-uri to provide the URI of a bound name. Otherwise, it should fail. The third rule of term2val transforms compound terms into contained objects.

The rules for model2tree mirror the rules for tree2model. We expect name-of to yield the name which establishes the binding to the linked object.

2.3   Connecting Spoofax and EMF

In Spoofax, lexical and context-free syntax are defined in SDF [9,26]. Name binding and scope rules are defined separately in NaBL [14]. From these definitions we generate metamodels in Ecore, EMF's metamodeling formalism [24]. Fig. 6 shows syntax definition, name binding rules and generated metamodel for a small data modeling language.

SDF and NaBL differ from the minimalistic grammar formalism in several ways. First, naming conventions are different. Since symbols are only optionally labeled in SDF, we generate missing labels either from sorts or from referred namespaces. We use annotated constructor names as production names. Since these are not required to be unique in SDF, we generate unique names where needed. Second, SDF supports special injection and bracket productions, which we model by inheritance. Third, SDF provides additional kinds of EBNF-like operators and allows to apply them not only to sorts, but on any symbol. We introduce intermediate sorts to break down such applications. Finally, NaBL separates name binding rules from productions. We weave productions and name binding rules based on their constructors.

Ecore differs from the minimalistic metamodel formalism as well. The only relevant differences are order and uniqueness of many-valued features. Since text is sequential, we generate ordered features. While references and containments are inherently unique in Ecore, we generate non-unique attributes. In a post-processing step, we simplify the generated metamodel. We fold linear inheritance chains, merge classes which share all their subclasses, and pull common features from subclasses into their parent class.

For the mapping between trees and models, we apply the previously shown transformations.Additionally, we provide a thin, generic Java layer which can convert between models as Spoofax terms and models as EMF objects.

3   Error Recovery

Error recovery is crucial for real-time synchronization between editors. Furthermore, it allows for persisting erroneous models using the textual syntax. We distinguish three kinds of errors which affect editor synchronization. *Parse errors* and *unresolved names* are discovered in the textual editor when the text is parsed to an AST which is afterwards statically analyzed. *Graphical syntax errors* occur in the graphical editor when a model does not satisfy lower bound constraints of its metamodel. Graphical editors relax this constraint to allow for incremental modeling. More specific, semantic errors do not affect synchronization and error marking for such errors is allowed in either the textual or graphical editor, or both.

Parse Errors. Modern IDEs parse text with every change that is made to it, ensuring rapid syntactic and semantic feedback as a program is edited. As text is often in a syntactically invalid state as it is edited, parse error recovery is needed to diagnose and report parse errors, and to construct a valid AST for syntactically invalid text. Therefore, Spoofax has strong support for parse error recovery [4]. It introduces additional recovery productions to grammars that make it possible to parse syntactically incorrect text with added or missing characters. These rules are automatically derived from the original grammar. Spoofax' parsing algorithm activates these rules only when syntax errors are encountered and uses layout information to improve the quality of recoveries for scoping structures, while still ensuring efficient parsing of erroneous text. This approach avoids the loss of AST parts when a correct text is changed into an incorrect one, which is crucial for real-time synchronization.

Unresolved names. Spoofax resolves names after parsing with an algorithm which is based on declarative name binding and scoping rules [14]. The algorithm is language-independent, handles multiple files, and works incrementally, which allows for efficient re-analysis after changes. During intermediate editing stages, not all references may be resolved. Fig. 7 illustrates this with a simple data model. It contains a property title of type Strin, which cannot be resolved.

Fig. 7. Recovery from a name resolution error and from a graphical syntax error

We recover from such errors during tree-to-model transformation (step ❷). Spoofax provides special URIs for unresolved references. When we discover such a URI, we do not fill the corresponding slot in the model. GMF handles such underspecified models and visualizes model elements with unfilled slots. In the example from Fig. 7, the property appears in the graphical editor without any type. The user can specify the missing type either by continue typing or by choosing the type in the properties view of the graphical editor.

Graphical syntax errors. During graphical editing, newly added model elements are typically underspecified. Since graphical editors do not enforce completion, a user might first create a number of such underspecified elements before she starts to complete them. To recover from such errors, the model-to-tree transformation needs to handle incomplete models (step ❺). A simple fix would be to map unfilled slots to empty strings in the AST. Step ❻ would add these empty strings at positions where the parser expects text for the missing element. The parser recovers from such errors, but might report the error at a different position, confusing the user. To overcome this problem, the model-to-tree transformation creates textual default values for unspecified attributes and references and ignores elements with unspecified containments.

Both attributes and references are represented by strings in text. If they are unspecified upon model-to-text transformation, we generate a default value that conforms to the lexical syntax. For example, if an integer is expected, we take default value 0, while if a string is expected, we take default value x (cf. Fig. 7). Note that in case of a reference, it is important not to choose an existing name, since this will connect every new model element to an existing one. The generation of default values introduces unresolved names and possibly semantic errors as well. These errors are marked until they are resolved by completing underspecified elements. Users may also switch to textual editing in the meantime, and resolve the errors by typing. The solution can be further improved by allowing users to specify default values in the syntax definition, as one may not prefer the 'default' defaults. Unspecified containments should ideally not be permitted by graphical editors. In the graphical Behavior Trees editor (Sect. 5), for example, we automatically create both an atomic sequence and a contained node upon using the node tool. However, this is not possible if multiple subtypes are allowed, in which case the user needs to manually indicate the type of the contained element. Therefore, we ignore elements with unspecified containments during model-to-tree transformation. This means that users are required to complete such an element

Fig. 8. Textual layout preservation and pretty-printing in reaction to a new property

before switching to the textual editor, or the element will be destroyed upon the next text-to-model transformation.

4 Layout Preservation

Textual layout consists of comments and whitespace, while graphical layout consists of positions and sizes of graphical elements. This information needs to be preserved during editor synchronization. Our approach to layout preservation is based on merging in both directions (steps ③⑥). New ASTs or models are compared against their old version to calculate differences between them. Differences are then merged into the relevant representation, which causes the representation to be incrementally updated with changes from the other editor.

Textual Layout Preservation. Spoofax supports textual layout preservation for refactorings [5]. To achieve this, it combines origin tracking with pretty-printing. We reuse this feature to preserve textual layout when propagating changes from the graphical editor to text. Origin tracking relates nodes in an AST with text fragments. This information is propagated by transformations. It is lost when we transform a tree into a model, but it is still available in the AST of the textual editor. Pretty-printing considers this old AST and a new one generated by model-to-tree transformation. It compares both ASTs and preserves text corresponding to unchanged parts. Fragments corresponding to removed parts are removed from the text. New AST nodes are pretty-printed and inserted into the text. For this purpose, Spoofax generates pretty-printing rules from the syntax definition, which can be enhanced with user-defined rules [4].

Fig. 8 shows an example for the data modeling language that involves pretty-printing. First, a reference of type Author is added to the entity Book in the graphical editor. A new object is added to the underlying model and positional information for the connection anchors is added to the notation model. Model-to-tree transformation yields a new AST. Each of its subterms will match with a term in the old AST, except for the term corresponding to the new reference. This term is pretty-printed and inserted into the text. Comments and whitespace in the surrounding text are preserved.

The approach works in the presence of any type of syntactic or semantic error. However, it fails during a graphical cut-and-paste operation. Cutting destroys

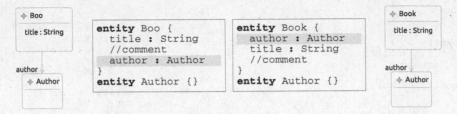

Fig. 9. Graphical layout preservation in reaction to a changed order of properties

the corresponding textual element and its associated layout. The element is recreated upon pasting, but its original layout is lost.

Graphical Layout Preservation. Spoofax re-parses text once it changes. Tree-to-model transformation turns the new AST into a model which is merged with the model from the graphical editor. We rely on EMF Compare [28,2] for comparing and merging models. Since old and new model will typically show much resemblance, difference calculation is very precise and changes that require merging are very small.

An example is given in Fig. 9 where we change the order of entities in the text. The text is parsed and a new AST is created that shows the reordering of two subterms. Tree-to-model transformation yields a new model which is compared against the old one. The only difference is a change in the order of the owned references of the `Module` object. We merge this into the old model, which result in a reordering of a list. Since the order of the entities is not graphically represented, GMF keeps the notation model and the diagram unchanged.

Fig. 9 shows another example in which we change the identifier of an entity. Many model merging approaches use identifiers of objects for matching. When an identifier changes, objects are no longer matched resulting in a deletion and re-creation. Layout of the deleted object is lost. EMF Compare takes not only identifiers but all slots of an object into account. It typically matches renamed elements and layout information can be preserved.

This is also shown in Fig. 9. Here, we change the name of entity `Boo` into `Book`. This change is reflected in the new AST and the new model. Since the name slots of the old and new `Entity` object show much resemblance and since both objects contain the same property, the objects match. During merging, only the value of the `name` attribute changes. During synchronization with the graphical editor (step ④), no information is added to the notation model, but the label corresponding to the attribute is re-rendered to show the new name.

The approach works in the presence of any type of semantic or graphical syntactic error. However, sometimes we cannot recover from a parse error, in which case only a partial AST is created. Synchronization will then destroy the graphical elements corresponding to the erroneous text region. Upon resolving the error, the graphical elements are recreated, but their original layout is lost. Furthermore, similarly to textual layout preservation, graphical layout preservation fails during textual cut-and-paste operations.

5   Case Study: Behavior Trees

A behavior tree (see Fig. 2 and Fig. 10 for examples) is a formal, tree-like graphical form that represents behavior of individual or networks of entities [7]. The Behavior Trees (BT) language has formed the base of Behavior Engineering (BE), an approach to systems development that supports the engineering of large-scale dependable software intensive systems [17].

Tooling support for BT initially focused on graphical editors only [27,22]. Recently, the language was extended with a formal textual syntax [3] and TextBE, a textual editor combined with a visualizer based on EMFText and SVG Eclipse, was introduced [17]. Although textual editing greatly reduced the time to create behavior tree models, TextBE is still limited in that it visualizes only on-save, which inhibits the expected interaction in an IDE, prevents manual layout of the graphical representation, which affects use cases like printing and sharing seriously, and does not provide navigation means between textual and graphical representation, which inhibits fast visual search. We applied our approach to BT in order to create an integrated textual and graphical editor. The editors synchronize in real-time, allow for manual and automated textual and graphical layout, preserve layout during synchronization, and support selection sharing to navigate between both representations.

Fig. 10 illustrates the robustness of the text-to-model transformation. First, the identifier of state Closed changes from 2 into 21. As a consequence, references to this state become unresolved and the label in the graphical model vanishes. Next, a semicolon is added after the node which results in a parse error. Though, a new model element appears since the semicolon indicates a following node. When we continue typing R1 C3 1, the graphical node is incrementally

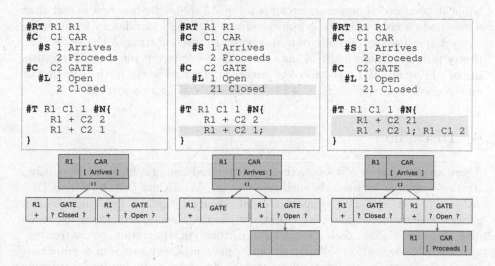

Fig. 10. Graphical layout preservation and auto-layout during textual editing and in the presence of parse errors and unresolved references.

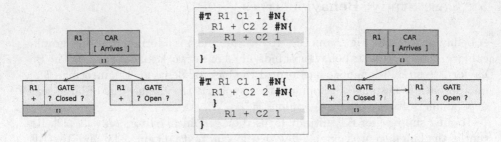

Fig. 11. Graphical layout preservation during textual drag-and-drop

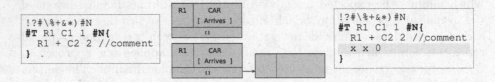

Fig. 12. Textual layout preservation and pretty-printing during graphical editing in the presence of both graphical and textual syntax errors

built up while its original assigned position is maintained. Finally, we update the broken reference by typing an additional 1. This resolves the reference such that the graphical representation shows the same label as before. Fig. 11 illustrates a more drastic change, where text is dragged from an inner scope and dropped in an outer scope. Graphically, connections between nodes change accordingly, while all positions of nodes are preserved. Fig. 12 shows the text before and after a new node is created in the graphical editor. Although mandatory features are not yet specified, we already obtain a textual representation of the node. The pretty printer automatically indents the node, while layout information consisting of whitespace and a comment is preserved. This all works in the presence of an erroneous text region (cf. !?#\%+&*)#N) which is also preserved.

6   Discussion

There are two classes of tools that support textual and graphical model editing. *Textual modeling frameworks* such as Xtext [8], MontiCore [15], EMFText [10], TCS [12], and TEF [19] support textual editing by parser generation and a generic tree-to-model mapping. First, we discuss their specification approach and then we discuss their support for editor synchronization, error-recovery and layout preservation. Similar to our approach, Xtext provides a grammar-based formalism and generates metamodels. However, name binding constructs provided by the formalism are limited. Scope and import rules, which can be declaratively defined in NaBL, need to be implemented in Java instead. This is a limitation of the other frameworks as well. MontiCore provides a formalism for describing both a grammar and a metamodel. While we automatically derive a set of abstract classes and an inheritance hierarchy from the textual syntax definition, MontiCore allows users to manually specify those. This provides more flexibility to influence the resulting metamodel. TEF requires the user to specify both grammar and metamodel, which is very redundant. EMFText and TCS take the opposite approach and start from a metamodel. TCS requires the user to specify templates, which are then used for parsing and pretty-printing. With EMFText, user-defined templates are optional, since it generates default ones based on the UML Human-Usable Textual Notation [23].

Of all the frameworks, only TEF merges textual and graphical models, while the others only inherit limited synchronization capabilities from EMF and GMF, where models are synchronized on save. Saving overwrites the previous model and breaks references from the notation model. A GMF edit policy then tries to repair references, which often leads to deletions followed by re-creations of notations and a loss of layout. All frameworks except TEF support textual layout preservation. However, in on-save synchronization multiple model changes are merged into the text at once, making the merging process imprecise such that layout is not always preserved correctly. All frameworks have only limited error recovery capabilities such that switching between textual and graphical editing is only possible if models are not broken. However, on-save synchronization does not introduce the problem of layout being destroyed when elements are temporarily lost due to parse errors or cut-and-paste operations. Our approach could possibly be improved by providing additional means to maintain such layout, or by delaying synchronization until parse errors don't result in partial ASTs anymore and cut-and-paste operations are completed.

Projectional editors as provided by MPS [6] or Intentional [21] support different views and different concrete syntax projections which are automatically synchronized since they all share the same abstract syntax model. Editing directly affects the abstract syntax, similar to graphical editing. However, typical textual operations such as indentation or rearranging are not possible, but can be simulated to a certain degree. Another notable tool that provides mappings between text and models is Enso [25], which requires the user to provide both a grammar and a metamodel that need to be kept consistent.

7   Conclusion

This paper presented an approach for robust real-time synchronization between textual and graphical editors. It recovers from errors during synchronization and preserves textual and graphical layout during editing, even in the presence of errors. It allows for a new type of highly interactive editors and has successfully been applied to the Behavior Trees modeling language.

References

1. Bravenboer, M., Kalleberg, K.T., Vermaas, R., Visser, E.: Stratego/XT 0.17. A language and toolset for program transformation. SCP 72(1-2), 52–70 (2008)
2. Brun, C., Pierantonio, A.: Model differences in the Eclipse Modeling Framework. In: UPGRADE, IX (April 2008)
3. Colvin, R., Hayes, I.J.: A semantics for Behavior Trees using CSP with specification commands. SCP 76(10), 891–914 (2011)
4. de Jonge, M., Nilsson-Nyman, E., Kats, L.C.L., Visser, E.: Natural and flexible error recovery for generated parsers. In: van den Brand, M., Gašević, D., Gray, J. (eds.) SLE 2009. LNCS, vol. 5969, pp. 204–223. Springer, Heidelberg (2010)
5. de Jonge, M., Visser, E.: An algorithm for layout preservation in refactoring transformations. In: Sloane, A., Aßmann, U. (eds.) SLE 2011. LNCS, vol. 6940, pp. 40–59. Springer, Heidelberg (2012)
6. Dmitriev, S.: Language oriented programming: The next programming paradigm (2004)
7. Dromey, R.G.: From requirements to design: Formalizing the key steps. In: SEFM, pp. 2–11 (2003)
8. Eysholdt, M., Behrens, H.: Xtext: implement your language faster than the quick and dirty way. In: OOPSLA, pp. 307–309 (2010)
9. Heering, J., Hendriks, P.R.H., Klint, P., Rekers, J.: The syntax definition formalism SDF - reference manual. SIGPLAN 24(11), 43–75 (1989)
10. Heidenreich, F., Johannes, J., Karol, S., Seifert, M., Wende, C.: Derivation and refinement of textual syntax for models. In: Paige, R.F., Hartman, A., Rensink, A. (eds.) ECMDA-FA 2009. LNCS, vol. 5562, pp. 114–129. Springer, Heidelberg (2009)
11. Hemel, Z., Kats, L.C.L., Groenewegen, D.M., Visser, E.: Code generation by model transformation: a case study in transformation modularity. SoSyM 9(3), 375–402 (2010)
12. Jouault, F., Bézivin, J., Kurtev, I.: TCS: a DSL for the specification of textual concrete syntaxes in model engineering. In: GPCE, pp. 249–254 (2006)
13. Kats, L.C.L., Visser, E.: The Spoofax language workbench: rules for declarative specification of languages and IDEs. In: OOPSLA, pp. 444–463 (2010)
14. Konat, G., Kats, L., Wachsmuth, G., Visser, E.: Declarative name binding and scope rules. In: Czarnecki, K., Hedin, G. (eds.) SLE 2012. LNCS, vol. 7745, pp. 311–331. Springer, Heidelberg (2013)
15. Krahn, H., Rumpe, B., Völkel, S.: Integrated definition of abstract and concrete syntax for textual languages. In: Engels, G., Opdyke, B., Schmidt, D.C., Weil, F. (eds.) MODELS 2007. LNCS, vol. 4735, pp. 286–300. Springer, Heidelberg (2007)
16. Mülder, A., Nyßen, A.: TMF meets GMF. Kombination textueller und grafischer Editoren. Eclipse Magazin 3, 74–78 (2011) (in German)
17. Myers, T.: TextBE: A textual editor for behavior engineering. In: ISSEC (2011)
18. Object Management Group. Meta Object Facility (MOF) 2.0 Query/View/Transformation Specification. Version 1.1 (January 2011)
19. Scheidgen, M.: Integrating content assist into textual modelling editors. In: Modellierung, pp. 121–131 (2008)
20. Scheidgen, M.: Textual modelling embedded into graphical modelling. In: Schieferdecker, I., Hartman, A. (eds.) ECMDA-FA 2008. LNCS, vol. 5095, pp. 153–168. Springer, Heidelberg (2008)

21. Simonyi, C.: The death of computer languages, the birth of intentional programming. In: NATO Science Committee Conference (1995)
22. Smith, C., Winter, K., Hayes, I.J., Dromey, R.G., Lindsay, P.A., Carrington, D.A.: An environment for building a system out of its requirements. In: ASE, pp. 398–399 (2004)
23. Steel, J., Raymond, K.: Generating human-usable textual notations for information models. In: EDOC, pp. 250–261 (2001)
24. Steinberg, D., Budinsky, F., Paternostro, M., Merks, E.: Eclipse Modeling Framework, 2nd edn. Addison-Wesley (2009)
25. van der Storm, T., Cook, W.R., Loh, A.: Object grammars: Compositional & bidirectional mapping between text and graphs. In: Czarnecki, K., Hedin, G. (eds.) SLE 2012. LNCS, vol. 7745, pp. 4–23. Springer, Heidelberg (2013)
26. Visser, E.: A family of syntax definition formalisms. Technical Report P9706, Programming Research Group, University of Amsterdam (August 1997)
27. Wen, L., Colvin, R., Lin, K., Seagrott, J., Yatapanage, N., Dromey, R.G.: "Integrare", a collaborative environment for behavior-oriented design. In: Luo, Y. (ed.) CDVE 2007. LNCS, vol. 4674, pp. 122–131. Springer, Heidelberg (2007)
28. Xing, Z., Stroulia, E.: UMLDiff: an algorithm for object-oriented design differencing. In: ASE, pp. 54–65 (2005)

Achieving Practical Genericity in Model Weaving through Extensibility[*]

Max E. Kramer[1], Jacques Klein[2], Jim R.H. Steel[3], Brice Morin[4], Jörg Kienzle[5], Olivier Barais[6], and Jean-Marc Jézéquel[6]

[1] Karlsruhe Institute of Technology, Karlsruhe
[2] University of Luxembourg, Luxembourg
[3] The University of Queensland, Brisbane
[4] SINTEF ICT, Oslo
[5] McGill University, Montréal
[6] IRISA-INRIA, Triskell, Rennes

Abstract. Many tasks in Model-Driven Engineering (MDE) involve cross-cutting model modifications that are bound to certain conditions. These transformation tasks may affect numerous model elements and appear in different forms, such as refactoring, model completions or aspect-oriented model weaving. Although the operations at the heart of these tasks are domain-independent, generic solutions that can easily be used and customized are rare. General-purpose model transformation languages as well as existing model weavers exhibit metamodel-specific restrictions and introduce accidental complexity. In this paper, we present a model weaver that addresses these problems using an extensible approach that is defined for metamodelling languages and therefore generic. Through examples of different formalisms we illustrate how our weaver manages homogeneous in-place model transformations that may involve the duplication, merge, and removal of model elements in a generic way. Possibilities to extend and customize our weaver are exemplified for the non-software domain of Building Information Modelling (BIM).

1   Introduction and Motivation

In Model-Driven Engineering (MDE), various activities require the modification of several areas of a model that satisfy specific properties. Such activities may take the shape of refactoring tasks or search-and-replace tasks similar to those supported in textual editors of Integrated Development Environments (IDEs). Others appear as model-completion transformations or aspect-oriented model weaving. These activities are composed of atomic add, change, and remove operations similar to Create, Read, Update, Delete (CRUD) operations of databases. Although these operations are problem-independent, generic solutions that can be *easily* reused and customized for arbitrary domains are rare. Existing solutions

---

[*] This work is supported by the Fonds National de la Recherche (FNR), Luxembourg, under the MITER project C10/IS/783852.

K. Duddy and G. Kappel (Eds.): ICMT 2013, LNCS 7909, pp. 108–124, 2013.

are restricted to certain types of models, do not support conditional application of changes, ignore domain-specific properties, or introduce accidental complexity.

General-purpose model-to-model transformation languages, for example, have not been designed specifically for homogeneous in-place refinement transformations, but support a multitude of scenarios. As a result, domain experts wanting to add or change model details have to make efforts to master these powerful, yet general-purpose, transformation languages. They have to reason about languge technicalities that are not central to their task, such as copying elements.

Model weaving approaches provide specific constructs for model changes that cross-cut the system's main decomposition. Currently available model weavers, however, tend to complicate these simple tasks just as general-purpose transformation languages do. The complexity results from the need for detailed weaving instructions, preparatory transformations of input models to weaving-supporting formalisms, or incomplete automation. Nevertheless, industrial domain-specific applications of model weaving, e.g. for communication infrastructure [4] or robustness modelling [1], suggest that these shortcomings can be overcome.

This paper presents a generic, extensible, and practical model weaver, called GeKo [5], together with a demonstration of its use in different domains. Our approach is generic because it is defined on top of a metamodelling language. It can be applied to all instances of arbitrary metamodels that were defined using this metamodelling language. Our approach is extensible because domain-specific solutions can be used without modifications of the generic core weaving logic. Finally, it is practical because it can be used together with existing MDE tools. It is not necessary to learn new notations or to understand new frameworks in order to apply the weaver. The presented approach evolved from earlier work on generic model weaving [22]. We added extension support, automated customization steps and improved the join point detection mechanism, the weaving implementation and the formalization. Our weaver was used to integrate building specification information into models of buildings. It is currently being integrated into the Palladio [3] IDE for model-driven development of component-based systems.

The contributions of this paper are:

- The presentation of a generic model weaver proving that practical generic model weaving can be defined on the level of metamodelling languages.
- The illustration of an extension mechanism for this weaver, showing that little work is needed to customize the generic approach to specific domains.
- The detailed description of challenging weaving scenarios for examples of two formalisms that illustrate the atomic metamodel-independent operations.

The remainder of this paper is structured as follows. Section 2 provides the background for our work. In Section 3, we present the key characteristics and the individual weaving phases. Section 4 explains how we ensure that our concepts and implementations are generic and extensible. The customization capabilities are illustrated in Section 5 through an application of our approach to Building Information Modelling (BIM). Section 6 details the generic realisation of atomic duplication, merge, and removal operations during model composition. Section 7 presents related work and Section 8 draws some final conclusions.

2   Foundations

2.1   Model Weaving and Aspect-Oriented Modelling

Aspect-Oriented Modelling (AOM) provides explicit language constructs for cross-cutting concerns. Many AOM techniques use constructs similar to those of Aspect-Oriented Programming (AOP). A *pointcut* describes at which points of a model an aspect should be applied. An *advice* defines what should be done whenever a part of a model matches the description of a pointcut. Together, pointcut and advice form an *aspect*. The points in a base model that match a pointcut are called *join points*. After identification of these points, the changes described in an advice can be executed at these points. This process of incorporating advice information into a base model is called *model weaving*. Other approaches to model composition, e.g. [6], do not provide new constructs such as pointcuts as they merge models expressed using the same notation.

2.2   Building Information Modelling

The term Building Information Modelling (BIM) [7] refers to models of buildings that contain semantic information in addition to three-dimensional geometric information. BIM started to replace two-dimensional models in the last decade, but is still not completely widespread [10]. Most BIM design tools use proprietary formats to represent and render models. For interoperability these tools usually provide import and export functionalities for a standard format called Industry Foundation Classes (IFC) [11]. The weaver presented in this paper was used together with a framework that bridges the technological spaces of BIM and MDE [27] in order to apply MDE techniques to models of buildings. Such an application of MDE presents challenges in terms of scalability and integration as many stakeholders use partial models of significant size and complexity.

A common technique to avoid adding the same details at several places in a model of a building is to define them in a document called a *building specification*. As building specifications, like all natural-language texts, can be ambiguous and open to different interpretations, it is hard to use them in automated processes. Nevertheless, building specifications and models are used as the main inputs for analysis tasks like cost estimation. These analyses would be easier if cross-cutting specification concerns were directly woven into models of buildings [17].

3   Overview

In this section we introduce our approach to model weaving. First, we describe five key features that characterise our approach in addition to the genericity and extensibility explained in Section 4. Then, we outline the main weaving phases.

3.1   Key Characteristics

Asymmetric Weaving of Ordinary Models. In our approach, aspects that are defined by a pointcut model and an advice model are woven into a base model. This kind of approach is called asymmetric as the arguments have different *roles* (base, pointcut and advice), in contrast to symmetric approaches, such as [6], which weave entities that are not distinguished using *roles* or types.

Implicit Join Points allow Direct Use. Our approach uses implicit join points that are identified using a join point detection mechanism. This means that points at which a model should be changed can be defined using an ordinary model snippet, which serves as a detection pattern. No preparatory steps, such as manually annotating a model or executing transformations that mark elements to be changed, are needed as is the case for other approaches [13,26].

Aspect Definition using Familiar Syntax. In our approach, pointcut and advice models are defined using relaxed versions of the original metamodel. In these metamodels, constraints, such as lower bounds and abstract metaclasses, are relaxed in order to allow the definition of incomplete model snippets. Such a relaxed metamodel is a supertype of the original metamodel as every model conforming to the original metamodel also conforms to the relaxed metamodel. Therefore, aspects can be defined with existing tools that only have to be slightly modified in order to support instantiations of abstract metaclasses and allow violations of lower bounds. Relaxed metamodels were previously presented [24], but they have not been realised in an automated, metamodel-independent way.

Declarative Mapping from Pointcut to Advice. In our approach, users declaratively define which elements of the pointcut correspond to which elements of the advice. This indirect weaving specification relieves the user from the need to explicitly specify weaving steps as they are inferred from the mapping. In most cases the mapping can even be determined automatically. In contrast to declarative transformation languages like QVT-R, this mapping is metamodel-independent. The foundations of such declarative weaving instructions have been presented previously [22], and continue to be a unique feature of GeKo.

Metamodel-independent Operations. Our generic model weaver is able to process instances of arbitrary metamodels. This is possible because weaving operations are based on the properties of the metamodel to which the model conforms. These metamodel properties are automatically retrieved for every metamodel and not hard-coded for a specific metamodel. They can be attributes, which store primitive types, or references to complex types. Attributes and references are part of various metamodelling languages, such as the standard EMOF 2.0 or KM3 [12]. Therefore, our approach can even be used for different metamodelling languages. Metamodel-independent operations have already been proposed [22], but have never been realised in a completely generic way. Our current implementation [5] is based on the metamodelling language *Ecore*, which is a variant of EMOF 2.0.

3.2 Weaving Phases

Our approach consists of five different phases, shown in Fig. 1. Six out of the seven extension points discussed in Section 4 are also displayed.

0) Loading Makes the relevant base, pointcut, and advice models available.

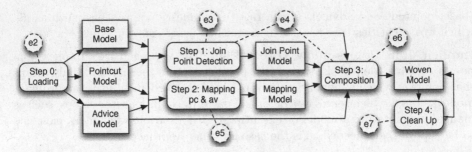

Fig. 1. The models, phases, and major extension points of the weaving process

1) Join Point Detection. The first phase of weaving identifies all locations of the base model that match the model snippets defined in the pointcut model. As an intermediate result, we obtain for each matched location a one-to-one mapping from pointcut elements to base elements, which we call *join points*. Depending on the structure and size of base and pointcut models, this preparatory step can dominate the overall time required for weaving. For this reason, we decouple it completely from the other phases of weaving. This allows for different matching algorithms as well as for domain-specific pointcut matching optimisations that are independent of the remaining weaving steps.

In our current implementation, join point detection is fully automated by generating rules targeting the business logic integration platform Drools, which implements the Rete algorithm [8]. This is similar to the SmartAdapters approach [23]. The main difference, however, is that we do not generate advice instantiation rules but decoupled this from the advice-independent join point detection in order to separate steps that are subject to different evolution pressure.

2) Inferring a Pointcut to Advice Mapping. In order to know how elements before weaving correspond to elements after the weaving we need a mapping from pointcut to advice elements. This mapping is a model consisting of entries that list references to pointcut and advice elements. It can be defined independent of the way the pointcut and advice model itself are defined. To relieve the user from as much complexity as possible, the weaver automatically infers the mapping and skips ambiguous cases. Unambiguity is given, if every pointcut element matches at most one advice element of the same type having the same primitive attributes. Fortunately, this happens to be the case for many weaving scenarios such as the one presented in Fig. 2. The mapping inference algorithm matches pointcut elements to advice elements that exhibit all attributes of the pointcut element. Therefore, it rather produces false negatives than false positives. If an automatically inferred mapping is incomplete, only the remaining unmapped elements have to be mapped manually. As the m-to-n mapping may relate multiple pointcut elements with multiple advice elements, it may induce duplication and merge operations, which are discussed in detail in Section 6.2 and Section 6.3.

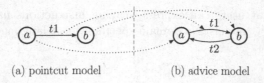

(a) pointcut model   (b) advice model

Fig. 2. An example of a pointcut and advice model with an unambiguous mapping (dotted arrows) from pointcut to advice elements that can be automatically inferred.

3) Model Composition. The central weaving phase composes the base and advice models by merging the property values of their elements. Property values of the advice are used to replace or complete base property values, but removal operations are deferred to the last phase. At the end of the composition phase, newly introduced elements are added to containers using the involved containment references. A detailed description of the composition phase is given in Section 6.

4) Removal and Clean-up. In the last phase of weaving, base elements that correspond to pointcut elements, but that do not correspond to any advice elements, are removed. In order to keep the model consistent, references to these elements need to be removed as well. If model elements violate the lower bounds of reference properties as a result of these removals, then they are removed as well. This is necessary to guarantee that woven models still conform to their metamodel. An example for this removal of inconsistencies is presented in Section 6.4.

4 Genericity and Extensibility

In this section we explain the techniques used in order to provide a generic and extensible approach, which can be customized for arbitrary metamodels.

4.1 Genericity

The key design decision that makes our approach generic is to transform models solely by operations formulated on the meta-metamodel level. These operations allow us to add, change, and remove elements of a metamodel instance using the properties of the metamodel that in turn conforms to a meta-metamodel. Let us illustrate this using a small example. Suppose a single join point element j in a base model matches a pointcut element p that corresponds to an advice element v. Such a match leads to a woven model in which j exhibits the properties of v. In order to perform this weaving it is irrelevant whether the model elements j and v are entities of a UML diagram or elements of a construction plan of a building. It is sufficient to inspect and update the values of the properties that are defined in the metamodel for the metaclasses of j and v.

To make this metamodel-independent approach work, we give users the ability to formulate pointcut and advice model snippets as instances of automatically derived metamodel variants with relaxed constraints. We already described the derivation and use of these relaxed metamodels in Section 3.1. A convenient consequence is that users can express weaving instructions using the familiar syntax for ordinary models. No domain-specific aspect languages are needed.

4.2 Extensibility

Our generic approach may not handle all weaving circumstances for all meta-models in the way desired by its users. Therefore, we give users the ability to reuse parts of our generic weaver and to customize them to obtain a domain-specific weaver. In this section, we briefly present the customization capabilities and in Section 5 we show an exemplary customization for the domain of BIM.

Some of the extension points that we provide can be used to change the default weaving behaviour of GeKo. Others can be used to perform additional work before or after general weaving operations. In some cases we provide two extension points for the same task in order to give users the ability to provide simple as well as more elaborate extensions. In the current implementation of our approach the customization possibilities are realised as Eclipse extension points that can be extended without directly modifying the original plug-ins.

We will now briefly describe the customization facilities in their order of use:

EP 1: During the preparatory derivation of relaxed metamodels for pointcut and advice models the default generator model can be modified. It specifies how Java classes that realise the metaclasses of the metamodel are generated.

EP 2: The process of loading and storing models before and after the actual weaving can be customized using a simple and a detailed extension point.

EP 3: Join point detection can be completely customized as its result is an ordinary one-to-one mapping from pointcut to base elements for every join point.

EP 4: It is possible to ignore specific properties of metaclasses during join point detection and model comparison using another extension point.

EP 5: For the automatic inference of a mapping from pointcut elements to advice elements the calculation of unique identifiers can be customized. These identifiers are used to match pointcut elements to advice elements.

EP 6: The introduction of new base elements corresponding to advice model elements that do not have associated pointcut elements can be customized.

EP 7: The determination of containment references can be customized for advice elements that are not unambiguously contained in another element.

All of these extension points, except EP 3 and EP 5, are used for the BIM customization of our weaver, which we present in the next section. EP 3 is required, for example, when model semantics have to be considered during join point detection. For behavioural models, such as sequence diagrams, it is possible that join points do not appear explicitly with the same syntax in the base model. In the presence of loops, for example, the first part of the join point can appear in a first iteration of the loop, whereas the second part of the join point occurs on a second iteration of the loop [14]. In such a case, the join point detection mechanism has to be extended to account for the semantics of such elements.

5   Customizing GeKo to Support BIM Weaving

To give the reader a better idea of the extension capabilities of our generic approach we present a set of weaver extensions for IFC models of buildings.

The first two extensions to our model weaver are necessary because we cannot use default XMI serialisation for IFC models. We load IFC models serialised in ASCII text files as instances of an Ecore metamodel using a technological bridge [27]. In our first extension (EP 1) we propagate the IFC-specific changes in the bridge's code generator into the code generator for the relaxed pointcut and advice metamodels. The second extension (EP 2) customizes the resource loader to retrieve content model elements from wrapping elements that model the serialisation format. Because the serialisation and the domain metamodel are defined using Ecore, we do not have to provide all loading and storing infrastructure but can reuse most of the generic facilities of GeKo and EMF.

The third extension (EP 4) ensures that the weaver ignores specific values of properties of metaclasses during join point detection and model comparison. Specifically, when creating a pointcut model and specifying that a property's value is irrelevant, it is important to avoid that the default value specified by IFC is applied. During join point detection, there are certain properties, such as globally unique identifiers, which cannot be omitted from the pointcut (for reasons specific to the IFC metamodel) but which we do not wish to detect in join points. The third extension allows us to ignore values for these properties.

The fourth extension (EP 6) ensures that model elements that are not convenient to express in the aspect are included in the woven model. For example, every IFC element is required to include an "owner history", which details the person responsible for making changes to the model. It is inconvenient to repeat this information for every pointcut and advice element, so this extension makes it possible to have this information propagated implicitly.

The last extension (EP 7) for IFC models applies at the very end of the weaving process. It ensures that all elements added to the base model during the weaving that are not yet contained in any building element are added to the main container using the correct containment reference. This extension illustrates an advantage of our approach resulting from the decision to support pointcut and advice definition using incomplete model snippets. IFC models may exhibit deeply nested hierarchies. A window, for example, may be part of a hierarchy that starts with a storey and includes a building container, building, site container, site, project container, and project. If pointcut and advice models were complete models, the whole hierarchy beginning with the building project would have to be specified. In our approach, however, it is possible to refer to arbitrarily nested elements at the first level of pointcut and advice models. If new elements are added during the weaving, we can use information available at the join points to hook these new elements into the containment hierarchy.

Given the practical experience of providing a set of domain-specific extensions to our own generic approach, we are convinced that this strategy is generally suitable for modifying domain-specific models. The fact that less than 10% additional code (0.5 KLOC customization code, 5.1 KLOC generic code)

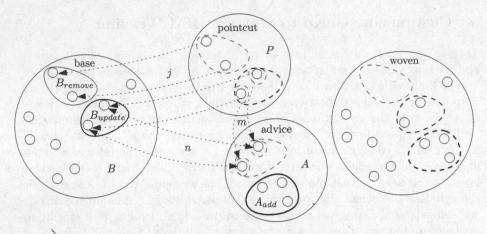

Fig. 3. Formalisation visualisation showing involved models, sets and mappings

was needed to customize the weaver for IFC models suggests that applying our generic approach requires less effort than the development of domain-specific model weavers. This, however, needs to be confirmed by future experiments that involve new extensions for other DSMLs.

6   Composition: Duplication, Merge and Removal

This section illustrates some model composition operations executed during the application of our generic weaving approach. First, we provide a short description of the formalisation upon which all composition operations are built. Second, we exemplify duplication, merge and removal operations using examples for Labelled Transition Systems (LTS) and Building Information Modelling (BIM). We chose a well-known formalism to ease the understanding and provide examples from the construction domain to illustrate the metamodel-independence of the operations.

6.1   Weaving Formalisation

We present the essential concepts of a set-theoretic formalisation of our approach. The input to our weaving algorithm is a set of base-model elements B, a set of pointcut-model elements P, and a set of advice-model elements A. From these, a join point mapping from pointcut to base elements $j : P \rightarrow B$, and a mapping from pointcut to advice elements $m : 2^P \rightarrow 2^A$ are calculated as intermediate results in steps 1) and 2) of our weaving process (see Section 3.2). Finally, the woven model is obtained using three sets and a bidirectional m-to-n mapping that we present in this section. A visualisation of the presented formalisation is displayed in Fig. 3. The interested reader is referred to an initial [22] and complete [15] description of our formalisation.

The first set contains all base-model elements that have to be removed during the weaving. These are all elements of the base model that correspond to an element of the pointcut model with no corresponding element in the advice model. More formally, given B, P, A, j and m as defined above, we define $B_{remove} := \{b \in B \mid \exists p \in P : j(p) = b \wedge m(\{p\}) = \emptyset\}$.

We define a second set that contains all base-model elements to be updated during the weaving. These are all base elements that correspond to at least one pointcut element with a corresponding advice element. In the same context as B_{remove} we define $B_{update} := \{b \in B \mid \exists p \in P : j(p) = b \wedge m(\{p\}) \neq \emptyset\}$.

The third set contains all advice-model elements that have to be added to the base model during the weaving. It is independent of a join point and contains all advice elements that correspond to no pointcut model element. More formally, given the input as above, we define $A_{add} := \{a \in A \mid \nexists p \in P : a \in m(\{p\})\}$.

The bidirectional m-to-n mapping relates base-model elements with the corresponding advice-model elements using the detected join-point mapping from pointcut to base elements and the mapping from pointcut to advice elements. In the same context as for B_{remove} and B_{update} we define the mapping $n_{base-advice}$ as $b \mapsto \{a \in A \mid \exists p \in P : j(p) = b \wedge a \in m(\{p\})\}$ and the mapping $n_{advice-base}$ as $a \mapsto \{b \in B \mid \exists p \in P : j(p) = b \wedge a \in m(\{p\})\}$ as compositions of j and m.

Our approach is inspired by graph transformations but different: In contrast to other approaches [28,20] our formalisation and implementation [5] uses sets that directly contain model elements. No translation to nodes, edges and their types and attributes is performed. Relations between set members are only handled different than other attributes after removal operations. The mapping from pointcut to advice elements can also be non-injective and not right-unique.

6.2   Duplication

The first weaving scenario that we present involves the duplication of a base model element. Such a duplication is needed if a pointcut element corresponds to more than one advice element (m is non-injective). The consequence for each join point is as follows: All the base elements representing the advice elements that are involved in the duplication have to be updated. After the duplication, these base elements have to exhibit all properties of the base element that corresponds to the pointcut element of the duplication. This is achieved by introducing the attribute and reference values of the base element that corresponds to the pointcut element into the base elements that correspond to the advice elements.

Fig. 4 illustrates such a duplication with example models of a LTS. The pointcut element b corresponds to the two advice elements $b1, b2$ (Fig. 4(b)). The only possible join point maps this pointcut element b to the base element b. More formally, $n_{base-advice}(b) = \{b_1, b_2\}$. As a result, all incoming transitions $t1$ and all outgoing transitions $t3, t4$ of b are duplicated for $b1$ and $b2$ during the weaving (Fig. 4(c)). The transition $tnew$ from $b1$ to $b2$ is newly introduced independent of this duplication operation as $tnew \in A_{add}$.

Fig. 5 illustrates a duplication scenario for models of buildings. The purpose of the aspect is to duplicate cable ports. In IFC (see Section 2.2) a cable port is represented as an `IfcPort` that is related via an `IfcRelConnectsPortToElement` to an `IfcFlowSegment` that is typed using `IfcCableSegmentType` (Fig. 5.a). To

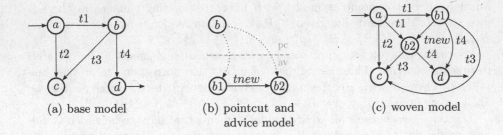

(a) base model   (b) pointcut and   (c) woven model
                            advice model

Fig. 4. Weaving an aspect into a LTS while duplicating the base element b

achieve a duplication of such ports, the advice model (Fig. 5.b) contains the same elements as the pointcut model and an additional IfcPort together with an additional relation. The mapping from pointcut to advice elements relates the single `IfcPort` of the pointcut to both `IfcPorts` of the advice and the single `IfcRelConnectsPortToElement` to both instances of the advice. All other pointcut and advice elements have a one-to-one correspondence. We do not visualise this mapping or a woven example as this would require too much space.

6.3 Merge

A scenario that can be seen as the dual to duplication occurs if more than one pointcut element corresponds to an advice element (m is not right-unique). The resulting merge has to ensure that the relevant advice elements exhibit all properties of all corresponding pointcut elements. This is realised by introducing all attribute and reference values of the base elements corresponding to the pointcut elements into the base element corresponding to the advice element.

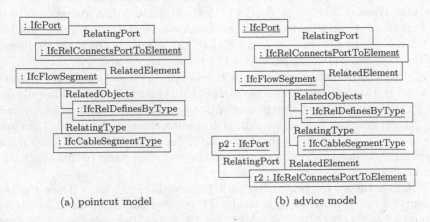

(a) pointcut model   (b) advice model

Fig. 5. An example aspect for IFC models which duplicates cable ports

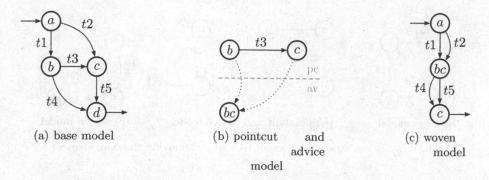

Fig. 6. Weaving an aspect into a LTS while merging the base elements b and c

The merge weaving scenario is illustrated for LTS in Fig. 6. The two pointcut elements b and c correspond to the advice element bc (Fig. 6(b)). The only possible join point maps these pointcut elements b and c to the elements with the same names in the base model. More formally $n_{base-advice}(b) = \{bc\} = n_{base-advice}(c)$. During the weaving of this example b's incoming transition $t1$ and c's incoming transition $t2$ are merged into the resulting element of the woven model bc (Fig. 6(c)). The same applies for b's outgoing transition $t4$ and c's outgoing transition $t5$. Independent of this merge operation the transition $t3$ from b to c is removed as it is bound to the transition $t3$ of the pointcut model but has no correspondence in the advice model ($t3 \in B_{remove}$).

A similar merge scenario for IFC models is shown in Fig. 7. The aspect ensures that every door with an unspecified fire rating obtains the properties of a fire resistant door. To achieve this, the property set that contains the unspecified fire rating value (and other property values which should be preserved) is merged

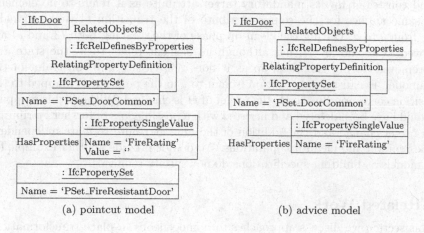

Fig. 7. An example aspect for IFC models which merges properties

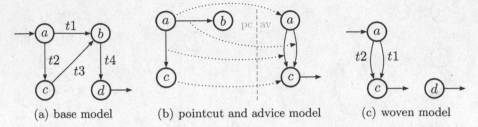

| (a) base model | (b) pointcut and advice model | (c) woven model |

Fig. 8. Weaving an aspect for a small LTS while removing the base element b

with a property set of fire resistance properties. Instead of listing all these properties (e.g. fire rating = "AS 1905.1", smoke stop = true), the corresponding property sets are listed in the pointcut and mapped to a single property set in the advice.

6.4 Removal

The last scenario that we discuss in detail involves the removal of base elements and illustrates the final clean-up phase. As explained in Section 6.1, a base element has to be removed during the weaving at a join point if this join point binds the base element to a pointcut element without a correspondence in the advice. After removing these unmatched elements it may be that other base elements that referred to a removed element violate lower bound constraints of the metamodel. Therefore, we have to detect these inconsistent elements and remove them too. Because this removal of inconsistencies can produce new inconsistencies, we have to continue the clean-up until all constraints are satisfied.

We illustrate a removal scenario using LTS example models in Fig. 8. The pointcut model element b corresponds to no advice-model element (Fig. 8(b)). Thus $b \in B_{remove}$ and therefore b is removed from the woven model (Fig. 8(c)). As a result, the transition $t3$ that originally went from c to b violates the lower-bound constraint for its mandatory target attribute as it refers to no element. The same applies for the source attribute of the transition $t4$ that originally went from b to d. During the clean-up phase of the weaving both $t3$ and $t4$ are removed. Note, however, that although no element refers to it, the state d is not removed during the clean-up as it does not violate any constraint of the metamodel. Because the transition from a to b in the pointcut is mapped to the transition corresponding to $t1$, the target of $t1$ is changed. Without this mapping $t1$ would have been deleted and inserted with a possible loss of further attributes. This target change and the addition of the final attribute to c are independent of the removal and clean-up operations. We do not provide another example for IFC models as building specifications do not specify removals.

7 Related Work

In this section we discuss approaches to homogeneous in-place transformations that are generic in the sense that they can be applied to different metamodels.

SmartAdapters is a model weaving technique for which join points had to be specified manually in the initial version. First, it had to be tailored to specific metamodels, such as Java Programs [19] and Class Diagrams [18]. Then, it has been generalised to support arbitrary metamodels [21]. Later efforts focused on its use for adapting component models at runtime so that initially generic weaving functionality can no longer be separated from advanced concepts for component-based systems. Despite this specialisation, SmartAdapters shares various concepts with GeKo. A major difference, however, is the representation of weaving instructions. In addition to a declarative pointcut and advice model, SmartAdapters needs a *composition protocol* with imperative weaving instructions. It supports sophisticated weaving operations that cannot be expressed with GeKo, but it also requires explicit definitions for very basic weaving tasks.

MATA [28] is a concept for generic model weaving based on graph transformations. It converts a base model into an attributed type graph, applies graph rules obtained from composition rules, and converts the resulting graph back to the original model type. Composition rules are defined as left-hand-side (pointcut) and right-hand side (advice), but can also be expressed in a single diagram. Although the approach is conceptually generic, we are only aware of an application in which composition rules are defined using the concrete syntax of the UML. An aspect is defined using a UML profile with stereotypes to mark elements that have to be created, matched, or deleted. In contrast to our approach, MATA does not directly operate on the input models but requires conversions and does not provide extension possibilities for domain-specific weaving.

Almazara [25] is a model weaver that generates graph-based model transformations from Join Point Designation Diagrams (JPDDs) using transformation templates. These diagrams are defined using a UML Profile and support various selection criteria, such as indirect relationships. The generated transformations collect runtime information, evaluate dynamic selection constraints and realise the weaving. This is very different from snippet-replacing approaches as it heavily integrates matching and weaving. Although JPDDs provide specialised constructs for behavioural weaving, the authors state that Almazara can be used with any modelling language. We are, however, not aware of such non-UML applications.

The Atlas Model Weaver (AMW) was developed to establish links between models that can be stored as so called *weaving models*. The links are created semi-automatically and can be used for comparing, tracing, or matching related elements. Published applications of AMW [6] use the links for heterogeneous model transformations and model comparison, but they can also be used to weave elements into a model instance. An unpublished example [2], in which attributes are woven into metaclasses, shows that join points have to be specified manually as no means are provided for pointcut definition or join point detection.

The Reuseware Composition Framework [9] provides a generic mechanism for composing modelling languages. In order to compose languages they either have to be manually extended so that they represent a component description language or a non-invasive extension has to be provided using OCL-expressions. The authors state that it is possible to reuse much composition logic once a language was made composable. Nevertheless, they do not describe an automated way to retrieve such language extensions. Furthermore, the focus of Reuseware is rather permanent language modularity than transitional composition of instances.

The Epsilon Merging Language (EML) [16] can be used to merge heterogeneous models using a syntax that is similar to declarative model transformation languages like QVT-R. These general-purpose languages support various transformation scenarios and are not specialized for in-place asymmetric homogeneous weaving according to property-based conditions. As a result, basic weaving operations, such as merging two instances of the same metaclass, have to be redefined for every application domain. This disadvantage can be mitigated using advanced transformation approaches. Higher-Order Transformations (HOTs) [13], for example, adapt transformation patterns to a domain and to individual model parts. Similarly, Generic Model Transformations [26] provide transformation templates that can be bound to specific metamodels. These approaches only support restricted pattern matching and need to be explicitly instantiated. Furthermore, users have to express transformations using constructs of the approaches and cannot describe their tasks solely with concepts of their domain.

We summarize our discussion of related work in three points. First, only our approach offers a declarative and domain-specific notation for homogeneous in-place transformations that is automatically derived in a generic way. Second, no other approach reduces the verbosity and complexity of weaving instructions and sophisticated weaving scenarios such as duplication or merge like we do it with pointcut to advice mappings. Last, related work neither separates matching from modifying logic to allow for combinations of different approaches nor provides it explicit extension points to support domain-specific customizations.

8   Conclusions and Future Work

In this paper we have presented GeKo, a generic model weaver working purely on metamodelling language constructs. We have shown that GeKo is both practical and generic because it uses declarative aspects formulated in existing notations and because it can be applied on instances of any kind of well-defined metamodel. With a selection of extension points for the refinement of weaving behaviour we have also shown that GeKo is easily extensible. This feature is crucial for a generic approach, in that it allows for customizations for domain-specific needs while reusing generic core operations. Finally, we have shown how the formalisation of GeKo allows the management of challenging weaving scenarios such as duplication, merge, and removal. With examples based on BIM and LTS we have illustrated that the operations induced by related pointcut and advice snippets can solve the problems of these scenarios in a generic way.

Further application of GeKo to weaving problems in other domains will assist in evaluating the sufficiency and usefulness of currently available extension points, and, if necessary, the identification of new ones. Also, it will be interesting to investigate alternative engines and concepts for the detection of join points, e.g. to ensure scalability in the presence of large base models and numerous join points or to allow for join point detection based on pointcut semantics.

References

1. Ali, S., Briand, L., Hemmati, H.: Modeling robustness behavior using aspect-oriented modeling to support robustness testing of industrial systems. Software and Systems Modeling, 1–38 (2011)
2. AMW Use Case: Aspect Oriented Modeling,
   http://www.eclipse.org/gmt/amw/usecases/AOM/
3. Becker, S., Koziolek, H., Reussner, R.: The Palladio component model for model-driven performance prediction. Journal of Systems and Software 82, 3–22 (2009)
4. Cottenier, T., van den Berg, A., Elrad, T.: The motorola WEAVR: Model weaving in a large industrial context. In: Proceedings of the 5th International Conference on Aspect-Oriented Software Development (AOSD 2006). ACM (2006)
5. Current prototype,
   http://code.google.com/a/eclipselabs.org/p/geko-model-weaver
6. Didonet Del Fabro, M., Valduriez, P.: Towards the efficient development of model transformations using model weaving and matching transformations. Software and Systems Modeling 8, 305–324 (2009)
7. Eastman, C., Teicholz, P., Sacks, R., Liston, K.: BIM Handbook. Wiley (2011)
8. Forgy, C.L.: Rete: A fast algorithm for the many pattern/many object pattern match problem. Artificial Intelligence 19(1), 17–37 (1982)
9. Heidenreich, F., Henriksson, J., Johannes, J., Zschaler, S.: On language-independent model modularisation. In: Katz, S., Ossher, H., France, R., Jézéquel, J.-M. (eds.) Transactions on AOSD VI. LNCS, vol. 5560, pp. 39–82. Springer, Heidelberg (2009)
10. Howard, R., Björk, B.C.: Building information modelling - experts' views on standardisation and industry deployment. Advanced Engineering Informatics 22(2), 271–280 (2008)
11. Industry Foundation Classes (IFC2x Platform), ISO/PAS Standard 16739:2005
12. Jouault, F., Bézivin, J.: KM3: A DSL for metamodel specification. In: Gorrieri, R., Wehrheim, H. (eds.) FMOODS 2006. LNCS, vol. 4037, pp. 171–185. Springer, Heidelberg (2006)
13. Kapova, L., Reussner, R.: Application of advanced model-driven techniques in performance engineering. In: Aldini, A., Bernardo, M., Bononi, L., Cortellessa, V. (eds.) EPEW 2010. LNCS, vol. 6342, pp. 17–36. Springer, Heidelberg (2010)
14. Klein, J., Hélouet, L., Jézéquel, J.M.: Semantic-based weaving of scenarios. In: Proceedings of the 5th International Conference on Aspect-Oriented Software Development (AOSD 2006). ACM (2006)
15. Klein, J., Kramer, M.E., Steel, J.R.H., Morin, B., Kienzle, J., Barais, O., Jézéquel, J.M.: On the formalisation of geko: a generic aspect models weaver. Technical Report (2012)
16. Kolovos, D.S., Paige, R.F., Polack, F.A.C.: Merging models with the epsilon merging language (EML). In: Wang, J., Whittle, J., Harel, D., Reggio, G. (eds.) MoDELS 2006. LNCS, vol. 4199, pp. 215–229. Springer, Heidelberg (2006)
17. Kramer, M.E., Klein, J., Steel, J.R.: Building specifications as a domain-specific aspect language. In: Proceedings of the Seventh Workshop on Domain-Specific Aspect Languages, DSAL 2012, pp. 29–32. ACM (2012)

18. Lahire, P., Morin, B., Vanwormhoudt, G., Gaignard, A., Barais, O., Jézéquel, J.M.: Introducing variability into aspect-oriented modeling approaches. In: Engels, G., Opdyke, B., Schmidt, D.C., Weil, F. (eds.) MODELS 2007. LNCS, vol. 4735, pp. 498–513. Springer, Heidelberg (2007)
19. Lahire, P., Quintian, L.: New perspective to improve reusability in object-oriented languages. Journal of Object Technology (ETH Zurich) 5(1), 117–138 (2006)
20. Mehner, K., Monga, M., Taentzer, G.: Analysis of aspect-oriented model weaving. In: Rashid, A., Ossher, H. (eds.) Transactions on AOSD V. LNCS, vol. 5490, pp. 235–263. Springer, Heidelberg (2009)
21. Morin, B., Barais, O., Jézéquel, J.M., Ramos, R.: Towards a generic aspect-oriented modeling framework. In: Models and Aspects Workshop, ECOOP 2007 (2007)
22. Morin, B., Klein, J., Barais, O., Jézéquel, J.M.: A generic weaver for supporting product lines. In: Proc. of the 13th International Workshop on Early Aspects at ICSE 2008, EA 2008, pp. 11–18. ACM (2008)
23. Morin, B., Klein, J., Kienzle, J., Jézéquel, J.M.: Flexible model element introduction policies for aspect-oriented modeling. In: Petriu, D.C., Rouquette, N., Haugen, Ø. (eds.) MODELS 2010, Part II. LNCS, vol. 6395, pp. 63–77. Springer, Heidelberg (2010)
24. Ramos, R., Barais, O., Jézéquel, J.M.: Matching model-snippets. In: Engels, G., Opdyke, B., Schmidt, D.C., Weil, F. (eds.) MODELS 2007. LNCS, vol. 4735, pp. 121–135. Springer, Heidelberg (2007)
25. Sánchez, P., Fuentes, L., Stein, D., Hanenberg, S., Unland, R.: Aspect-oriented model weaving beyond model composition and model transformation. In: Czarnecki, K., Ober, I., Bruel, J.-M., Uhl, A., Völter, M. (eds.) MODELS 2008. LNCS, vol. 5301, pp. 766–781. Springer, Heidelberg (2008)
26. Sánchez Cuadrado, J., Guerra, E., de Lara, J.: Generic model transformations: write once, reuse everywhere. In: Cabot, J., Visser, E. (eds.) ICMT 2011. LNCS, vol. 6707, pp. 62–77. Springer, Heidelberg (2011)
27. Steel, J., Duddy, K., Drogemuller, R.: A transformation workbench for building information models. In: Cabot, J., Visser, E. (eds.) ICMT 2011. LNCS, vol. 6707, pp. 93–107. Springer, Heidelberg (2011)
28. Whittle, J., Jayaraman, P.: Mata: A tool for aspect-oriented modeling based on graph transformation. In: Giese, H. (ed.) MODELS 2008. LNCS, vol. 5002, pp. 16–27. Springer, Heidelberg (2008)

A Rete Network Construction Algorithm
for Incremental Pattern Matching

Gergely Varró* and Frederik Deckwerth**

Technische Universität Darmstadt,
Real-Time Systems Lab,
D-64283 Merckstraße 25, Darmstadt, Germany
{gergely.varro,frederik.deckwerth}@es.tu-darmstadt.de

Abstract. Incremental graph pattern matching by Rete networks can
be used in many industrial, model-driven development and network analysis scenarios including rule-based model transformation, on-the-fly consistency validation, or motif recognition. The runtime performance of
such an incremental pattern matcher depends on the topology of the
Rete network, which is built at compile time. In this paper, we propose
a new, dynamic programming based algorithm to produce a high quality
network topology according to a customizable cost function and a user-
defined quantitative optimization target. Additionally, the Rete network
construction algorithm is evaluated by using runtime measurements.

Keywords: incremental graph pattern matching, search plan generation
algorithm, Rete network construction.

1 Introduction

The model-driven development and the network analysis domains both have
industrial scenarios, such as (i) checking the application conditions in rule-based
model transformation tools [1], or (ii) recognition of motifs [2,3] (i.e., subgraph
structures) in social, financial, transportation or communication networks, which
can be described as a general pattern matching problem.

In this context, a pattern consists of constraints, which place restrictions on
variables. The pattern matching process determines a mapping of variables to the
elements of the underlying model in such a way that the assigned model elements
must fulfill all constraints. An assignment, which involves all the variables of a
pattern, is collectively called a match.

When motif recognition, which aims at collecting statistics about the appear-
ance of characteristic patterns (i.e., subgraph structures) to analyze and improve
(e.g., communication) networks, is carried out by a pattern matching engine, two
specialties can be identified which are challenging from an implementation aspect
due to their significant impact on performance. On one hand, motifs frequently

* Co-funded by the DFG as part of the CRC 1053 MAKI.
** Supported by CASED. (www.cased.de)

K. Duddy and G. Kappel (Eds.): ICMT 2013, LNCS 7909, pp. 125–140, 2013.

and considerably *share subpatterns*, whose common handling can spare a substantial amount of memory. On the other hand, the motif searching process is invoked and executed *several times* on network graphs which are only *slightly altered* between two invocations. This observation opens up the possibility of using incremental pattern matchers which store matches in a cache, and update these matches incrementally in a change propagation process triggered by notifications about changes in the model (i.e., network graph).

Many sophisticated incremental pattern matchers [4,5,6] are implemented as Rete networks [7] which are directed acyclic graphs consisting of data processing nodes that are connected to each other by edges. Each node represents a (sub)pattern and stores the corresponding matches, while edges can send events about match set modifications. At compile time, the incremental pattern matcher builds a Rete network by using the pattern specifications. At runtime, each node continuously tracks the actual set of matches. When the network receives notifications about model changes, these modifications are processed by and propagated through the nodes. When the propagation is terminated, the network stores the matches for the patterns according to the altered model.

In the state-of-the-art Rete-based incremental pattern matching engines, the recognition of shared subpatterns, which can strongly influence the runtime memory consumption, is carried out at compile time during the construction of the Rete network by hard-wired algorithm implementations, whose design is based on the qualitative judgement of highly-qualified, experienced professionals. This approach hinders (i) the reengineering of the network builder module, (ii) the introduction of quantitative performance metrics, and (iii) the flexible selection of different optimization targets.

In this paper, we propose a new, dynamic programming based algorithm to construct a Rete network which has a high quality according to a customizable cost function and a user-defined quantitative optimization target. The algorithm automatically recognizes isomorphic subpatterns which can be represented by a single data processing node, and additionally, it favours those network topologies, in which a *large number* of these isomorphic subpatterns are handled *as early as possible*. Finally, the effects of the Rete network construction algorithm are quantitatively evaluated by using runtime measurements.

The remainder of the paper is structured as follows: Section 2 introduces basic modeling and pattern specification concepts. The incremental pattern matching process is described in Sec. 3, while Sec. 4 presents the new Rete network construction algorithm. Section 5 gives a quantitative performance assessment. Related approaches are discussed in Sec. 6, and Sec. 7 concludes our paper.

2   Metamodel, Model and Pattern Specification

2.1   Metamodels and Models

A *metamodel* represents the core concepts of a domain. In this paper, our approach is demonstrated on a real-world running example from the network analysis domain [2] whose metamodel is depicted in Fig. 1(a). *Classes* are the nodes in the metamodel. Our example domain consists of a single class MotifNode.[1] *References* are the edges between classes which can be uni- or bidirectionally navigable as indicated by the arrows at the end points. A navigable end is labelled with a *role name* and a *multiplicity* which restricts the number of targets that can be reached via the given reference. In our example, a MotifNode can be connected to an arbitrary number of MotifNodes via bidirectional motifEdges.

Figure 1(b) depicts a *model* from the domain, whose nodes and edges are called *objects* and *links*, respectively. The model shows an instance consisting of three objects of type MotifNode connected by two links of type motifEdge.

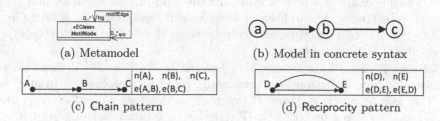

(a) Metamodel   (b) Model in concrete syntax

(c) Chain pattern   (d) Reciprocity pattern

Fig. 1. Metamodel, model and 2 patterns from the motif recognition scenario

2.2 Pattern Specification

A user of the pattern matcher specifies a set of patterns $\mathcal{P}$. As defined in [8,9], a *pattern* $P = (V_P, C_P, t_P, p_P)$ is a set of constraints C_P over a set of variables V_P. A *variable* $v \in V_P$ is a placeholder for an object in a model. A *constraint* $c \in C_P$ specifies a condition (of a *constraint type* $t_P(c)$) on a set of variables (which are also referred to as *parameters* in this context) that must be fulfilled by the objects which are assigned to the parameters. A pattern must be free of undeclared parameters and unused variables.

No undeclared parameters. The parameters of a constraint c must be variables from the set V_P, formally, $\forall c \in C_P, \forall i \le ar(t_P(c)) : p_P(c, i) \in V_P$, where $p_P(c, i)$ denotes the ith parameter of constraint c and the inequality $i \le ar(t_P(c))$ expresses that a constraint c of (constraint) type $t_P(c)$ has an arity $ar(t_P(c))$ number of parameters.

No unused variables. Each variable v must occur in at least one constraint as parameter, formally, $\forall v \in V_P, \exists c \in C_P, \exists i \le ar(t_P(c)) : p_P(c, i) = v$.

Metamodel-Specific Constraint Types: Constraint type n maintains a reference to class MotifNode in the metamodel. Constraints of type n prescribe that their single parameter must be mapped to objects of type MotifNode. Constraint

---

[1] The intentionally simple metamodel enables a compact data structure representation throughout the paper, which was required due to space limitations. However, this choice yields at the same time to the algorithmically most challenging situation (due to the high complexity of isomorphism checks in „untyped" graphs).

type e refers to association motifEdge. Constraints of type e require a link of type motifEdge that connects the source and the target object assigned to the first and second parameter, respectively.

Example. Figures 1(c) and 1(d) show two sample patterns in visual and textual syntax. The Chain pattern (Fig. 1(c)) has 3 variables (A, B, C), 3 unary constraints of type n, and 2 binary constraints of type e. Constraints of type n and e are depicted by nodes and edges in graphical syntax, respectively. E.g., n(A) prescribes that objects assigned to variable A must be of class MotifNode.

Pattern related concepts. A *morphism* $m = (m_V, m_C)$ is a function on patterns which consists of a pair of functions m_V and m_C on variables and constraints, respectively. A morphism m is *constraint type preserving* if $\forall c \in C_P$: $t_{m(P)}(m_C(c)) = t_P(c)$; and *parameter preserving* if $\forall c \in C_P, \forall i \leq ar(t_P(c))$: $p_{m(P)}(m_C(c), i) = m_V(p_P(c, i))$.

Patterns P and P' are *isomorphic* (denoted by $\triangleq(P) = P'$) if there exists a constraint type and parameter preserving, bijective morphism $\triangleq$ from P to P'. The *join of patterns* P_l *and* P_r *on join variables* $v_{x_1}, \ldots, v_{x_q} \in V_{P_l}$, and $v_{y_1}, \ldots, v_{y_q} \in V_{P_r}$ is a pattern with $|V_{P_l}| + |V_{P_r}| - q$ variables and $|C_{P_l}| + |C_{P_r}|$ constraints which is produced by a morphism pair $\bowtie^l$ and $\bowtie^r$ as follows. Each corresponding pair (v_{x_z}, v_{y_z}) of the q join variables is mapped to a (shared) new variable v'_z (i.e., $\bowtie^l_V(v_{x_z}) = \bowtie^r_V(v_{y_z}) = v'_z$). Each non-join variable v_x and v_y of pattern P_l and P_r are mapped to a new variable v'_x and v'_y by $\bowtie^l$ and $\bowtie^r$, respectively. Formally, $\bowtie^l_V(v_x) = v'_x$ and $\bowtie^r_V(v_y) = v'_y$. A new constraint c'_l (c'_r) is assigned to each constraint c_l (c_r) from pattern P_l (P_r) by $\bowtie^l_C$ ($\bowtie^r_C$) in a constraint type and parameter preserving manner.

A *subpattern* P' *of pattern* P consists of a subset of constraints of pattern P together with the variables occurring in the selected constraints as parameters. Two subpatterns P_1 and P_2 of a pattern P are *unifiable* if they have common variables. These common variables are referred to as *unifiable variables*. Two subpatterns of a pattern are *independent* if they do not share any constraints. The *union* of two independent subpatterns P_1 and P_2 of a pattern (denoted by $P_1 \cup P_2$) is produced by independently computing the union of the variables ($V_{P_1 \cup P_2} := V_{P_1} \cup V_{P_2}$) and the constraints ($C_{P_1 \cup P_2} := C_{P_1} \cup C_{P_2}$) of the two subpatterns and using *identity* morphisms id^l and id^r which map P_1 to $P_1 \cup P_2$ and P_2 to $P_1 \cup P_2$, respectively, in a constraint type and parameter preserving manner. A set of subpatterns of a pattern constitutes a *partition* if they are pairwise independent, and their union produces the pattern itself. In the following, the subpatterns of a pattern constituting a partition are called *components*.

Note that union is performed on components of a given pattern, and results in another component of the same pattern which will replace the operands in the partition. In contrast, a join operates on arbitrary patterns, and yields to a new pattern which is unrelated to the operand patterns. In the context of a join operation, each of the operands and the result pattern has its own variable set.

Example. Figure 2(b) is used to exemplify the concepts of this section. Nodes with s labels in the center (on white background) represent patterns. Each pattern

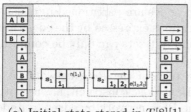
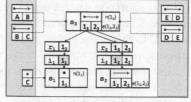

(a) Initial state stored in $T[8][1]$ (b) State inserted into $T[4][1]$

Fig. 2. Illustration of pattern related concepts and the algorithm execution ($k = 1$)

has its own, distinguished set of variables which are marked by indexed integers. The pattern in s_3 is the join of the patterns in s_1 and s_2 on join variables 1_1 and 1_2. In this case, function $\bowtie_V^l$ maps variable 1_1 to 1_3, while $\bowtie_V^r$ assigns variables 1_3 and 2_3 to 1_2 and 2_2, respectively. Constraints $n(1_1)$ and $e(1_2, 2_2)$ are mapped by $\bowtie_C^l$ and $\bowtie_C^r$ to $n(1_3)$ and $e(1_3, 2_3)$, respectively. The patterns on the left side (with grey background) show the components of the Chain (Fig. 1(c)) pattern which share variables labelled by capital letters with the latter pattern. The union of these components can be computed along the (unifiable) variables with the same name resulting in the Chain pattern. The components of the Reciprocity (Fig. 1(d)) pattern are shown on the right side.

3   Incremental Pattern Matching Process

As [9] states, *pattern matching* is the process of determining mappings for all variables in a given pattern, such that all constraints in the pattern are fulfilled. The mappings of variables to objects are collectively called a *match* which can be a *complete match* when all the variables are mapped, or a *partial match* in all other cases.[2] The overall process of *incremental pattern matching* is as follows:

Compile time tasks. At compile time, a Rete network [7], whose structure is presented in Sec. 3.1, is built from the pattern specifications by a network construction algorithm which will be discussed in details in Sec. 4.

Runtime behaviour. At runtime, the Rete network continuously tracks (i) the complete matches for all patterns in the underlying model and (ii) those partial matches that are needed for the calculation of the complete matches. These matches are stored in the Rete network and incrementally updated in a change propagation process which is triggered by notifications about model changes as presented in Sec. 3.2.

3.1   Rete Network

A *Rete network* is a directed acyclic graph whose nodes are data processing units which are organized into a parent-child relationship by the edges (considering the

---

[2] A match maps only pattern variables to model objects, while a morphism maps variables *and* constraints of a pattern to their counterparts in another pattern.

traditional source-to-target direction). The nodes are partitioned into skeletons $\mathcal{S}$, indexers $\mathcal{I}$, and remappers $\mathcal{R}$. The connections expressed by the edges are also restricted, because skeletons, remappers, and indexers can only be connected to remappers, indexers, and skeletons, respectively.

A *skeleton* calculates matches for a pattern in the Rete network. A *basic skeleton*, which corresponds to a pattern with a *single* constraint, has no outgoing edges. A *joined skeleton* is connected in the Rete network by edges to its left r_l and right r_r child remappers, and it represents a pattern with *several* constraints which is assembled from 2 smaller patterns, whose (great-grandchild) skeletons can be reached in the Rete network via paths (of length 3) along the left and right child remappers of the joined skeleton, respectively.

A *remapper* maintains an array-based mapping from the variables of its grand-child skeleton to the variables of its parent joined skeleton to support the match computation performed in the latter node.

An *indexer* stores the matches produced by its child skeleton in a table. Each field of this table contains the mapping of a variable (represented by a column) to an object according to the match (symbolized by a row). The matches are sorted according to the values that were assigned to a subsequence of variables (the so-called *indexed variables*) of the child skeleton. The skeleton and its indexed variables uniquely identify the corresponding indexer in the Rete network.

Example. Figure 3 depicts two sample Rete networks, which track the matches of the patterns of Figs. 1(c) and 1(d) on the model of Fig. 1(b). The identifiers of skeletons s, indexers i and remappers r are marked in the (leftmost) rectangles in the node headers. The pattern represented by a skeleton is shown in the header as well. In Fig. 3(b), basic skeleton s_1 corresponds to the pattern which has a single unary constraint of type n on parameter 1_1. This skeleton produces matches for the Rete network which map variable 1_1 to all MotifNodes from the model. These matches are stored sorted according to the values assigned to indexed variable 1_1 (shown by the grey column) in indexer i_1. MotifEdges are entered into the Rete network in skeleton s_2 and stored in indexer i_2. This indexer sorts the motifEdges according to their source objects, as only variable 1_2 is indexed. Joined skeleton s_3 carries out a join of patterns in skeletons s_1 and s_2 on join variables 1_1 and 1_2. To perform this operation, (i) join variables 1_1 and 1_2 have to be indexed in the grandchild indexers i_1 and i_2, respectively, (ii) variable 1_1 of skeleton s_1 has to be remapped by (left child) remapper r_1 according to $\bowtie^l$ to variable 1_3 of skeleton s_3, and similarly (iii) variables 1_2 and 2_2 must be remapped by (right child) remapper r_2 according to $\bowtie^r$ to variables 1_3 and 2_3, respectively. Joined skeleton s_4 joins patterns in skeletons s_1 and s_3 on join variables 1_1 and 2_3. Note that this join operation only involves variable 2_3 from skeleton s_3, consequently, indexer i_3 must only index this variable. Skeletons s_5 and s_6 represent patterns which are isomorphic to the Chain and the Reciprocity pattern, respectively. As a consequence, the matches produced by skeleton s_5 are the complete matches for the Chain pattern (in the left grey framed table), while skeleton s_6 creates no complete matches for the Reciprocity pattern. Note that skeleton s_6 joins the pattern in skeleton s_3 via two distinct paths by using join variables 1_3 and 2_3 in

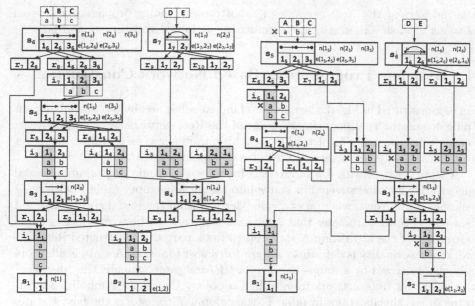

(a) Rete network with 7 indexers   (b) Rete network with 6 indexers

Fig. 3. Sample Rete networks

the left branch, and 2_3 and 1_3 in the right branch. As the left and right paths both involve 2 join variables, indexers i_4 and i_5 must use both join variables 1_3 and 2_3 for indexing (however, in a different order).

3.2 Incremental Pattern Matching at Runtime with Rete Network

To demonstrate the runtime behaviour of a Rete network in an incremental setting, let us suppose that the Rete network is already filled with matches computed from the initial content of the underlying model. More specifically, (i) indexers store the (partial or complete) matches calculated by their child skeleton, (ii) basic skeletons provide access for the Rete network to the model, and (iii) the top-most joined skeletons (i.e., without skeleton ancestors) already produced the complete matches for the corresponding patterns.

When the underlying model is altered, the Rete network is notified about this model change. This notification triggers a bottom-up change propagation process, which passes *match deltas* (i.e., representing match additions or deletions) from basic skeletons towards the top-most joined skeletons. As a common behaviour in this process, each node carries out 3 steps, namely, it (i) receives a match delta from one of its child nodes as input, (ii) performs data processing which might result in new match deltas as output, and (iii) optionally propagates all the output match deltas to all of its parent nodes.

Example. If the link between objects a and b is removed from the model of Fig. 1(b), then the matches marked by (red) crosses in Fig. 3(b) are deleted from the indexers of the Rete network in a bottom-up change propagation process starting at basic skeleton s_2 and terminating at joined skeletons s_5 and s_6.

4   Dynamic Programming Based Network Construction

As demonstrated in Fig. 3, the number of indexers has an obvious and significant influence on the runtime memory usage of the Rete network. As a consequence, our network construction algorithm uses this parameter as an optimization target to quantitatively characterize Rete network topologies.

A Rete network with few indexers is built by a dynamic programming based algorithm which iteratively fills states into an initially empty table T with $n+1$ columns and k rows, where n is a value derived from the initial state and $k \geq 1$ is a user-defined parameter that influences the trade-off between efficiency and optimality of the algorithm. A *state* represents a partially constructed Rete network, whose quality is defined by an *arbitrary* cost function. A state is additionally characterized by a *unification point (UP) indicator* which is the "distance" of the partial Rete network from a final topology that must symbolize all patterns in the specification. In table T, the column $T[col]$ stores the best k states (in an increasing cost order), whose UP indicator is col, while $T[col][row]$ is the rowth best from these states.

The main distinguishing feature of the algorithm is that the table *only stores a constant number* of states *in each column*, immediately discarding costly network topologies, which are not among the best k solutions, and implicitly all their possible continuations. The algorithm itself shares its core idea (and its two outermost loops) with the technique presented in [10] which was used for generating search plans for batch pattern matchers, but the current approach uses *completely different data structures* in the optimization process.

Algorithm data structures. A *state* S contains a Rete network RN_S, sets of components $Comp_S$ and skeleton patterns $Skel_S$, and an isomorphism function iso_S. Each pattern P in the specification will be represented in the component set $Comp_S$ of state S by a partition of its subpatterns which are called *components of pattern P in state S* (denoted by $Comp_S^P$) in the following. The component set $Comp_S$ is the collection of all components of all patterns in state S. A *skeleton pattern* P_s corresponds to skeleton s in the Rete network RN_S, and it represents a set of isomorphic components which are mapped to skeleton pattern P_s by the *isomorphism function* iso_S. The skeleton patterns that have a corresponding skeleton in network RN_S are contained in set $Skel_S$. The cost c_S of a state S can be *arbitrarily* defined. In this paper, the number of indexers $|\mathcal{I}_{RN_S}|$ in the Rete network RN_S is used as a cost function.

Unification points. A *unification point (UP) on variable v* is a situation, when variable v is unifiable by a pair of components of a pattern P in a state S. To compactly characterize the number of UPs on variable v, a *unification point indicator* upi_S^v *for variable v* is introduced as the number of those components of pattern P in state S which contain variable v. The *unification point indicator*

upi_S *of a state* S is calculated as $\sum_{P \in \mathcal{P}} \sum_{v \in V_P}(upi_S^v - 1)$. The subtraction is only required to be able to evaluate the term $\sum_{v \in V_P}(upi_S^v - 1)$ to 0, if and only if each variable of pattern P appears in a single component from the set Comp_S.

Example. Figure 2 depicts two states from the Rete network construction process. The tables on the left and right sides of each state (on the area with grey background) represent the components, whose union always results in the Chain and Reciprocity patterns, respectively. These components are mapped by the isomorphism function iso_S (denoted by the dashed lines) to the (jointly depicted) skeleton patterns and Rete network in the middle. Note that a skeleton pattern always unambiguously corresponds to a skeleton. The two states have 0 and 2 indexers, respectively, which are used as costs of the states. In Fig. 2(a), the UP indicators for variables B, D, E are 3, as each of these variables appears in 3 components, while the UP indicators for variables A and C are 2. The UP indicator of the state itself is $3 \cdot (3 - 1) + 2 \cdot (2 - 1) = 8$.

Initialization. Each pattern P in the specification is split into components $\mathsf{C}_1^P, \ldots, \mathsf{C}_{|C_P|}^P$ with *single* constraints which trivially constitute a partition of pattern P. Components $\mathsf{C}_1^P, \ldots, \mathsf{C}_{|C_P|}^P$ of each pattern P are added to the set Comp_{S_0}. For each constraint type t appearing in any of the patterns, a skeleton s_t and a corresponding skeleton pattern P_{s_t} are added to the Rete network RN_{S_0} and skeleton pattern set Skel_{S_0}, respectively. The skeleton pattern P_{s_t} has $ar(t)$ new variables and one constraint of type t with the newly created variables as parameters. In this way, all components C consisting of a single constraint of type t, which are obviously isomorphic, can be represented by skeleton pattern P_{s_t} which is registered into the isomorphism function as $\mathsf{iso}_{S_0}(\mathsf{C}) = P_{s_t}$.

Algorithm. Algorithm 1 determines the UP indicator upi_{S_0} of the initial state S_0 (line 1), and stores this state S_0 in $T[n][1]$ (line 2). Then, the table is traversed by processing columns in a decreasing order (lines 3–11). In contrast, the inner loop (lines 4–10) proceeds in an increasing state cost order starting from the best state $T[col][1]$ in each column $T[col]$. For each stored state S, the possible extensions Δ_{Skel} of the skeleton pattern set Skel_S are determined by `calculateDeltas` (line 6) which are used by `calculateNextStates` (line 7) to produce all continuations of state S. Each next state S' (lines 7–9) is conditionally inserted into the column $T[upi_{S'}]$ identified by the corresponding UP indicator $upi_{S'}$ in the procedure `conditionalInsert` (line 8) if the next state S' is among the k best states in the column $T[upi_{S'}]$. When the three loops terminate, the algorithm returns the Rete network $RN_{T[0][1]}$ (line 12).

The basic idea when producing all continuations of a state S (lines 6–7) is that unifiable components are aimed to be replaced by their union. As (i) isomorphic components are represented by a single skeleton pattern in state S (and a corresponding skeleton in the Rete network RN_S), and (ii) the union of components can be expressed by a new skeleton pattern, which is the join of the skeleton patterns of the unifiable components, a single join operation can also characterize the unification of numerous component pairs from the set Comp_S.

Algorithm 1. The procedure `calculateReteNetwork`(S_0, k)

```
1: n := upi_{S_0}
2: T[n][1] := S_0
3: for (col := n to 1) do
4:     for (row := 1 to k) do
5:         S := T[col][row] // current state S
6:         Δ_Skel := calculateDeltas(S)
7:         for each (S' ∈ calculateNextStates(S, Δ_Skel)) do
8:             conditionalInsert(T[upi_{S'}], S')
9:         end for
10:    end for
11: end for
12: return RN_{T[0][1]}
```

In order to support effective subpattern sharing in the Rete network, *a single join should represent as many unifications as possible.* This can only be achieved if the complete set of applicable joins and their corresponding unifications are determined in advance, and the actual computation of next' states is delayed.

Section 4.1. The procedure `calculateDeltas`(S) iterates through all unifiable components of all patterns in state S, and for each unification, a corresponding join is determined in such a manner that the union of the components is isomorphic to the result of the join. In other words, the set of applicable joins (i.e., the skeleton deltas in Sec. 4.1) is calculated together with a grouping of unifications (i.e., the component deltas in Sec. 4.1), in which each group contains those unifications that can be characterized by a single join.

Section 4.2. The procedure `calculateNextStates`(S, Δ_{Skel}) iterates through all applicable joins, and for each corresponding group, all those independent subsets are calculated which do not share any unifications. The unifications in these subsets can be used for preparing the next states.

The procedure `conditionalInsert`$(T[upi_{S'}], S')$ calculates index **c** which marks the position at which state S' should be inserted based on its cost. Index **c** is set to $k + 1$ if state S' is not among the best k states. Formally, **c** is the smallest index for which $c_{S'} < c_{T[upi_{S'}][\mathbf{c}]}$ holds (or $T[upi_{S'}][\mathbf{c}] = \texttt{null}$). If $\mathbf{c} < k + 1$, then state $T[upi_{S'}][k]$ is removed, elements between $T[upi_{S'}][\mathbf{c}]$ and $T[upi_{S'}][k-1]$ are shifted downward, and state S' is inserted at position **c**.

Example. Due to space limitations, Fig. 2 can only exemplify an incomplete, single iteration of the algorithm execution. The initial state (Fig. 2(a)) has a UP indicator 8. Consequently, table T (not shown in Fig. 2) has 8 columns, and the initial state is inserted into $T[8][1]$. When this state is processed by the procedure `calculateDeltas`(S), all unifiable component pairs are evaluated. During this evaluation, it is determined that e.g., (J1) if skeletons s_1 and s_2 are joined on variables 1_1 and 1_2 (see s_3 in Fig. 2(b)), then this join alone represents the unification of the component pairs (i) $n(A), e(A, B)$; (ii) $n(B), e(B, C)$;

(iii) $n(D), e(D, E)$; and (iv) $n(E), e(E, D)$. Three additional join possibilities (not shown in Fig. 2) are identified in the same stage, namely, (J2) skeletons s_1 and s_2 can be joined on variables 1_1 and 2_2 as well (resulting in a node with an incoming edge). Skeleton s_2 can be joined to itself (J3) either on variable sequences $1_2, 2_2$ and $2_2, 1_2$ (forming a cycle from the two edges), (J4) or on variables 2_2 and 1_2 (providing a chain from the two edges). The procedure `calculateDeltas`(S) computes the information exemplified on case (J1) for all the 4 joins, which is passed as Δ_{Skel} to the procedure `calculateNextStates`$(S, \Delta_{\mathsf{Skel}})$ in line 7 for further processing. The 4 unifiable component pairs of case (J1) have no constraints in common, consequently, these four unifications and the corresponding join can be directly used to build a next state (Fig. 2(b)), in which skeleton s_3 alone represents the 4 (isomorphic) components on the sides. Three additional next states are constructed for cases (J2)–(J4) as well. The next states prepared for cases (J1), (J3), and (J4) are inserted into empty slots $T[4][1]$, $T[6][1]$, and $T[7][1]$, respectively, according to their UP indicators, while the state created for case (J2) (again with UP indicator 4) is discarded (in line 8), as the state of Fig. 2(b) stored already in slot $T[4][1]$ has less indexers. When the three loops terminate, Alg. 1 returns the Rete network of Fig. 3(b) from the field $T[0][1]$.

4.1   Skeleton Pattern Delta Calculation

The procedure `calculateDeltas`(S) uses skeleton deltas and component deltas as new data structures to represent applicable, but delayed joins and unions, respectively. A *skeleton delta* consists of a set of component deltas $\Delta_{s'}$, a skeleton pattern $P_{s'}$ and a Rete network $RN_{s'}$. A *component delta* in the set $\Delta_{s'}$ contains two components C_l and C_r, and an isomorphism $\triangleq$ which maps the union $C_l \cup C_r$ of the components to the skeleton pattern $P_{s'}$.

The procedure `calculateDeltas`(S) (Algorithm 2) iterates through each pair C_l^P, C_r^P of unifiable components of pattern P in state S (lines 2–3). For each such pair, the method `createSkeletonPattern` (line 5) prepares a skeleton pattern $P_{s'}$ and an isomorphism $\triangleq$, such that $\triangleq$ maps the union of the components C_l^P and C_r^P to the skeleton pattern $P_{s'}$ (i.e., $\triangleq(C_l^P \cup C_r^P) = P_{s'}$). If the skeleton pattern $P_{s'}$ is already represented in the set Δ_{Skel} by another skeleton pattern P_{s*}, which is isomorphic to $P_{s'}$ according to an other morphism $\triangleq^*$ (line 6), then the component delta $(C_l^P, C_r^P, \triangleq \circ \triangleq^*)$ is simply added to the already stored set Δ_{s*} (line 7), as $C_l^P \cup C_r^P$ is isomorphic to skeleton pattern P_{s*} as well. Otherwise, a new Rete network $RN_{s'}$ is created by `createReteNetwork` (line 9), a new singleton set $\Delta_{s'}$ is prepared with the component delta $(C_l^P, C_r^P, \triangleq)$ (line 10), and the skeleton delta $(\Delta_{s'}, P_{s'}, RN_{s'})$ is added to the set Δ_{Skel} (line 11).

To describe the procedure `createSkeletonPattern`, let us suppose that components C_l^P and C_r^P are mapped by function isos_S to skeleton patterns P_{s_l} and P_{s_r}, respectively. Consequently, there exists an isomorphism $\triangleq^l$ ($\triangleq^r$) from component C_l^P (C_r^P) to skeleton pattern P_{s_l} (P_{s_r}). The new skeleton pattern $P_{s'}$ is the join of skeleton patterns P_{s_l} and P_{s_r} (by using $\bowtie^l$ and $\bowtie^r$), where the join variables in skeleton pattern P_{s_l} (P_{s_r}) are the images of the unifiable variables of components C_l^P and C_r^P according to isomorphism $\triangleq^l$ ($\triangleq^r$). The new

---

Algorithm 2. The procedure `calculateDeltas`(S)

1: $\Delta_{\mathsf{Skel}} := \emptyset$
2: **for each** $(P \in \mathcal{P})$ **do**
3:    **for each** $(C_l^P, C_r^P \in \mathsf{Comp}_S^P)$ **do**
4:       **if** $(C_l^P \neq C_r^P \wedge \texttt{areUnifiable}(C_l^P, C_r^P))$ **then**
5:          $(P_{s'}, \triangleq) := \texttt{createSkeletonPattern}(\mathsf{iso}_S, C_l^P, C_r^P)$
6:          **if** $(\exists(\Delta_{s*}, P_{s*}, RN_{s*}) \in \Delta_{\mathsf{Skel}}, \exists \triangleq^* : \triangleq^*(P_{s'}) = P_{s*})$ **then**
7:            $\Delta_{s*} := \Delta_{s*} \cup \left\{ (C_l^P, C_r^P, \triangleq \circ \triangleq^*) \right\}$
8:          **else**
9:            $RN_{s'} := \texttt{createReteNetwork}(RN_S, \mathsf{iso}_S, C_l^P, C_r^P)$
10:            $\Delta_{s'} := \left\{ (C_l^P, C_r^P, \triangleq) \right\}$
11:            $\Delta_{\mathsf{Skel}} := \Delta_{\mathsf{Skel}} \cup \{ (\Delta_{s'}, P_{s'}, RN_{s'}) \}$
12:          **end if**
13:       **end if**
14:    **end for**
15: **end for**
16: **return** Δ_{Skel}

---

isomorphism $\triangleq$ can be defined as a composition of morphisms $\bowtie^{l,r}$ and $\triangleq^{l,r}$, namely, $\forall v \in V_{C_l^P} : \triangleq_V(v) := \bowtie_V^l(\triangleq_V^l(v)), \forall c \in C_{C_l^P} : \triangleq_C(c) := \bowtie_C^l(\triangleq_C^l(c))$, $\forall v \in V_{C_r^P} : \triangleq_V(v) := \bowtie_V^r(\triangleq_V^r(v))$, and $\forall c \in C_{C_r^P} : \triangleq_C(c) := \bowtie_C^r(\triangleq_C^r(c))$.

The procedure `createReteNetwork` creates a new Rete network $RN_{s'}$ by adding a new skeleton s' and its left r_l and right r_r remappers (plus the corresponding edges) to the old network RN_S. Indexer i_l (i_r) is either reused from RN_S if RN_S already contained it as a parent of skeleton s_l (s_r), or newly created. The edges between these indexers and skeletons are handled analogously. As the exact internal parameterization of network nodes is easily derivable from morphisms $\bowtie^l$, $\bowtie^r$, $\triangleq^l$, and $\triangleq^r$, it is not discussed here due to space limitations.

4.2 Next State Calculation

The procedure `calculateNextStates`$(S, \Delta_{\mathsf{Skel}})$ (Algorithm 3) iterates through all skeleton deltas $(\Delta_{s'}, P_{s'}, RN_{s'})$ in the set Δ_{Skel} (line 2). In order to clarify the role of the inner loop (lines 3–8), let us examine its body (lines 4–7) first. The new Rete network $RN_{S'}$ simply uses the network $RN_{s'}$ from the skeleton delta (line 4). The skeleton pattern $P_{s'}$ is added to the skeleton pattern set Skel_S of state S to produce the new one (line 5). The procedure `calculateComponents` (line 6) creates a new component set $\mathsf{Comp}_{S'}$ from the old one Comp_S by replacing the components C_l and C_r of each component delta $(C_l, C_r, \triangleq)$ from the set $\Delta_{s'}^I$ with their union $C_l \cup C_r$. The new isomorphism function $\mathsf{iso}_{S'}$ retains the mappings of those components from the old one iso_S that do not appear in any component deltas from the set $\Delta_{s'}^I$, while the union $C_l \cup C_r$ of component pairs mentioned in a component delta $(C_l, C_r, \triangleq)$ is mapped to skeleton pattern $P_{s'}$ (i.e., $\mathsf{iso}_{S'}(C_l \cup C_r) = P_{s'}$). A new state $S' = (RN_{S'}, \mathsf{Skel}_{S'}, \mathsf{Comp}_{S'}, \mathsf{iso}_{S'})$ is added to the set Δ_S representing the possible continuations of state S (line 7).

Algorithm 3. The procedure `calculateNextStates`$(S, \Delta_{\mathsf{Skel}})$

1: $\Delta_S := \emptyset$
2: **for each** $((\Delta_{s'}, P_{s'}, RN_{s'}) \in \Delta_{\mathsf{Skel}})$ **do**
3:   **for each** $(\Delta_{s'}^I \in \texttt{allMaximalIndependentSets}\,(\Delta_{s'}))$ **do**
4:     $RN_{S'} := RN_{s'}$
5:     $\mathsf{Skel}_{S'} := \mathsf{Skel}_S \cup \{\,P_{s'}\,\}$
6:     $(\mathsf{Comp}_{S'}, \mathsf{iso}_{S'}) := \texttt{calculateComponents}(S, \Delta_{s'}^I)$
7:     $\Delta_S := \Delta_S \cup \{\,(RN_{S'}, \mathsf{Skel}_{S'}, \mathsf{Comp}_{S'}, \mathsf{iso}_{S'})\,\}$
8:   **end for**
9: **end for**
10: **return** Δ_S

As the set $\mathsf{Comp}_{S'}$ must also contain *independent* components, the replacement in line 6 is only allowed if all component delta pairs $(C_l^{P_\alpha}, C_r^{P_\alpha}, \triangleq^{P_\alpha})$ and $(C_l^{P_\beta}, C_r^{P_\beta}, \triangleq^{P_\beta})$ from the set $\Delta_{s'}^I$ are independent, which means that they either originate from different patterns (i.e., $P_\alpha \neq P_\beta$), or they do not share any components (i.e., $C_{l,r}^{P_\alpha} \neq C_{l,r}^{P_\beta}$). As pairwise independence does not necessarily hold for the component deltas in set $\Delta_{s'}$, the method `allMaximalIndependentSets` carries out the Bron-Kerbosch algorithm [11] (line 3), and calculates all such subsets of $\Delta_{s'}$, whose (component delta) elements are pairwise independent.

5 Measurement Results

In this section, we quantitatively assess the effect of subpattern sharing on the number of indexers by comparing the case when our algorithm builds a *separate* Rete network for each pattern with the situation when isomorphic subpatterns are represented by shared skeletons (i.e., *combined* approach). For the evaluation, we used the patterns from [2], and the algorithm parameter k was set to 1.

The measurement results are presented in Table 1. A column header has to be interpreted in a *cumulative* manner including all patterns which appear in the headers of the *current and all the preceding* columns. A value in the first row shows the *sum* of the number of indexers[3] in those Rete networks that have been *separately* built for the patterns in the (current and its preceding) column headers. In contrast, a value in the second row presents the number of indexers[3] in the *single* Rete network that has been constructed by the *combined* approach which used the patterns in the (current and its preceding) column headers as input. The values in the third row express the memory reduction as the ratio of the values in the first two rows. Rows four and five denote the Rete network construction runtimes[4] for the separate and combined approach, respectively, while the sixth row depicts the ratio of the values from the previous two rows.

---

[3] The parent indexers of the basic skeletons were not included in either case, as their functionality (e.g., navigation on edges) is provided by the underlying modeling layer.

[4] The runtime values are averages of 10 user time measurements performed on a 1.57 GHz Intel Core2 Duo CPU with Windows XP Professional SP 3 and Java 1.7.

Table 1. Measurement results

	Pattern	FeedForward	FeedBack	Caro	DoubleCross	InStar	OutStar	Reciprocity
Indexers [#]	Separate	4	8	13	17	21	25	27
	Combined	4	5	7	11	14	20	21
Ratio	Combined / Separate	1.00	0.63	0.54	0.65	0.67	0.80	0.78
Runtime [ms]	Separate	12.500	14.063	23.438	28.126	79.689	134.377	134.377
	Combined	10.938	21.875	56.250	106.250	428.125	770.313	843.750
Ratio	Combined / Separate	0.88	1.56	2.40	3.78	5.37	5.73	6.28

The most important conclusion from Table 1 is that the combined approach uses 20–46% less indexers than the separate approach for the price of an increase in the algorithm runtime by a factor of 1–6 which is not surprising as the combined approach has to operate on tables that are wider by approximately the same factor. For a correct interpretation, it should be noted that the number of indexers influences the memory consumption at runtime, while the algorithm is executed only once at compile time.

6   Related Work

Motif recognition algorithms. The state-of-the-art motif recognition algorithms are excellently surveyed in [12]. These are batch techniques which match all non-isomorphic (graph) patterns up to a certain size, in contrast to our incremental approach, which builds a Rete network only for the (more general, constraint-based) patterns in the specification (and for a small part of their subpatterns). In the rest of this section, which is still knowingly incomplete, only Rete network based incremental approaches are mentioned.

Rete network construction in rule-based systems. As Rete networks were used first in rule-based systems, different network topologies have been analyzed in many papers from the artificial intelligence domain including [13], which recognized that linear structures can be replaced by (balanced) tree-based ones. However, this report provided neither cost functions to characterize the quality of a Rete network, nor algorithms to find good topologies.

A graph based Rete network description was proposed in [14] together with cost functions that could be used as optimization targets in a network construction process. Furthermore, the author gives conditions for network optimality according to the different cost metrics, in contrast to our dynamic programming based approach, which could only produce provenly optimal solution if the number of rows was not limited by the constant parameter k. On the other hand, no network construction algorithm is discussed in [14].

Rete network construction in incremental pattern matchers. Incremental graph pattern matching with Rete networks [7] was examined decades ago in [4] which already described an advanced network compilation algorithm (beyond the presentation of the runtime behaviour of the Rete network). This approach processed pattern specifications one-by-one, and it was able to reuse network nodes in a restricted manner, namely, if a subpattern was isomorphic to another one from a previous pattern, for which a network node had *actually* been generated earlier in the construction procedure. In this sense, the recognition of isomorphic parts in two patterns depends on the order, in which the subpatterns of the first pattern had been processed. However, [4] gives no hint how such an order can be found.

Another sophisticated, Rete network based incremental graph pattern matching engine [6] has recently been used for state space exploration purposes in graph transformation systems. In this setup, the standard Rete approach was extended by graph transformation related concepts such as quantifiers, nested conditions, and negative application conditions. Additionally, disconnected graph patterns could also be handled. Regarding the Rete network construction, [6] uses the same technique as [4] with all its strengths and flaws.

IncQuery [5,15] is also a high quality pattern matcher that uses Rete networks for incremental query evaluation. Queries can be defined by graph patterns which can be reused and composed in a highly flexible manner. If isomorphic subpatterns are identified as standalone patterns, then they can be handled by a single node which can be reused by different compositions leading to the original patterns, but the *automated identification of isomorphic subpatterns is not yet supported* in contrast to our approach. As another difference, the *constructed Rete network has always a linear topology* in IncQuery, while our algorithm can produce a balanced net structure as well. Considering the Chain and the Reciprocity patterns, the Rete network of Fig. 3(b) can only be constructed in IncQuery if the user *manually* specifies skeletons s_3 and s_4 as patterns and the complete network structure by pattern compositions.

7   Conclusion

In this paper, we proposed a novel algorithm based on dynamic programming to construct Rete networks for incremental graph pattern matching purposes. The cost function and the optimization target used by the algorithm can be easily replaced and customized. As the basic idea of the proposed algorithm is similar to the technique presented in [10] for batch pattern matching, our *fully implemented* network building approach can be easily integrated into the search plan generation module of the Democles tool which will be able to handle batch and incremental scenarios in an integrated manner.

As an evaluation from the aspect of applicability, the proposed algorithm can (i) use model-sensitive costs (originating from model statistics), (ii) handle n-ary constraints in pattern specifications, and (iii) be further customized by setting parameter k which influences the trade-off between efficiency and optimality.

The most important future task is to assess the effects of network topologies on the runtime performance characteristics of the pattern matcher in industrial application scenarios by using different cost functions and optimization targets in the proposed network construction algorithm.

References

1. Jouault, F., Kurtev, I.: Transforming models with ATL. In: Bruel, J.-M. (ed.) MoDELS 2005. LNCS, vol. 3844, pp. 128–138. Springer, Heidelberg (2006)
2. von Landesberger, T., Görner, M., Rehner, R., Schreck, T.: A system for interactive visual analysis of large graphs using motifs in graph editing and aggregation. In: Magnor, M.A., Rosenhahn, B., Theisel, H. (eds.) Proceedings of the Vision, Modeling, and Visualization Workshop, DNB, pp. 331–339 (2009)
3. Krumov, L., Schweizer, I., Bradler, D., Strufe, T.: Leveraging network motifs for the adaptation of structured peer-to-peer-networks. In: IEEE Proceedings of the Global Communications Conference, pp. 1–5 (2010)
4. Bunke, H., Glauser, T., Tran, T.-H.: An efficient implementation of graph grammar based on the RETE-matching algorithm. In: Ehrig, H., Kreowski, H.-J., Rozenberg, G. (eds.) Graph Grammars 1990. LNCS, vol. 532, pp. 174–189. Springer, Heidelberg (1991)
5. Bergmann, G., Ökrös, A., Ráth, I., Varró, D., Varró, G.: Incremental pattern matching in the VIATRA model transformation system. In: Proc. of the 3rd Int. Workshop on Graph and Model Transformation, pp. 25–32. ACM (2008)
6. Ghamarian, A.H., Jalali, A., Rensink, A.: Incremental pattern matching in graph-based state space exploration. In: de Lara, J., Varró, D. (eds.) Proc. of the 4th International Workshop on Graph-Based Tools. ECEASST, vol. 32 (2010)
7. Forgy, C.L.: RETE: A fast algorithm for the many pattern/many object match problem. Artificial Intelligence 19, 17–37 (1982)
8. Horváth, Á., Varró, G., Varró, D.: Generic search plans for matching advanced graph patterns. In: Workshop on Graph Transformation and Visual Modeling Techniques, vol. 6, ECEASST (2007)
9. Varró, G., Anjorin, A., Schürr, A.: Unification of compiled and interpreter-based pattern matching techniques. In: Vallecillo, A., Tolvanen, J.-P., Kindler, E., Störrle, H., Kolovos, D. (eds.) ECMFA 2012. LNCS, vol. 7349, pp. 368–383. Springer, Heidelberg (2012)
10. Varró, G., Deckwerth, F., Wieber, M., Schürr, A.: An algorithm for generating model-sensitive search plans for EMF models. In: Hu, Z., de Lara, J. (eds.) ICMT 2012. LNCS, vol. 7307, pp. 224–239. Springer, Heidelberg (2012)
11. Bron, C., Kerbosch, J.: Algorithm 457: Finding all cliques of an undirected graph. Communications of the ACM 16(9), 575–577 (1973)
12. Wong, E., Baur, B., Quader, S., Huang, C.-H.: Biological network motif detection: Principles and practice. Briefings in Bioinformatics 13(2), 202–215 (2012)
13. Perlin, M.W.: Transforming conjunctive match into RETE: A call-graph caching approach. Technical Report 2054, Carnegie Mellon University (1991)
14. Tan, J.S.E., Srivastava, J., Shekhar, S.: On the construction of efficient match networks. Technical Report 91, University of Houston (1991)
15. Bergmann, G., Horváth, Á., Ráth, I., Varró, D., Balogh, A., Balogh, Z., Ökrös, A.: Incremental evaluation of model queries over EMF models. In: Petriu, D.C., Rouquette, N., Haugen, Ø. (eds.) MODELS 2010, Part I. LNCS, vol. 6394, pp. 76–90. Springer, Heidelberg (2010)

Interactive Visual Analytics
for Efficient Maintenance of Model Transformations

Andreas Rentschler, Qais Noorshams, Lucia Happe, and Ralf Reussner

Karlsruhe Institute of Technology (KIT), Karlsruhe, Germany
{rentschler,noorshams,kapova,reussner}@kit.edu

Abstract. Maintaining model transformations remains a demanding task due to the sheer amount of metamodel elements and transformation rules that need to be understood. Several established techniques for software maintenance have been ported to model transformation development. Most available techniques proactively help to design and implement maintainable transformations, yet however, a growing number of legacy transformations needs to be maintained. Interactive visualization techniques to support model transformation maintenance still do not exist. We propose an interactive visual analytics process for understanding model transformations for maintenance. Data and control dependencies are statically analyzed and displayed in an interactive graph-based view with cross-view navigation and task-oriented filter criteria. We present results of an empirical study, where we asked programmers to carry out typical maintenance tasks on a real-world transformation in QVT-O. Subjects using our view located relevant code spots significantly more efficiently.

1 Introduction

Model transformations are of key importance in model-driven software development (MDSD). With the growing application of model-driven techniques in industry, maintenance costs of transformations move into a stronger focus.

During the life-cycle of a model-driven software system, transformations have to be adapted to evolving models, requirements, and technologies. Many established techniques to achieve maintainable software exist, including software quality metrics, program analysis, software testing, and modular programming. In recent years, substantial effort has been expended in porting such techniques to the specific field of model transformation development. The *program comprehension* community studies the way humans understand source code and how tools and techniques can support maintenance [1]. *Program analysis techniques* assist software maintainers in understanding unknown code and detecting code anomalies. When understanding a program, most parts are irrelevant as they do not contribute to a particular functional or non-functional concern. Slices can be automatically computed by statically analyzing the data and control flow of a program (static program slicing), or for a certain input to a program (dynamic program slicing). *Software visualization tools* [2] combine program analysis with information visualization techniques to create various displays of software structure, behavior, and evolution. In the recent past, approaches for detecting code anomalies and visualizing data and control flow had been transferred to the world of model transformation development, as well.

K. Duddy and G. Kappel (Eds.): ICMT 2013, LNCS 7909, pp. 141–157, 2013.
© Springer-Verlag Berlin Heidelberg 2013

Comprehension of programs with computations on complex data structures has rarely been studied so far. Existing static analysis approaches to support model transformation maintenance do not integrate data and control flow [3], and proposed graphical representations of dependencies [4] are too complex to effectively support understanding for a particular task. None of the approaches has been empirically validated. What is needed is a *visual analytics approach* [5] that allows for task-oriented data reduction and interaction between data and users in order to discover knowledge.

In this paper, we propose an interactive visual analytics process to understand model transformations for maintenance. One part of the process is to statically analyze model transformations for their data and control dependencies. Task-oriented filtering aligns the level of detail to a variety of comprehension and maintenance tasks. Results are displayed in an interactive graphical view with cross-view navigation and dynamic selection of filter criteria. To the best of our knowledge, this is the first validated approach to interactively support maintenance of model transformations.

In a qualitative and quantitative study, we asked programmers to carry out maintenance tasks on a real-world transformation in QVT-Operational (QVT-O). Programmers using our editor extension located relevant code spots significantly more efficiently than programmers without the extension.

To sum it up, this paper makes the following contributions.

- We define an interactive visual analytics process to support understanding of model transformations for maintenance.
- We define a generic dependency model for model transformations, unifying control and data flow information in a graph-like structure.
- We propose a set of task-oriented filter rules to exclude details from the dependency graph that can be considered irrelevant to carry out a certain maintenance activity.
- We present results from an empirical experiment to see how task-oriented dependency graphs improve the efficiency for locating features in a transformation.

This paper is structured as follows. First, we present a motivating example in Section 2. In Section 3, we introduce our visualization process, in Section 4 a model for a generic dependency graph, and in Section 5 task-oriented filtering. Section 6 illustrates how the approach had been empirically validated. In Section 7 related work is discussed. Finally, Section 8 presents conclusions and proposes directions for future work.

2 Motivating Example

Consider a QVT-O implementation of the UML2RDBMS example scenario. One rule, `Attribute2Column`, is mapping elements of type `Attribute` to elements of type `Column`:

```
mapping Attribute::Attribute2Column() : Column
merges Attribute::IdAttribute2AutogenColumn {
    result.name := self.name;
    result.type := UmlTypeToDbtype(self.type.name);
}
```

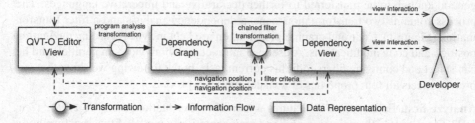

Fig. 1. Visual analytics process

By means of two practical scenarios, a comprehension scenario and a maintenance scenario, we demonstrate that even in an editor as advanced as that of Eclipse QVT-O, there is little support to cope with a transformation's inherent complexity.

Comprehension scenario. In this first scenario, we want to trace a bug resulting in missing Column objects in the target model. As a first step, we want to understand the context in which a rule Attribute2Column is used. In the QVT-O editor under Eclipse, we need to start a text-based search by the rule's name. If the transformation is modularized, we need to repeat the search in any other module with an import of the rule's containing module. To detect occurences, it is important to know that in QVT-O, keywords disjuncts, merges, inherits and map all have call-semantics.

Maintenance scenario. In the second scenario, we want to add a third attribute to class Column. Before we do so, it is useful to know about further locations in the program where Column or possible subclasses are instantiated. Again, we need to carry out a text-based search by the class name on all existing modules. In QVT-O, there are three ways to instantiate objects: implicitly via a mapping, or explicitly via the object operator, or by calling the corresponding constructor via new operator.

From these two scenarios it is clear that developers, especially those who are less familiar with QVT-O concepts, need to invest a lot of effort to identify relevant control and data dependencies in complex transformation programs. Program analysis techniques can automatically extract dependencies and present these graphically. However, large dependency graphs are difficult to read. In the next section of this paper, we propose a visual analytics process which takes the burden off developers to visualize only those dependencies which are considered as relevant for a particular activity.

3 Methodology Overview

To solve the information overload problem, *visual analytics processes* combine analytical approaches together with advanced visualization techniques. They can be characterized by four properties [6]:

"Analyse First – Show the Important – Zoom, Filter and Analyse Further – Details on Demand"

We define an interactive visualization process which adheres to these principles. In this paper, we apply our approach to the QVT-O language. However, our concepts are general enough to be transferred to further declarative and imperative languages. The process contains two transformation steps, a dependency analysis and a filter transformation (Figure 1). Code and graph representation are kept in sync regarding navigation position and code modifications. A user can interact with both views in parallel, and he can select and configure filters to fit his current task. In the following we show that our process meets all four properties of a visual analytics process.

Analyze first. Eclipse QVT-O features a textual representation, the *QVT editor view*. QVT-O automatically maintains a second representation, a model of the transformation and referenced metamodels. This model adheres to the QVT specification [7], thus offering a standardized interface for code analysis. The leftmost transformation in our process extracts data and control dependencies from the QVT model. Static control and data flow analysis results in an instance of a *dependency graph model*. This model is presented in Section 4.

Show the important. We already showed in the motivating example that, depending on what maintenance task is performed, a different subset of elements and element types available in the graph is required for reasoning. Which elements will be filtered out is configurable by the user. In Section 5, we explain our concept of *task-oriented filters* and we further define a set of useful types of filters.

Zoom, filter and analyse further. Humans are capable to only perceive a small subset of information at a time. Thus, we provide filters which remove any information out of focus. Depending on the task to be solved, a user's focus may lie on a certain method in the program, on a particular type of dependencies, or on a higher abstraction level. Because each view is limited regarding the information conveyed, *interaction* is needed. A feedback loop is established by dynamic filters, which can be quickly exchanged and configured, and which react on changes to the editing location. In Figure 1, filter dynamics are reflected by information flows leading to the filter transformation. Views are navigable, as pointed out by interactions between the developer and the views.

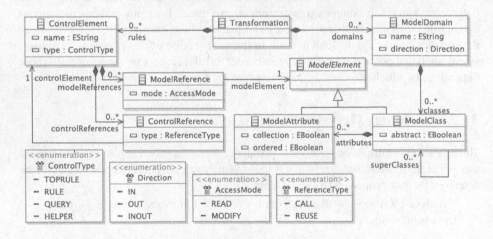

Fig. 2. Dependency graph model

Details on demand. Occasionally, if maintainers require full details, the dependency view enables users to navigate to the underlying program code of a mapping or the actual definition of a data element. This kind of feature is called *cross-view navigation* and is illustrated in Figure 1 by an information flow pointing back to the editor view.

4   Dependency Graph Model

An important step in the visualization process is to analyze rule-based model transformations for control units, data units, and interdependencies. Control-units are transformation rules and other top-level constructs to specify behavior, for example query functions and helper methods in QVT-O. Data units are metamodeling concepts, classes, attributes, and references. Figure 2 shows how we defined these concepts in the Ecore metamodeling language. In the model, a transformation (`Transformation`) consists of control elements (`ControlElement`) and metamodel domains (`ModelDomain`). Each domain refers to a metamodel name and has a direction (`IN`, `OUT`, or `INOUT`). Control elements have references (`ControlReference`) to other rules for reuse purposes (`inherits` or `merges` in QVT-O), tagged `REUSE`, but also for calls (`map` or `disjuncts` in QVT-O), tagged `CALL`. Control elements are typed. In QVT-O a `mapping` equals a `RULE`, method `main` equals `TOPRULE`, query and helper functions correspond to `QUERY` and `HELPER`. A control element can have data dependencies, represented by instances of `ModelReference`. Referencing a model element (`ModelElement`) can be either read-only (`READ`), or the referenced model element

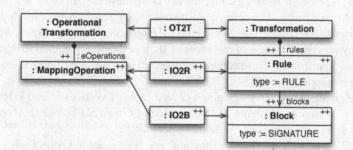

(a) Constructing an instance of `Rule` from a QVT-O mapping operation

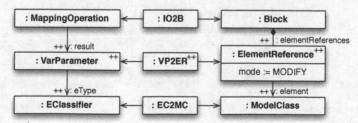

(b) Constructing an `ElementReference` instance from a QVT-O mapping's result parameter

Fig. 3. Constructing dependency graphs from QVT-O transformations

can be instantiated or its content modified (MODIFY for both cases). The model differentiates between access to a class and access to an attribute or reference (ModelClass and ModelAttribute). Like in Java, there is no distinction between references and attributes. Classes can further reference super classes. Any model element belongs to exactly one domain.

A graph model instance is constructed from instances of QVT-O's abstract syntax metamodel [7]. Figure 3 demonstrates by two exemplary triple graph grammar (TGG) rules in compact notation [8], how QVT-O mappings correspond to rules in the graph, and result parameters are represented by element references with write access mode.

For our implementation and in this paper, we decided to visualize dependency graphs as node-link diagrams (NLDs). An illustrative mapping between graph elements and notational elements is given in Figure 4.

5   Task-Oriented Filtering

Dependency graphs of model transformations can be huge, bearing the danger that useful information gets lost when studied by humans. Our idea is to identify and remove details which are irrelevant for performing a particular task before display. In this section, we present three filter functions and four useful combinations thereof.

As prerequisite for defining the filter functions, we formalize our dependency graph as follows: Let $ControlElement$, $ModelClass$, and $ModelAttribute$ be sets that represent instances of metamodel classes of the same name, respectively. Furthermore, let $ModelElement := ModelClass \cup ModelAttribute$ denote the set of ModelElement instances, i.e., the set containing instances of ModelClass and ModelAttribute. For referenced instances, let functions $modelReferences$, $modelElement$, $controlReferences$, $controlElement$, $superClasses$, $attributes$ be defined by representing sets of instances of their respectively named metamodel reference. When applied to sets, functions are applied element-wise and the result is the union of each mapping.

Then, we create the dependency graph G as a tuple of vertices V and Edges E, i.e., $G = (V, E)$. V and E elements are created using $ControlElement$, $ModelClass$, and $ModelAttribute$ elements by defining sets $V^{ControlElement}$, $V^{ModelClass}$, and $V^{ModelAttribute}$, as well as bijective functions ϕ_X (i.e., mapping rules), where

$$\phi_{ControlElement} : ControlElement \rightarrow V^{ControlElement}$$

$$\phi_{ModelClass} : ModelClass \rightarrow V^{ModelClass}$$

$$\phi_{ModelAttribute} : ModelAttribute \rightarrow V^{ModelAttribute}$$

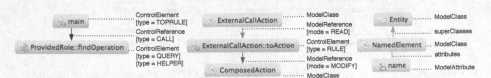

Fig. 4. Notational elements

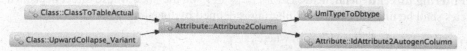

(a) Control dependencies for QVT-O mapping `Attribute2Column`

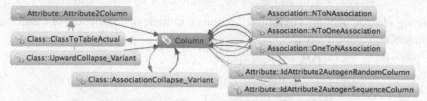

(b) Data and control dependencies for class `Column`

Fig. 5. Filtered dependency graphs for the introductory example

We imply $V^{ControlElement}$, $V^{ModelClass}$, $V^{ModelAttribute}$ are pairwise disjunct by construction and define $V := V^{ControlElement} \dot{\cup} V^{ModelClass} \dot{\cup} V^{ModelAttribute}$. We further define $V^{ModelElement} := V^{ModelClass} \dot{\cup} V^{ModelAttribute}$. To obtain E elements, where $E \subseteq V \times V$, we use the following four derivation rules:[1]

$\forall r_1, r_2 \in ControlElement :$
$\quad r_2 \in (controlElement \circ controlReferences)(r_1) \Longleftrightarrow$
$\quad (\phi_{ControlElement}(r_1), \phi_{ControlElement}(r_2)) \in E$

$\forall r \in ControlElement, e \in ModelElement :$
$\quad e \in (modelElement \circ elementReferences)(r) \Longleftrightarrow$
$\quad (\phi_{ControlElement}(r), \phi_{ModelElement}(e)) \in E$

$\forall c_1, c_2 \in ModelClass :$
$\quad c_2 \in superClasses(c_1) \Longleftrightarrow (\phi_{ModelClass}(c_1), \phi_{ModelClass}(c_2)) \in E$

$\forall a \in ModelAttribute, c \in ModelClass :$
$\quad a \in modelAttributes(c) \Longleftrightarrow (\phi_{ModelAttribute}(a), \phi_{ModelClass}(c)) \in E$

Now we can define three filter functions on top of the computed graph structure G.

Filtering control nodes. We define a filtering function removing data dependencies by $f^{controlflow}(V, E) := (V', E')$, where

$$V' := V \setminus V^{ModelElement}$$
$$E' := E \setminus (V^{ControlElement} \times V^{ModelElement})$$
$$\setminus (V^{ModelClass} \times V^{ModelClass})$$
$$\setminus (V^{ModelClass} \times V^{ModelAttribute})$$

---

[1] The function composition operator "$\circ$" is defined as: $(g \circ f)(x) = g(f(x))$.

Filtering direct dependencies. Let $v_{current} \in V$ be the node whose direct dependencies shall be filtered. Contextual filtering is defined by function

$$f_{v_{current}}^{context}(V, E) := (V', E'), \text{ where}$$
$$V' := \{v \in V \mid (v, v_{current}) \in E \vee (v_{current}, v) \in E\} \cup \{v_{current}\}$$
$$E' := \{(v_1, v_2) \in E \mid v_1 = v_{current} \vee v_2 = v_{current}\}$$

Filtering classes without attributes. To reduce complexity, attributes of classes and dependencies can be filtered by

$$f^{classes}(V, E) := (V', E'), \text{ where}$$
$$V' := V \setminus V^{ModelAttribute}$$
$$E' := E \setminus (V^{ControlElement} \times V^{ModelAttribute})$$
$$\setminus (V^{ModelAttribute} \times V^{ModelClass})$$

These filter functions can be arbitrarily combined. However, the order in which functions are applied is relevant, and not all combinations can be conceived as useful. We define four filter combinations together with their primary field of application:

$$F1 := f^{controlflow}, \qquad\qquad F2 := (f_{v_{current}}^{context} \circ f^{controlflow}),$$
$$F3 := f_{v_{current}}^{context}, \qquad\qquad F4 := (f_{v_{current}}^{context} \circ f^{classes}).$$

F1: Show control dependencies of the whole transformation. Resulting view helps to initially grasp the overall control structures of an unknown transformation. The filter is useful for investigating transformations of smaller size.

F2: Show control dependencies in context of the currently selected control node. When navigating the rules, data dependencies are not always of interest. For the comprehension scenario from Section 2, this filter is the optimal choice. In context of mapping `Attribute2Column` the filter would yield the graph shown in Figure 5a. A developer quickly recognizes two rules calling mapping `Attribute2Column`. The filter helps at understanding larger transformation programs.

F3: Show control and data dependencies in context of the currently selected control or data node, $v_{current}$. When reading transformation rules, it makes sense to primarily concentrate on direct dependencies. In contrast to slicing criteria, only direct dependencies are displayed, both in forward and backward directions. In the maintenance scenario from Section 2, we apply the filter in context of class `Column` to show all operations modifying or reading the element. There are seven mappings modifying the element (incoming connections in Figure 5b. The filter helps to cope with change requests where details at the attribute-level are required to locate concerns.

F4: Show control and data dependencies in context of the currently selected control or data node, but remove information about accessed class attributes. The resulting view leaves only data dependencies at the class-level. This filter is useful for change requests where details at the class-level are sufficient to locate concerns.

6 Empirical Evaluation

To evaluate how our approach supports important maintenance tasks, we carried out a case study, where users had to identify code locations affected by typical change requests. For the case study, we implemented our approach for QVT-O under Eclipse.[2]

6.1 Design

The purpose of the study is to empirically show that our approach makes maintaining model transformations more efficient (process-related improvement), the outcome is of higher quality (product-related improvement), and the developer experiences less effort (improvement regarding user experience).

In order to accomplish our set goal, we explored the following three hypotheses:

H1: Effectiveness. Subjects who use dependency graphs locate affected places *more effectively* than equally classified subjects who do not use it.

H2: Time expenditure. Subjects who use dependency graphs are *faster* in performing the maintenance tasks than equally classified subjects who do not use it.

H3: Perceived strain. Subjects who use dependency graphs are *less strained* than equally classified subjects who do not use it.

We varied the availability of the tool (control variable) and took measurements to assess effectiveness, time consumption and perceived strain (response variables). We used the following metrics: To evaluate the effectiveness, we determined the numbers of false positives and false negatives of each given answer. Based on these, we used the f-measure with $\beta = 1$ to compute the harmonic mean value of precision and recall. The f-measure is a widely-used measure for assessing quality of information retrieval. It is also suitable for evaluating feature location tasks [9].

Subjects had been asked to record starting and ending time for each task, so we could calculate the actual time needed. Regarding the subjectively felt level of strain, we asked for the user's personally experienced difficulty level on six-level Likert items in the post-session questionnaire.

According to a classification scheme by Juzgado and Moreno [10], this experiment follows a *between-subjects design*. Its single dimension *tool usage* has two levels (with or without). It is a *quasi-experiment*, since assignment to groups had been done based on information determined from the pre-questionaire, rather than purely randomly.

The study had been carried out in an exam-style situation on 2 bachelor students, 12 master students and 8 experienced researchers, all of them reasonably trained in the tools and activities of model transformation development.

We decided for an example transformation from a large scientific project, the Palladio Research Project [11]. The project provides a set of methods and tools for predicting the reliability and performance of software architectures. The QVT-O transformation PCM2QPN transforms Palladio Component Model (PCM) instances to Queuing Petri Nets (QPN). It encompasses 2886 lines of code, plus 952 lines of code distributed over 4 library modules. We decided for QVT-Operational because of its stable integration

---

[2] The tool we implemented can be downloaded from
http://sdqweb.ipd.kit.edu/wiki/Transformation_Analysis.

into the Eclipse IDE, its adherence to a language standard, and its wide acceptance. There is one source metamodel, the Palladio Component Model (PCM), consisting of 154 classes, and SimQPN's Petri net model as target model, consisting of 20 classes.

Each subject was asked to understand certain aspects, and to locate concerns of a set of change requests to a correct set of code places. In software engineering, there are typically four types of maintenance tasks [12], preventive, corrective, perfective and adaptive. In accordance to this widely used classification, we name five classes of change requests:

Bug fix request (Corrective): This request is about finding a bug which is present in the transformation, either the program does not compile, or the output is wrong. For instance, as a reaction to modifications to the metamodels, developers need to adapt the transformation accordingly.

Feature request (Perfective): To match new functional requirements, new functionality needs to be added, or existing functionality needs to be changed or removed. Because changes may originate from or have impact on depending artifacts, feature requests may result not only in modification of a transformation but also of metamodels, models and documentation.

Non-functional improvement (Perfective): A perfective task can also target non-functional requirements, it can even have an impact that is orthogonal to code structure.

Refactoring request (Preventive): Refactoring means organizing code structure without adding or removing existing functionality. For instance, a class attribute could be pulled up, which can result in an attribute assignment being pulled up a rule inheritance chain accordingly.

Environmental change request (Adaptive): Transformation programs do not function in isolation. Input metamodels change, or language concepts are updated.

Subjects were asked to *not* perform the actual change, because of the limited time frame, and because people brought a varying level of knowledge and experience with QVT-O and the underlying Object Constraint Language (OCL). Subject had to handle the following seven tasks:[3]

T1: Comprehension task / Searching for keywords

"Where does the transformation create elements in the target model? Name one example for each of the three variants for element instantiation."

Subjects had to look for the keywords `constructor`, `object`, `mapping`. They were asked to name one example for each instantiation type, 3 locations in total. Note that for mappings, non-tool users had to check for a return type, with implicit instantiation semantics. Tool users could check write-access edges in the graph, but still had to check the underlying code for the actual used instantiation type. Filter 4 combined with cross-navigation was the optimal choice. This task served as a warm-up question.

T2: Comprehension task / Analyzing control flow

"Which call trace leads from the entry method to a method creating instances of

---

[3] The experiment's tasks can be understood without knowledge of the PCM and QPN metamodels.

ExternalCallAction? Do not use the debugger or execute instrumented code."
A manual depth-first search using the browsing history had to be conducted, in order to find paths in the overall control flow leading from the entry method's node to the target method. Non-tool users had to use text-based search and hyperlink navigation. Tool users could use Filter F2, after identifying the target method as a method having write-access to the named class (Filter F4). The trace was 8 methods deep, and included downcasts regarding the contextual type of a mapping.

T3: Refactoring request / Analyzing control flow.

"Name all unused methods."

Non-tool users were required to search for occurences of each method's name. The transformation's main file had 41 mappings, 117 helpers, and 10 queries. Tool users could check for unreferenced nodes in the general control-flow view (Filter F1). There were 12 unused methods in total, 7 mappings and 5 helpers.

T4: Non-functional improvement / Analyzing data element usage

"Assert statements need to be added to check consistency of created connections. Please name all methods that instantiate objects of type ConnectionType."

Subjects had to look for the keywords constructor, object, mapping, in conjunction with ConnectionType. Non-tool users had to use the search command. Tool users could rely on write-access dependencies (Filter F4). There were 33 instantiating methods in total, 30 mapping rules and 3 helper methods.

T5: Feature request / Analyzing data element usage

"A new subtype of AbstractAction is planned to be added to the source meta-model. Where are AbstractAction elements handled? Name all occurences."

Here, subjects had to check data dependencies. While non-tool users had to use the search command, tool users could select Filter F4 and check outgoing or incoming edges in context of class AbstractAction. The correct answer included 5 mappings and 5 queries, where 2 queries were located in an external module.

T6: Feature request / Analyzing data element usage

"Class ForkAction, subtype of AbstractAction, should be used as blue print for the new subtype of AbstractAction to be added. Where does the transformation handle the ForkAction element? Name all occurences."

The right answer encompasses 8 queries and 6 mappings. Tool users could check data dependencies in context of ForkAction (Filter F4), others had to do a text-based search for the name.

T7: Bug fix request / Analyzing data flow for unused class attributes

"Created target models contain objects of class Place with an uninitialized attribute departureDiscipline. Identify the buggy lines of code."

Only one single mapping did create elements of type Place without proper initialization. Tool users were able to use Filter F3 in context of class Place, and check attribute dependencies for each displayed method.

6.2 Execution

Students had participated in two practical training sessions on transformation development. Training was done within scope of a practical course on MDSD. Each session ended with graded exercise sheets. We sent our fellow researchers training material to brush up their knowledge of the QVT-O language.

Assignment to one of the two groups happened randomly. Beforehand, participants had to fill out a pre-session questionnaire, where they rated their own expertise level on a 5-point Likert item and stated their academic degree. Based on this information, we randomly swapped participants between both groups so that each group had 7 students and 4 researchers, and the mean expertise level for both groups was equally balanced.

The experiment started with a 30 minutes tutorial on how to use the tool. Each participant was assigned to one workstation with a preconfigured Eclipse IDE. Then, subjects were handed out the task sheets, they were asked to answer tasks in prescribed order, and to note down when they started and when they ended a task. Subjects could freely partition their available time to the tasks. Subjects could decide to end a task prematurely, without the option to resume later. After 75 minutes total, the experiment closed with a post-session questionnaire. Using a debugger or executing the code was not permitted.

6.3 Analysis

For analysis, none of the outliers had been removed from the data set.

H1: Effectiveness. For hypothesis H1 we investigated the f-measure. Boxplots in Figure 6a contrast program with control group on a per-task level. Applying Welch's one-tailed t-test to the f1-measures at the default significance level of $\alpha = 0.05$, tool users showed a significant improvement over non-tool users for tasks 2-6 ($p_2 = 0.015$, $p_3 = 0.001$, $p_4 = 0.047$, $p_5 = 0.003$, $p_6 = 0.034$). For tasks 1 and 6, Welch's two-tailed t-test did not reveal a significant difference ($p_1 = 0.160$, $p_7 = 0.283$). We are able to reject H1's corresponding null hypothesis for all tasks but task one and task seven.

H2: Time expenditure. For H2 we tested time consumption. Figure 6b shows boxplots for the consumed time per task and added up. Welch's t-test had been used to test for significancy. We can confirm hypothesis H2 only for task 3 with a one-tailed test revealing $p = 0.010$. For the other tasks, two-tailed tests did not indicate any significant difference between groups.

H3: Perceived strain. H3 was based on subjective data from the questionnaires. All answers were posed using 6-point Likert items, ranging from "strongly disagree" to "strongly agree". One question was if subjects would rate the tasks as difficult to solve (see Figure 6c for details). Further questions asked tool users if they think that the tool helps in understanding, debugging, refactoring, and extending a previously unknown transformation, based on their experience they gained at the respective task. Figure 6d shows respective boxplots. Mean values report that non-tool users found the tasks to be "rather hard", while tool users found the tasks to be "rather easy". Additionally, tool users rated the tool's usability for understanding, debugging, and refactoring a

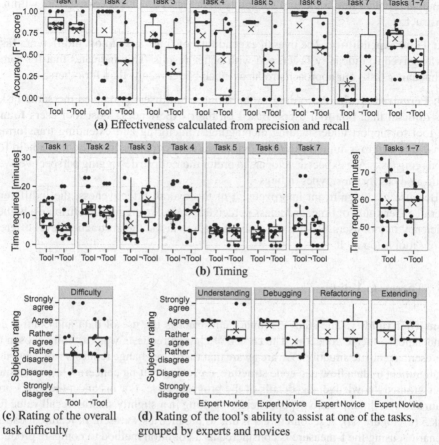

(a) Effectiveness calculated from precision and recall

(b) Timing

(c) Rating of the overall task difficulty

(d) Rating of the tool's ability to assist at one of the tasks, grouped by experts and novices

Fig. 6. Measured response variables[4]

transformation on a 6-level Likert item. On average, participants agreed that the tool helps in all four disciplines.

6.4 Discussion

H1: Effectiveness. Effectiveness is significantly improved for all tasks except the first and the last. For the first task, thought to be a warm-up exercise, we argue that even if tool users could profit from navigating the graph, they still had to check the underlying code for the keywords, making tool-based navigation only slightly better than a common text-based search. Many users did not find enough time for the last task, 4 out of 11 non-tool users and 3 out of 11 tool users did not even begin to process this task.

---

[4] In the boxplots, individual values are marked as dots jittered horizontally (and for discrete values also vertically) by a random value. A cross marks the mean, and a bar the median value.

A known problem lies in the tool's inability to detect attributes accessed from within a constructor.

H2: Time expenditure. The overall expenditure of time was almost indifferent. Task 3 was solved significantly faster, and with better results. This indicates that for some maintenance tasks our approach produces much better results than for others.

H3: Perceived strain. According to the ratings, tool users perceived the same tasks less difficult than non-tool users. Based on their experiences, most tool users found the tool to support understanding, debugging, refactoring and extending transformations, although to a limited extend. Novices were less convinced of the tool's help for debugging tasks. We expect developers to prefer the Eclipse debugging perspective over static analysis for most types of bugs.

Because of a significant improvement of the overall effectiveness, the indifferent overall expenditure of time, and a less perceived strain, we are able to attribute a higher efficiency to tool users. Results show that for some tasks, the abstraction level offered by our tool is too high.

6.5   Threats to Validity

Construct validity. The study's primary construct is the use of data and control dependencies to locate concerns. The choice of change requests was carefully chosen to represent a real-life situation. We are aware that there are change requests which are not in alignment to data flow and code structure, e.g. cross-cutting concerns, others require finer-grained knowledge, e.g. details of the program code. For instance, the tool's program analysis did miss two dependencies, resulting in a slightly smaller recall value for task 5 (cf. Figure 6a). A second threat is due to the metrics we used. In feature location scenarios, using the f-measure is considered as a common method to compare product-related quality [9]. Since people could freely partition their available time to the tasks, recorded times are not accurate, particularly towards the end. Subjective ratings need to be treated with care.

Internal validity. Blind testing was not possible, but people were assigned to one group at the latest possible time. Subjects were equally trained, advice had been given for each task on how to optimally use the tool and an alternative IDE feature. None of the subjects had been involved in the tool's development. We refrained from asking subjects to perform the actual maintenance task, because we expect the tool to show its particular strength in understanding code and locating concerns rather than in editing code.

External validity. Generalizability is threatened by the fact that we investigated only a single transformation written in a single transformation language. We are confident the transformation together with the two incorporated Ecore metamodels, the Palladio component model (PCM) and the queueing Petri-net model (QPN), reflect industrial quality standards. Program and model artifacts had been reviewed at least once. We also believe that our mix of novices and experts approximated to a real-world situation. We compared our tool to the bare Eclipse QVT-O environment, as we do not know of similar tools for QVT-O. Yet, by further equipping non-tool users with diagrammatic visualizations as those suggested by van Amstel et al. [4], we could check if our interactive approach would outcompete a static visualization approach.

7   Related Work

Program Analysis. Program analysis techniques are already applied to model transformations. Varro and his colleagues transfer graph transformations into Petri nets [13], where they are able to prove termination for many programs. Ujhelyi, Horvath and Varro analyze VIATRA2 VTCL programs for common errors in transformation programs [14]. The same authors suggest a dynamic backward slicing approach [15] to understand program behavior for a certain input. In comparison, our approach is based on static program analysis, aiming to support the process of understanding for maintenance rather than reasoning about program properties. Schönböck et al. use Petri nets to integrate data and control structures into a graphical view [16] to foster debuggability. Their approach is designed for declarative rule-based transformation languages and lacks validation.

Vieira and Ramalho developed a higher order transformation [3] to automatically extract dependencies from ATL transformations. Their objective is similar to ours, namely to assist developers inspecting transformation code. The unvalidated approach is ATL-specific, it lacks data dependencies and filters. A user interface is still missing.

Eclipse editors, including that for QVT-O, support hyperlinked syntax. However, control dependencies are not computed live, and navigation over calls is only possible in the forward direction. Learning about data dependencies from code requires good cognitive abilities and a thorough knowledge of all the relevant language concepts. Still, data dependencies derived from other methods can not directly be seen. Furthermore, it is not possible to directly learn about all the places a particular data element is accessed.

Program Visualization. Software visualization tools had been surveyed by Diehl in his book from 2007 [2]. Telea et al. make a comparison between hierarchical edge bundling (HEB) visualizations and classical node-link diagrams (NLDs) when used for comprehending C/C++ code [17]. Our graph notation can be classified as an NLD. Recently, van Amstel et al. have been conquering HEB diagrams for visualizing a transformation's data and control dependencies and metamodel coverage [4]. However, data and control dependencies are not integrated into a single view, and effectiveness and efficiency of static HEB diagrams for maintenance tasks remain to be validated.

8   Conclusions and Outlook

We demonstrated a novel approach to visualize data and control flow dependencies of metamodels and transformations using interactive node-link diagrams (NLDs). Efficiency of our approach has been shown in an experiment, where subjects using our approach were significantly more efficient and effective carrying out maintenance tasks. Results suggest that it is the large number of dependencies among metamodel elements and transformation rules that hampers understandability of model transformations.

Our study indicates that maintenance processes can be heavily improved by revealing dependency information to maintainers. Instead of utilizing program analysis techniques, transformation languages could proactively provide concepts to let programmers explicitly declare dependencies for program elements, e.g. rules and modules. Since prevalent module concepts are coined towards reuse rather than maintenance [18], we consider a module concept where dependencies can be declared upfront. For existing transformations, a module's dependencies can be derived automatically with our approach. A *clustering algorithm* based on dependency metrics could even propose suitable modular structures [19]. Next, we plan to try different types of visualizations, for example *filtered HEBs*. In future experiment runs, we would like to test transformations in further dialects, and compare our approach with other existing approaches. Additionally, analysis of OCL expressions [20] needs to be refined, as not all data dependencies are captured yet.

Acknowledgements. This research has been funded by the German Research Foundation (DFG) under grant No. RE 1674/5-1. We thank our experimentees for their valuable time.

References

1. Storey, M.A.D.: Theories, Tools and Research Methods in Program Comprehension: Past, Present and Future. Software Quality Journal 14(3), 187–208 (2006)
2. Diehl, S.: Software Visualization: Visualizing the Structure, Behaviour, and Evolution of Software. Springer (2007)
3. Vieira, A., Ramalho, F.: A Static Analyzer for Model Transformations. In: MtATL 2011. CEUR Workshop Proceedings, vol. 742, pp. 75–88. CEUR-WS.org (2011)
4. van Amstel, M.F., van den Brand, M.G.J.: Model Transformation Analysis: Staying Ahead of the Maintenance Nightmare. In: Cabot, J., Visser, E. (eds.) ICMT 2011. LNCS, vol. 6707, pp. 108–122. Springer, Heidelberg (2011)
5. Keim, D.A., Kohlhammer, J., Ellis, G., Mansmann, F.: Mastering the Information Age - Solving Problems with Visual Analytics. Eurographics Association (2010)
6. Keim, D.A., Mansmann, F., Schneidewind, J., Thomas, J., Ziegler, H.: Visual analytics: Scope and challenges. In: Simoff, S.J., Böhlen, M.H., Mazeika, A. (eds.) Visual Data Mining. LNCS, vol. 4404, pp. 76–90. Springer, Heidelberg (2008)
7. Object Management Group (OMG): MOF 2.0 Query/View/Transformation, version 1.1 (January 2011), http://www.omg.org/spec/QVT/1.1/PDF/
8. Kindler, E., Wagner, R.: Triple Graph Grammars: Concepts, Extensions, Implementations, and Application Scenarios. Technical Report TR-RI-07-284, Univ. of Paderborn (2007)
9. Wang, J., Peng, X., Xing, Z., Zhao, W.: An Exploratory Study of Feature Location Process: Distinct Phases, Recurring Patterns, and Elementary Actions.. In: ICSM 2011. IEEE (2011)
10. Juzgado, N.J., Moreno, A.M.: Basics of Software Engineering Experimentation. Kluwer Academic Publishers (2001)
11. Meier, P., Kounev, S., Koziolek, H.: Automated Transformation of Component-Based Software Architecture Models to Queueing Petri Nets. In: MASCOTS 2011, pp. 339–348. IEEE (2011)
12. Saleh, K.A.: Software Engineering. J Ross Publishing (2009)

13. Varró, D., Varró–Gyapay, S., Ehrig, H., Prange, U., Taentzer, G.: Termination Analysis of Model Transformations by Petri Nets. In: Corradini, A., Ehrig, H., Montanari, U., Ribeiro, L., Rozenberg, G. (eds.) ICGT 2006. LNCS, vol. 4178, pp. 260–274. Springer, Heidelberg (2006)
14. Ujhelyi, Z., Horváth, Á., Varró, D.: A Generic Static Analysis Framework for Model Transformation Programs. Technical report, Budapest Univ. of Technology and Economics (2009)
15. Ujhelyi, Z., Horváth, Á., Varró, D.: Dynamic Backward Slicing of Model Transformations. In: ICST 2012, pp. 1–10. IEEE (2012)
16. Schönböck, J., Kappel, G., Kusel, A., Retschitzegger, W., Schwinger, W., Wimmer, M.: Catch Me If You Can - Debugging Support for Model Transformations. In: Schürr, A., Selic, B. (eds.) MODELS 2009. LNCS, vol. 5795, pp. 5–20. Springer, Heidelberg (2009)
17. Telea, A., Hoogendorp, H., Ersoy, O., Reniers, D.: Extraction and Visualization of Call Dependencies for Large C/C++ Code Bases: A Comparative Study. In: VISSOFT 2009, pp. 81–88. IEEE (2009)
18. Wimmer, M., Kappel, G., Kusel, A., Retschitzegger, W., Schönböck, J., Schwinger, W.: Fact or Fiction – Reuse in Rule-Based Model-to-Model Transformation Languages. In: Hu, Z., de Lara, J. (eds.) ICMT 2012. LNCS, vol. 7307, pp. 280–295. Springer, Heidelberg (2012)
19. Dietrich, J., Yakovlev, V., McCartin, C., Jenson, G., Duchrow, M.: Cluster Analysis of Java Dependency Graphs. In: SoftVis 2008, pp. 91–94. ACM (2008)
20. Jeanneret, C., Glinz, M., Baudry, B.: Estimating Footprints of Model Operations. In: ICSE 2011, pp. 601–610. ACM (2011)

Checking Model Transformation Refinement

Fabian Büttner[1], Marina Egea[2], Esther Guerra[3], and Juan de Lara[3]

[1] École des Mines de Nantes - INRIA, France
fabian.buettner@inria.fr
[2] Atos Research & Innovation Dept., Madrid, Spain
marina.egea@atosresearch.eu
[3] Universidad Autónoma de Madrid, Spain
{Esther.Guerra,Juan.deLara}@uam.es

Abstract. Refinement is a central notion in computer science, meaning that some artefact S can be safely replaced by a refinement R, which preserves S's properties. Having available techniques and tools to check transformation refinement would enable (a) the reasoning on whether a transformation correctly implements some requirements, (b) whether a transformation implementation can be safely replaced by another one (e.g. when migrating from QVT-R to ATL), and (c) bring techniques from stepwise refinement for the engineering of model transformations.

In this paper, we propose an automated methodology and tool support to check transformation refinement. Our procedure admits heterogeneous specification (e.g. PaMoMo, Tracts, OCL) and implementation languages (e.g. ATL, QVT), relying on their translation to OCL as a common representation formalism and on the use of model finding tools.

1 Introduction

The raising complexity of languages, models and their associated transformations makes evident the need for engineering methods to develop model transformations [12]. Model transformations are software artefacts and, as such, should be developed using sound engineering principles. However, in current practice, transformations are normally directly encoded in some transformation language, with no explicit account for their *requirements*. These are of utmost importance, as they express *what* the transformation has to do, and can be used as a basis to assert correctness of transformation implementations. While many proposals for requirements gathering, representation and reasoning techniques have been proposed for general software engineering [15,23], their use is still the exception when developing model transformations.

Specifications play an important role in software engineering, and can be used in the development of model transformations in several ways. First, they make explicit what the transformation should do, and can be used as a basis for implementation. Specifications do not necessarily need to be complete, but can document the main requirements and properties expected of a transformation. Then, they can be used as oracle functions for testing implementations [11].

K. Duddy and G. Kappel (Eds.): ICMT 2013, LNCS 7909, pp. 158–173, 2013.
© Springer-Verlag Berlin Heidelberg 2013

In this setting, it is useful to know when a transformation T refines a specification S. Intuitively, this means that T can be used in place of S without breaking any assumption of the users of S. Some other times, we need to know whether a transformation T refines another transformation T' and can replace it. Fig. 1 gathers

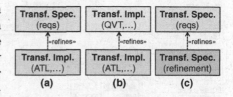

Fig. 1. Refinement scenarios

several scenarios where checking transformation refinement is useful. In (a), an implementation refines a requirements specification, hence ensuring correctness of the implementation with respect to the specification. In (b), a transformation implementation (e.g. in QVT) is refined by another one (e.g. in ATL) which can replace the former safely. This is especially useful if we want to migrate transformations, ensuring correctness of the migrated transformation. Finally, in (c), a specification refines another specification, which enables the application of stepwise refinement methodologies for transformation development.

In this paper, we tackle the previous scenarios by proposing an automated methodology to check transformation refinements. Our proposal relies on OCL as a common denominator for both specification languages (e.g. PAMoMo [13], Tracts [25] and OCL [18]) and transformation languages (e.g. QVT-R [21], triple graph grammars [22] and ATL [16]). For this purpose, we profit from previous works translating these languages into OCL [6,7,13,25]. Hence, transformation specifications and implementations are transformed into *transformation models* [4] and we use SAT/model finding [6] techniques to automatically find counterexamples that satisfy properties assumed by the specification, but are incorrectly implemented. While refinement has been previously tackled in [25], our work is novel in that it proposes an automated procedure for performing this checking, and is able to tackle heterogeneous specification and transformation languages by using OCL as the underlying language for reasoning.

Paper organization. Section 2 motivates the need for transformation refinement using an example. Section 3 introduces model transformation refinement. Section 4 details our methodology to check refinements. Section 5 provides more examples, Section 6 compares with related work and Section 7 concludes.

2   A Motivating Example

Assume we have gathered the requirements for the *Class2Relational* transformation, and want to use them as a blueprint to check whether an implementation correctly addresses them. Fig. 2 shows part of a specification of the requirements using the PAMoMo specification language [13], though we could choose any other transformation specification language instead (like Tracts or OCL).

PAMoMo is a formal, pattern-based, declarative, bidirectional specification language that can be used to describe correctness requirements of transformations and of their input and output models in an implementation-independent

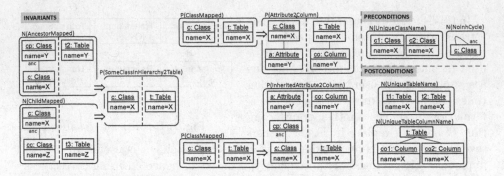

Fig. 2. A specification for the *Class2Relational* transformation

way. These requirements may correspond to *pre-/postconditions* that input/output models should fulfill, as well as transformation *invariants* (i.e. requirements that the output model resulting from a particular input model should satisfy).

Preconditions, postconditions, and invariants are represented as graph patterns, which can be positive to specify expected model fragments, or negative to specify forbidden ones. They can have attached a logical formula stating extra conditions, typically (but not solely) constraining the attribute values in the graph pattern. Optionally, patterns can define one enabling condition and any number of disabling conditions, to reduce the scope of the pattern to the locations where the enabling condition is met, and the disabling conditions are not. The interested reader can find the formalization of these concepts in [13,14].

Fig. 2 shows to the left three invariants that our *Class2Relational* transformation should fulfill. This specification is very general, in the sense that it gathers only the minimal requirements that any implementation of the *Class2Relational* should satisfy, leaving room for different transformation strategies. In particular, the specification only requires the transformation of at least one class in every class hierarchy, allowing freedom as to how many classes per hierarchy to transform (being 1 the minimum). This condition is checked by invariant *SomeClassInHierarchy2Table*, which states that if a class *c* does not have ancestors or children that have been transformed (disabling conditions *AncestorMapped* and *ChildMapped* respectively), then *c* should be transformed into a table (invariant *SomeClassInHierarchy2Table*). In the invariant, assigning the same variable to different attributes accounts for ensuring equality of their values, like *X*, which is assigned to the name of both the class *c* and the table *t*, meaning that both objects should have the same name. Moreover, relation *anc* is the transitive closure of the inheritance relation. Altogether, this invariant states that at least one class in each hierarchy should be transformed. The remaining invariants in this specification handle the correct transformation of attributes. To its right, invariant *Attribute2Column* states that if a class *c* is transformed (enabling condition *ClassMapped*), then its owned attributes should be converted into columns of the table. Below, invariant *InheritedAttribute2Column* states that all inherited attributes should be transformed into columns as well. Finally, another invariant (omitted for reasons of space) states that attributes of non-mapped children classes should also be transformed for their mapped ancestors.

Fig. 2 shows to the right some pre- and postconditions for the input/output models. Whereas the shown invariants are positive and therefore their satisfaction is demanded, the shown pre- and postconditions are negative, indicating forbidden situations. Thus, precondition *UniqueClassName* forbids duplicated class names for input models, and *NoInhCycle* forbids having inheritance cycles. Three additional preconditions, not shown for space constraints, forbid duplicate attribute names in the same class, either defined locally or inherited. Similarly, postcondition *UniqueTableName* forbids duplicated table names in output models, and *UniqueTableColumnName* forbids two equally named columns in the same table. Note that although this is not the case, we could also define negative invariants, as well as positive pre- and postconditions, in specifications.

Developers can use the specification in Fig. 2 as a guide to implement the transformation in their favorite language. As an example, Listing 1 shows a possible implementation in ATL. The strategy followed is transforming each class and, in the generated table, creating columns coming from the attributes defined in the class or its ancestor classes (checked in line 10). The specification would also admit other transformation strategies, like mapping only top classes or only leaf classes. Note that the implementation transforms packages into schemas in lines 3–4, though the specification does not state how to handle them (there is just a multiplicity constraint saying that classes are always in a package).

```
1  module AllClasses; create OUT : SimpleRelational from IN : SimpleClass;
2
3  rule P2S { from p : SimpleClass!Package
4            to s : SimpleRelational!Schema }
5
6  rule C2T { from c : SimpleClass!Class
7            to t : SimpleRelational!Table ( name <− c.name, schema <− c.package ) }
8
9  rule A2A { from ua : SimpleClass!Attribute,
10              c : SimpleClass!Class ( c = ua.owner or c.ancestors()−>includes(ua.owner) )
11            to col : SimpleRelation!Column ( name <− ua.name, owner <− ua.owner ) }
```

Listing 1. Transformation implementation using ATL (*"AllClasses.atl"*)

Then, the question arises whether the implemented transformation is a refinement of the specification, i.e., whether for any valid input model (satisfying the preconditions), its transformation yields a model satisfying the invariants and postconditions of the specification. As we will see in Section 4, the answer to this question is *no* because this implementation does not guarantee the invariant *InheritedAttributeToColumn*, since the rule A2A contains a little bug (which we will uncover in Section 4.1). While finding this bug can be done manually by testing, in this paper we propose an automated procedure to detect the postconditions and invariants of the specification that are not satisfied.

Other scenarios for checking refinement are also of practical use. For example, if we want to migrate this transformation into QVT-R, we might want to ensure that the target transformation is compatible with the original one. The next section discusses the notion of *transformation refinement*, while Section 4 presents our approach to automatically assess the scenarios identified in Fig. 1.

3   Model Transformation Refinement

Conceptually, a model-to-model transformation S from a source metamodel $\mathcal{M}_{src}$ to a target metamodel $\mathcal{M}_{tar}$ can be represented by a relation $Sem(S)$ between pairs of source and target models of the metamodels[1].

$$Sem(S) = \{(M_{src}, M_{tar}) : M_{src} \ S \ M_{tar}, \text{ where}$$
$$M_{src} \text{ is a model of } \mathcal{M}_{src}, \text{ and } M_{tar} \text{ is a model of } \mathcal{M}_{tar}\}$$

A relation S does not need to be functional, i.e., the same source model may be related with several target models. In this way, we support both deterministic and non-deterministic transformations. Based on this characterization, we can express a refinement relation of a transformation.

Def. 1 (Refinement) *Given two transformation specifications S, S' between a source metamodel $\mathcal{M}_{src}$, and a target metamodel $\mathcal{M}_{tar}$. S' refines S iff the following conditions hold:*

$$\forall M_{src}, M_{tar} : ((M_{src}, M_{tar}) \in Sem(S') \ \wedge \ \exists M'_{tar} : (M_{src}, M'_{tar}) \in Sem(S))$$
$$\Rightarrow (M_{src}, M_{tar}) \in Sem(S) \tag{1}$$

$$\forall M_{src}, M_{tar} : (M_{src}, M_{tar}) \in Sem(S) \Rightarrow (\exists M'_{tar} : (M_{src}, M'_{tar}) \in Sem(S')) \tag{2}$$

The second condition specifies the executability of S': S' must accept all inputs that S accepts. The first condition requires that S' behaves consistent to S on those inputs. Fig. 3 illustrates this relationship using a set notation. The source models accepted by S are given by set $Dom(S)$ (its domain, i.e., the models in the source metamodel of S). The definition domain of S is the set $Ran(S)$ (its range, made of the models in the target metamodel of S). Models are represented as dots, pairs of models in $Sem(S)$ are joined by a solid arrow, and pairs of models in $Sem(S')$ are joined by dashed arrows. Fig. 3(a) shows a valid refinement as the upper pair in $Sem(S')$ is also in $Sem(S)$. Since refinement is not concerned with source models not considered by S, the lower source model is allowed to be related with any target model in $Sem(S')$. Fig. 3(b) is not a refinement because the pair in $Sem(S')$ is not in $Sem(S)$, while the source model of this pair is in $Dom(S)$. Fig. 3(c) is not a refinement, as $Sem(S')$ misses one source model of $Dom(S)$. Altogether, the figure illustrates that the domain of S' should include the domain of S and be consistent with the elements in the domain of S.

For the sake of simplicity, we assume that S and S' share the same metamodels. In practice, S may focus on the most important aspects of a transformation, while a refinement S' may be defined in more detail and over larger source/target metamodels. Provided that the metamodels for S' are subtypes of the metamodels of S [24], we can always silently extent the metamodels for S to those of S' in Definition 1.

---

[1] Notice that we are assuming source-to-target transformations.

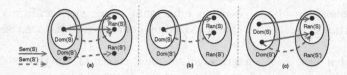

Fig. 3. Valid (a) and invalid (b, c) refinements

Some approaches, like model transformation contracts [9,14], characterize the semantics of a transformation S from a source to a target metamodel by means of three types of constraints: preconditions (Pre_S), invariants (Inv_S) and postconditions ($Post_S$). We capture this semantics in Def. 2. In the definition, we represent by Pre_S the set of preconditions pre_i that the source models of S must fulfill, and use $Pre_S(M_{src})$ to indicate that the model M_{src} fulfills all the preconditions of S, i.e., $pre_1(M_{src}) \wedge \ldots \wedge pre_n(M_{src})$. We use a similar notation for invariants and postconditions as well. For this kind of transformations, assuming that their conditions can be translated into first-order logic, we can restate Def. 1 in terms of characterizing predicates as follows.

Def. 2 (Contract-based transformation specification) *Let S be a contract-based transformation specification from a source metamodel M_{src} to a target metamodel M_{tar}. The relation set $Sem(S)$ defined by S can be characterized by three types of predicates that represent S's preconditions, invariants and postconditions (the contract of S) in the following way*

$$Sem(S) = \{(M_{src}, M_{tar}) : (M_{src} \in \mathcal{M}_{src}) \wedge (M_{tar} \in \mathcal{M}_{tar}) \wedge$$
$$Pre_S(M_{src}) \wedge Inv_S(M_{src}, M_{tar}) \wedge Post_S(M_{tar})\} \tag{3}$$

with the additional condition that $\forall (M_{src} \in \mathcal{M}_{src})$

$$(Pre_S(M_{src}) \Rightarrow \exists(M_{tar} \in \mathcal{M}_{tar}) : Inv_S(M_{src}, M_{tar}) \wedge Post_S(M_{tar})) \tag{4}$$

Prop. 1 (Refinement for contract-based transformation specifications) *Let S and S' be contract-based transformation specifications from a source metamodel M_{src} to a target metamodel M_{tar}. S' refines S iff the following conditions hold*

$$\forall (M_{src} \in \mathcal{M}_{src}, M_{tar} \in \mathcal{M}_{tar})(Pre_S(M_{src}) \wedge Inv_{S'}(M_{src}, M_{tar}) \wedge$$
$$Post_{S'}(M_{tar})) \Rightarrow (Inv_S(M_{src}, M_{tar}) \wedge Post_S(M_{tar})) \tag{5}$$

$$\forall (M_{src} \in \mathcal{M}_{src})(Pre_S(M_{src}) \Rightarrow Pre_{S'}(M_{src})) \tag{6}$$

Proof. We can show that using Def. 2, conditions (1) and (2) hold iff conditions (5) and (6) hold. The proof is included in the extended version of this paper[2].

---

[2] http://www.emn.fr/z-info/atlanmod/index.php/ICMT_2013_Refinement

This proposition allows checking refinement using satisfiability solving for transformations that can be characterized by contracts, as the next section will show.

Notice that Def. 2 characterizes an 'angelic' choice [3] for the executability: given a valid source model (w.r.t. Pre_S), there must be at least one target model such that Inv_S and $Post_S$ hold. We do not require that Pre_S and Inv_S always imply $Post_S$, like one often expects an implementation to imply a postcondition in program verification. In our context, Inv_S is part of the specification, just as Pre_S and $Post_S$.

Strong refinement. We demanded above that a refining transformation specification S' must accept all input models that the refined transformation S accepts (specified by Pre_S), and that the output models of S' for those inputs are valid w.r.t. Inv_S, and $Post_S$. We did not characterize the effect of S' for input models not fulfilling Pre_S. However, if we think of $Post_S$ as a contract that *any* transformation execution needs to fulfill, it makes sense to define a new notion of refinement that we call *strong refinement*. Thus, S' is a strong refinement of S iff it is a refinement and $\forall(M_{src} \in \mathcal{M}_{src}, M_{tar} \in \mathcal{M}_{tar})$

$$((Pre_{S'}(M_{src}) \wedge Inv_{S'}(M_{src}, M_{tar}) \wedge Post_{S'}(M_{tar})) \Rightarrow Post_S(M_{tar})) \tag{7}$$

Previous works [25] have approached transformation refinement from a testing perspective. Hence, given a set of (manually created) input models, developers might discover an implementation result violating some postcondition or invariant, but cannot prove refinement. In the next section, we provide a stronger, automated methodology based on constraint solving to perform the checking.

4   Checking Refinement Using OCL Model Finders

Our methodology for checking transformation refinement builds on the fact that transformations in several declarative languages can be translated into a unified representation using OCL contracts. This unified representation, called *transformation model* [4], can be easily checked and analyzed using readily available OCL model finders. In short, the source and target metamodels are merged, and OCL constraints over this merged metamodel expresses the transformation semantics.

While such contracts are not directly executable, they are well-suited for automated checking of transformation properties as they allow expressing conditions covering the source and target models of the transformation at the same time. The checking can be done using a model finder, i.e., a satisfiability checker for metamodels, to verify the absence of counter examples for a given property. This way, for example, we have shown in [6] how to check if an ATL transformation can create output models that violate given constraints. Thus, we propose to generate and combine the OCL contracts for two transformation specifications in order to analyze the refinement relation between them following Prop. 1.

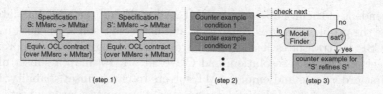

Fig. 4. Steps in the methodology to check refinement

Fig. 4 shows the steps in our refinement checking methodology: (1) generation of the OCL contracts from both specifications S and S', (2) generation of counter example conditions, and (3) checking unsatisfiability of the counter-example conditions with an OCL model finder. Next, we detail these steps.

(1) Generation of OCL transformation contracts. First, each of the specifications S and S' is translated into equivalent sets of OCL constraints, $cons(S)$ and $cons(S')$, over the combination of the source and target metamodels, M_{src} and M_{tar}. Namely, $cons(S) = precons(S) \cup invcons(S) \cup postcons(S)$, where $precons(S)$, $invcons(S)$, and $postcons(S)$ are OCL encodings of Pre_S, Inv_S, and $Post_S$, fulfilling the conditions explained in Def. 2. Thus, in this setting we have $(M_{src}, M_{tar}) \in Sem(S)$ iff the evaluation of the constraints in $cons(S)$ over M_{src} combined with M_{tar} is true (and analogously for S').

Generators of such sets of OCL constraints have been described for several declarative, rule-based, specification/implementation transformation languages, including PAMOMO [13], QVT-R [7], triple grammars [7] and ATL [6].

(2) Generation of counter-example conditions. In order to check the two conditions for refinement of Prop. 1, we need that $invcons(S) \wedge postcons(S)$ is implied by $precons(S) \wedge invcons(S') \wedge postcons(S')$ and that $precons(S')$ is implied by $precons(S)$ for every instance of M_{src} combined with M_{tar}. This can be expressed as the following counter-example conditions that must all be unsatisfiable:

1. For each constraint c in $invcons(S) \cup postcons(S)$, the set of constraints $precons(S) \cup invcons(S') \cup postcons(S') \cup \{negated(c)\}$ must be unsatisfiable.
2. For each constraint c in $precons(S')$, the set of constraints $precons(S) \cup \{negated(c)\}$ must be unsatisfiable.
3. (For strong refinement) For each constraint c in $Post_S$, the set of constraints $precons(S') \cup invcons(S') \cup postcons(S') \cup \{negated(c)\}$ must be unsatisfiable.

If none of the counter-example conditions in 1–2 (1–3) is satisfiable, then S' refines (strongly refines) S.

(3) Satisfiability checking of counter-example conditions. We use OCL model finders to check the counter-example conditions. There are several approaches for checking the satisfiability of OCL constraints, and our methodology is independent of them. For example, UML2Alloy [1] and the USE Validator [17] translate the problem into relational logic and use a SAT solver to check it, while UMLtoCSP [8] translates it into a constraint-logic program. The approach of Queralt et al. [20] uses resolution, and Clavel et. al [10] map a subset of OCL into a first-order logic and employ SMT solvers to check unsatisfiability. In this paper, we have used the USE Validator because it supports a large subset of OCL and because the underlying SAT solver provides robust performance for a variety of problems. This tool performs model finding within given search bounds, using finite ranges for the number of objects, links and attribute values. Thus, when a counter example is found, we have proven that there is no refinement; if no counter example is found, we only know that the refinement is guaranteed up to the search bounds. However, not finding a counterexample is a strong indication of refinement if wide enough bounds are chosen for the search.

4.1 Running Example

In Sect. 2, we presented a specification of the *Class2Relational* transformation using PAMoMo (cf. Fig. 2), as well as a possible implementation of the *All-Classes* strategy using ATL (cf. Listing 1). Next, we illustrate our methodology by checking whether *AllClasses* refines *Class2Relational*.

(1) Generation of OCL transformation contracts. First, we generate the OCL contracts for *Class2Relational* and *AllClasses*. Following the compilation and tool support presented in [14], we generate one OCL invariant from each PAMoMo pattern. Listing 2 shows the OCL invariants for precondition *Unique-ClassName*, invariant *Attribute2Column* and postcondition *UniqueTableColumn-Name*. These constraints belong to the sets *precons(Class2Relational)*, *invcons(Class2Relational)* and *postcons(Class2Relational)*, respectively. Notice that we silently assume a singleton class *GlobalContext* which hosts all OCL invariants. We refer the reader to [14] for a detailed presentation of this compilation scheme, and just highlight that the OCL expressions derived from preconditions only constrain the source models, those from postconditions only constrain the target models, and those from invariants constrain both.

```
1  context GlobalContext inv Pamomo_Pre_UniqueClassName:
2  not Class.allInstances()->exists(c1 | Class.allInstances()->exists(c2 | c2<>c1 and c1.name=c2.name))
3
4  context GlobalContext inv Pamomo_Inv_Attribute2Column:
5  Class.allInstances()->forAll(c |
6    Attribute.allInstances()->forAll(a | c.atts->includes(a) implies
7      Table.allInstances()->forAll(t | c.name=t.name implies
8        Column.allInstances()->exists(co | t.cols->includes(co) and a.name=co.name))))
9
10 context GlobalContext inv Pamomo_Pos_UniqueTableColumnName:
11 not Table.allInstances()->exists(t |
12   Column.allInstances()->exists(c1 | t.cols->includes(c1) and
13     Column.allInstances()->exists(c2 | c2 <> c1 and t.cols->includes(c2) and c1.name=c2.name)))
```

Listing 2. Some OCL invariants generated from the PAMoMo specification.

Then, we derive an OCL contract for the ATL implementation, following the rules and tool described in [6]. In this case, *precons(AllClasses)* and *postcons*(*AllClasses*) only contain the source and target metamodel integrity constraints, like multiplicity constraints. Listing 3 shows some OCL constraints in *invcons*(*AllClasses*). They control the matching of source objects, the creation of target objects and the bindings of properties in the target objects (see [6] for details).

```
 1  context Attribute inv ATL_MATCH_A2A:
 2     Attribute.allInstances()−>forAll(l_ua |
 3        Class.allInstances()−>forAll(l_c | (l_c.ancestors()−>includes(l_ua.owner)) implies
 4           A2A.allInstances()−>one(l_A2A | l_A2A.ua = l_ua and l_A2A.c = l_c)))
 5
 6  context A2A inv ATL_MATCH_A2A_COND: self.c.ancestors()−>includes(self.ua.owner)
 7
 8  context C2T inv ATL_BIND_C2T_t_name: self.t.name=self.c.name
 9  context A2A inv ATL_BIND_A2A_col_name: self.col.name=self.ua.name
10  context A2A inv ATL_BIND_A2A_col_owner: self.col.owner=self.c.c2t.t
11
12  context Column inv ATL_CREATE_Column: self.a2a−>size()=1
```

Listing 3. OCL invariants generated from the ATL rule *A2A*.

Notice that the mapping used for ATL [6] imposes a limitation for *invcons*(*AllClasses*): The OCL constraints use additional trace classes connecting the source and target objects in the transformation model. This means that we can use these constraints only in their positive form in the counter-example conditions, because for the negation we would need to express "there is no valid instance of the trace classes such that...", which is not available in OCL. In practice, this means that, using this OCL compilation, we can check whether an ATL specification refines any other transformation specification, but not the opposite. The compilations for PAMOMO and QVT-R do not have this limitation.

(2) Generation of counter-example conditions. From the full version of *Class2Relational* (Fig. 2 only shows an excerpt), we obtain 7 OCL invariants in *precons* (5 coming from PAMOMO preconditions and 2 from multiplicity constraints), 4 invariants in *postcons* (2 and 2), and 4 invariants in *invcons*. From the ATL version of *AllClasses*, we obtain 2 invariants in each *precons* and *postcons* for the multiplicity constraints, and 10 invariants in *invcons* characterizing the ATL rules. This gives 4 counter-example conditions to check for the first condition in Prop. 1, as explained on page 165, plus 2 cases for the second. If we want to check for strong refinement, we have 4 more counter-example conditions.

(3) Satisfiability checking of counter-example conditions. Checking the 10 counter-example conditions, for example with the USE Validator, yields the counter example shown in Fig. 5(a). The counter example satisfies all invariants that characterize *AllClasses* (hence it is a model of a valid ATL execution), but the OCL expression derived from the PAMOMO invariant *InheritedAttribute2Column* is violated (hence this pair of models is not in *Sem*(*Class2Relational*)). In particular, the problem is that the attribute inherited by *class1* is not attached to *table1*, but it is incorrectly attached to

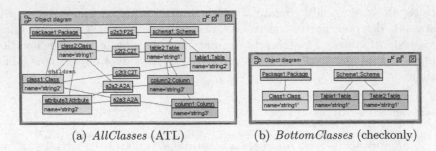

(a) *AllClasses* (ATL)   (b) *BottomClasses* (checkonly)

Fig. 5. Refinement counter examples, checking against *Class2Relational*

table2. Consequently, the instance is a counter example for postcondition *UniqueTableColumnName* as well.

If we examine the rule *A2A* in Listing 1 based on this counter example, we discover that the binding `owner<-ua.owner` is incorrect and should be changed to `owner<-c`. Fixing this error and checking the updated counter-example conditions again yields no counter example. Thus, the fixed version of *AllClasses* is a refinement of *Class2Relational*.

The ATL transformation is not a strong refinement of the PAMOMO specification though, since without demanding unique names in the source, ATL does not establish uniqueness of names in the target.

4.2 Tool Support

For the first step in Fig. 4, the generation of transformation models, we have automated generators available for PAMOMO and ATL. So far, the generation from QVT-R is performed manually. For the second step, we have created a prototype to automate the construction of the counter-example conditions. For the third step, we call the USE Validator [17] to find refinement counter examples.

5 Further Examples

In this section, we discuss some more results for the case study. We have considered a 'zoo' of various specifications of *Class2Relational* using different languages (PAMOMO, ATL and QVT-R) and following three strategies (mapping all classes, only top classes, or only bottom classes). We have applied our methodology to check refinement for each pair of specifications (110 counter-example conditions in total). Fig. 6 shows the results. The absence of an arrow indicates no refinement (except for ATL, which can only be checked on the implementation side of the refinement relation). The details for all strategies are online[3], here we just highlight some interesting points.

We have considered two PAMOMO specifications: *Class2Relational* (the running example), and a refinement of this called *TopOrAll* which demands a 'uniform' mapping either of all classes in the source model, or only of the top ones.

---

[3] http://www.emn.fr/z-info/atlanmod/index.php/ICMT_2013_Refinement

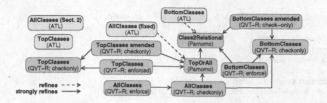

Fig. 6. Refinements between strategies (transitively reachable links are omitted)

The ATL implementation of the *TopClasses* strategy does not refine the *Class2Relational* specification. This strategy translates each top class into a table, and the attributes of the top class and its subclasses into columns of the table. However, if two subclasses of a top class have an attribute with the same name (which is not excluded by the preconditions of *Class2Relational*) then the generated table gets two columns with the same name, violating the postcondition *UniqueTableColumnName*. By contrast, the ATL versions of *All-Classes* (discussed in the previous section) and of *BottomClasses* are refinements of *Class2Relational*. *AllClasses* even refines the stronger specification *TopOrAll*.

Our methodology is also applicable to QVT-R. A QVT-R transformation S can be used in *enforce* mode to create a target model from scratch starting from a source model[4], or in *checkonly* mode to check the relation between an existing pair of models. Hence, we distinguish the sets $SEM_{ENF}(S)$ of source models and target models generated by S, and $SEM_{CHK}(S)$ of accepted pairs of source and target models. We will see that they are not equal.

Listing 4 shows the QVT-R implementation of the *BottomClasses* strategy. Interestingly, using this implementation in enforce mode is a refinement of the *Class2Relational* specification, but using it in checkonly mode is not. This is because the checkonly mode checks for the elements that should be created by the enforce mode, but the target model can contain more elements. The problem is that these extra elements can violate invariants or postconditions from the requirements specification. For example, Fig. 5(b) shows a refinement counter example violating the postcondition *UniqueClassName*, while satisfying the QVT-R transformation in checkonly mode.

```
1  transformation BottomClasses (source : SimpleClass, target : SimpleRelational) {
2    key SimpleRelational::Table {name};
3    key SimpleRelational::Column {owner, name};
4
5    top relation PackageToSchema {
6      checkonly domain source p : SimpleClass::Package {};
7      enforce domain target s : SimpleRelational::Schema {}; }
8
9    top relation ClassToTable {
10     cn : String;
11     checkonly domain source c : SimpleClass::Class {
12       package = p : SimpleClass::Package {}, name = cn };
13     enforce domain target t : SimpleRelational::Table {
14       schema = s : SimpleRelational::Schema {}, name = cn };
15     when { c.children−>size()=0 and PackageToSchema(p, s); }
```

---

[4] QVT-R also supports the incremental scenario, but we leave it out here.

```
16      where { AttributeToColumn(c, t); SuperAttributeToColumn(c, t); } }
17
18   relation AttributeToColumn {
19      an : String;
20      checkonly domain source c : SimpleClass::Class {
21         atts = a : SimpleClass::Attribute { name = an } };
22      enforce domain target t : SimpleRelational::Table {
23         cols = cl : SimpleRelational::Column { name = an } }; }
24
25   relation SuperAttributeToColumn {
26      checkonly domain source c : SimpleClass::Class {
27         package = p : SimpleClass::Package { classes = sc : SimpleClass::Class {} } };
28      enforce domain target t : SimpleRelational::Table {};
29      when { c.ancestors()->includes(sc); }
30      where { AttributeToColumn(sc, t); } }
31 }
```

Listing 4. QVT-R implementation of the *BottomClasses* strategy.

In order to make the checkonly transformation a refinement of *Class2Relational*, we need to include a top-level relation stating that non-bottom classes do not have an associated table. This extra relation is non-constructive and is not concerned with the creation of target elements, but with their absence. As ATL can only be used in enforce mode, this constraint is built-in into ATL.

Finally, the 'check-before-enforce' semantics of QVT-R prevents the creation of new objects if equivalent ones exist in the target. The equivalence criteria for objects are given through keys. By setting an appropriate key for columns (see line 3 in Listing 4) we avoid having repeated columns in tables. This is why the enforce mode of the QVT-R transformation for the *TopClasses* strategy correctly refines the *ClassToRelational* specification (whereas the ATL implementation does not, as explained above).

Regarding performance, for the examples considered so far, solving times using the USE Validator have not been an issue (within a few seconds for a default search bound of 0..5 objects per class). It remains as future work to evaluate the scalability on larger examples.

6   Related Work

To our knowledge, the only work addressing transformation refinement is [25]. Its authors use Tracts to build transformation contracts. Tracts are OCL invariants that can be used to specify preconditions, postconditions and transformation invariants. The authors introduce the following notion of refinement: a Tract S' refines another one S if S' has weaker preconditions, but stronger invariants and postconditions $((Pre_S \Rightarrow Pre_{S'}) \land (Inv_{S'} \Rightarrow Inv_S) \land (Post_{S'} \Rightarrow Post_S))$. This is a safe approximation to replaceability as in Def. 1, while our Prop. 1 exactly characterizes this notion. Moreover, we also distinguish *strong refinement*.

Regarding refinement checking, in [25], refinement is checked by building a suitable set of input test models and testing S' against S's pre/postconditions and invariants. This approach has two drawbacks. First, it is based on testing and on the manual creation of input test models. Secondly, it assumes that S' is an executable implementation which can be used for testing. As we have seen in this paper, S' might be a non-executable specification.

Our checking procedure ensures correctness criteria for the refining transformation. In this respect, the work in [19] provides a means to verify a transformation against verification properties, assuming that both are given by patterns, in the line of PAMOMO patterns. Verification properties are restricted to be positive. The checking implies generating all minimal glueings of the transformation patterns, and checking them against the verification property. In such restricted case, the verification is finitely terminating. We plan to investigate the glueing minimality conditions to provide suitable search bounds for the solver.

The use of OCL to define transformation contracts was proposed in [9]. This idea was extended in [4] with the aim to build transformation models as a declarative means to capture the transformation semantics. Transformation models with OCL constraints were used for transformation verification using model finders in [2,6,7]. None of these works propose checking transformation refinement.

7   Conclusions and Future Work

In this paper, we have presented a methodology and tool support to check transformation refinement. Refinement is useful to check whether an implementation is correct with respect to a specification, to ensure replaceability of implementations (e.g. when migrating a transformation), and to apply step-wise refinement techniques to transformation development.

Our methodology can be applied to check refinement between transformations in any specification or implementation language for which a translation to an OCL transformation model exists. To our knowledge, such translations exist for PAMOMO, QVT-R, TGGs, and for a subset of ATL without imperative code blocks. One limitation of the OCL contract-based approach is that recursive rules cannot be generally mapped into OCL contracts, since OCL has no fix-point operator. For example, the QVT-R-to-OCL translation in [7] would, for recursive rules, yield recursive helper operations. For bounded verification, however, such definitions can be still statically unfolded up to a given depth.

Our methodology is actually independent of OCL. For example, it would apply to transformations contracts specified in first order logic, too, like in [5]. That would open up further possibilities for symbolic reasoning. Our lightweight methodology permits checking transformation correctness; however, as it relies on bounded model finding, formally, our method can only disprove refinement. Using wide enough bounds can provide high confidence in refinement, though. Another possibility would be to prove implications from the invariants and postconditions of S' to those of S; however, this would require the use of theorem provers, with less automation. We will explore this path in future work. Finally, we also plan to combine the constraints coming from the implementation and the specification to derive models for testing, in the style of [11].

Acknowledgements.   Research partially funded by the Nouvelles Équipes Program of the Pays de la Loire Region (France), the EU project NESSoS

(FP7 256890), the Spanish Ministry of Economy and Competitivity (project "Go Lite" TIN2011-24139), the R&D programme of the Madrid Region (project "e-Madrid" S2009/TIC-1650).

References

1. Anastasakis, K., Bordbar, B., Georg, G., Ray, I.: On challenges of model transformation from UML to Alloy. Software and Systems Modeling 9(1), 69–86 (2010)
2. Anastasakis, K., Bordbar, B., Küster, J.M.: Analysis of model transformations via alloy. In: MODEVVA 2007 (2007)
3. Back, R.-J., von Wright, J.: Refinement Calculus: A Systematic Introduction. Graduate Texts in Computer Science. Springer, Berlin (1998)
4. Bézivin, J., Büttner, F., Gogolla, M., Jouault, F., Kurtev, I., Lindow, A.: Model transformations? Transformation models! In: Wang, J., Whittle, J., Harel, D., Reggio, G. (eds.) MoDELS 2006. LNCS, vol. 4199, pp. 440–453. Springer, Heidelberg (2006)
5. Büttner, F., Egea, M., Cabot, J.: On verifying ATL transformations using 'off-the-shelf' SMT solvers. In: France, R.B., Kazmeier, J., Breu, R., Atkinson, C. (eds.) MODELS 2012. LNCS, vol. 7590, pp. 432–448. Springer, Heidelberg (2012)
6. Büttner, F., Egea, M., Cabot, J., Gogolla, M.: Verification of ATL transformations using transformation models and model finders. In: Aoki, T., Taguchi, K. (eds.) ICFEM 2012. LNCS, vol. 7635, pp. 198–213. Springer, Heidelberg (2012)
7. Cabot, J., Clarisó, R., Guerra, E., de Lara, J.: Verification and validation of declarative model-to-model transformations through invariants. Journal of Systems and Software 83(2), 283–302 (2010)
8. Cabot, J., Clarisó, R., Riera, D.: UMLtoCSP: a tool for the formal verification of UML/OCL models using constraint programming. In: ASE 2007, ACM (2007)
9. Cariou, E., Marvie, R., Seinturier, L., Duchien, L.: OCL for the specification of model transformation contracts. In: OCL Workshop, vol. 12, pp. 69–83 (2004)
10. Clavel, M., Egea, M., de Dios, M.A.G.: Checking Unsatisfiability for OCL Constraints. Electronic Communications of the EASST 24, 1–13 (2009)
11. Guerra, E.: Specification-driven test generation for model transformations. In: Hu, Z., de Lara, J. (eds.) ICMT 2012. LNCS, vol. 7307, pp. 40–55. Springer, Heidelberg (2012)
12. Guerra, E., de Lara, J., Kolovos, D., Paige, R., dos Santos, O.: Engineering model transformations with transML. Software and Systems Modeling (2012) (in press)
13. Guerra, E., de Lara, J., Kolovos, D.S., Paige, R.F.: A visual specification language for model-to-model transformations. In: VL/HCC 2010, pp. 119–126. IEEE CS (2010)
14. Guerra, E., de Lara, J., Wimmer, M., Kappel, G., Kusel, A., Retschitzegger, W., Schönböck, J., Schwinger, W.: Automated verification of model transformations based on visual contracts. Autom. Softw. Eng. 20(1), 5–46 (2013)
15. Jackson, D.: Software Abstractions - Logic, Language, and Analysis. MIT (2012)
16. Jouault, F., Allilaire, F., Bézivin, J., Kurtev, I.: ATL: A model transformation tool. Sci. Comp. Pr. 72(1-2), 31–39 (2008)
17. Kuhlmann, M., Hamann, L., Gogolla, M.: Extensive validation of OCL models by integrating SAT solving into USE. In: Bishop, J., Vallecillo, A. (eds.) TOOLS 2011. LNCS, vol. 6705, pp. 290–306. Springer, Heidelberg (2011)
18. OMG OCL Specification, version 2.3.1 (Document formal/2012-01-01) (2012)

19. Orejas, F., Wirsing, M.: On the specification and verification of model transformations. In: Palsberg, J. (ed.) Mosses Festschrift. LNCS, vol. 5700, pp. 140–161. Springer, Heidelberg (2009)
20. Queralt, A., Teniente, E.: Verification and validation of UML conceptual schemas with OCL constraints. TOSEM 21(2), 13 (2012)
21. QVT (2005), http://www.omg.org/spec/QVT/1.0/PDF/ (last accessed November 2010)
22. Schürr, A.: Specification of graph translators with triple graph grammars. In: Mayr, E.W., Schmidt, G., Tinhofer, G. (eds.) WG 1994. LNCS, vol. 903, pp. 151–163. Springer, Heidelberg (1995)
23. Spivey, J.M.: An introduction to Z and formal specifications. Softw. Eng. J. 4(1), 40–50 (1989)
24. Steel, J., Jézéquel, J.-M.: On model typing. SoSyM 6(4), 401–413 (2007)
25. Vallecillo, A., Gogolla, M.: Typing model transformations using Tracts. In: Hu, Z., de Lara, J. (eds.) ICMT 2012. LNCS, vol. 7307, pp. 56–71. Springer, Heidelberg (2012)

Complete Specification Coverage in Automatically Generated Conformance Test Cases for TGG Implementations

Stephan Hildebrandt, Leen Lambers, and Holger Giese

Hasso Plattner Institute, Prof.-Dr.-Helmert-Str. 2-3, 14482 Potsdam, Germany
{stephan.hildebrandt,leen.lambers,holger.giese}@hpi.uni-potsdam.de

Abstract. Model transformations can be specified using an operational or a relational approach. For a relational approach, an operationalization must be derived from the transformation specification using approved formal concepts, so that the operationalization conforms to the specification. A conforming operationalization transforms a source model S to a target model T, which is moreover related to S according to the relational transformation specification. The conformance of an operationalization with its relational specification must be tested since it is not certain that the formal concepts have been correctly realized by the implementation. Moreover, transformation implementations often perform optimizations, which may violate conformance.

The Triple Graph Grammar (TGG) approach is an important representative of relational model transformations. This paper presents an extension of an existing automatic conformance testing framework for TGG implementations. This testing framework exploits the grammar character of TGGs to automatically generate test input models together with their expected result so that a complete oracle is obtained. The extension uses dependencies implicitly present in a TGG to generate minimal test cases covering all rules and dependencies in the TGG specification if the TGG is well-formed. In comparison to the previous random approach, this guided approach allows more efficient generation of higher quality test cases and, therefore, more thorough conformance testing of TGG implementations. The approach is evaluated using several TGGs, including one stemming from an industrial case study.

1 Introduction

Model transformations are an important part of every MDE approach. Therefore, their correctness has to be guaranteed. In a relational model transformation approach, errors may arise from faulty operationalizations, i.e. operationalizations that do not conform to the transformation specification. *Conformance* means that a source model S, which is transformed to a target model T by a transformation implementation, is also related to T according to the relational specification (and vice versa if the specification is bidirectional).

The *Triple Graph Grammar* [14] (TGG) approach is an important representative of *relational model transformation approaches*. To a certain extent, the

K. Duddy and G. Kappel (Eds.): ICMT 2013, LNCS 7909, pp. 174–188, 2013.

conformance of a TGG and a corresponding operationalization can be proven by formal reasoning [14,9,5]. In general, though, it is not certain whether implementations have realized each formal concept describing a conforming operationalization correctly. Moreover, usually, TGG formalizations neither cover every technicality that TGG implementations rely on, nor cover each additional optimization that augments the efficiency of the model transformation execution. Therefore, conformance testing of the implementation is required.

A framework for *automatic conformance testing* of TGG implementations was already presented [10], which automatically generates and executes test cases. A test case consists of a source (test input) and an expected target model (test oracle). The testing framework generates random test cases, executes the TGG implementation under test to transform the source model, and compares the created target model with the expected target model. If a difference is detected, a conformance error has been found. The framework's test case generation approach makes use of the *grammar* character of TGGs. TGG rules are randomly applied to create a source and expected target model simultaneously.

To assess the quality of a test case, the framework measures *specification coverage*, which consists of *rule coverage* and *rule dependency coverage*. Rule coverage is the percentage of TGG rules that were applied when building a particular test case. Likewise, rule dependency coverage is the percentage of covered *produce-use* dependencies between TGG rules. The aim of generating test cases is to achieve complete specification coverage. However, when evaluating the random generation approach [10] with several TGGs, complete specification coverage could not be achieved for complex TGGs. If a TGG contains very complex rules, the random generation approach is unlikely to generate test cases covering such rules.

Therefore, this paper presents a different test case generation approach, which generates test cases *guided by dependencies* between TGG rules. In practice, these test cases also achieve complete specification coverage for complex TGGs. Moreover, the test cases are as small as possible, which helps in finding the cause of conformance errors.

This paper is structured as follows: First, Sec. 2 presents the basic principles of TGGs and a running example. Sec. 3 briefly describes the existing conformance testing framework. The new dependency-guided generation approach and its completeness and minimality properties are explained in Sec. 4. An evaluation of the approach follows in Sec. 5, related work is discussed in Sec. 6 and Sec. 7 concludes the paper.

2   Triple Graph Grammars in a Nutshell

Triple Graph Grammars are a relational approach to bidirectional model transformation and model synchronization [14]. TGGs combine three conventional graph grammars for the source, target and correspondence models. The correspondence model explicitly stores correspondence relationships between source and target model elements. Fig. 1 shows the metamodels of *Block Diagrams*,

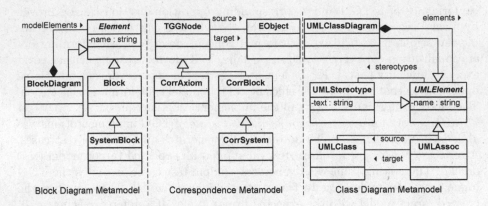

Fig. 1. Example Metamodels

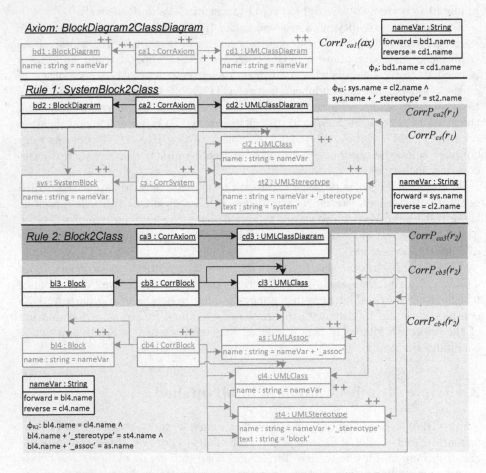

Fig. 2. Example TGG relating Block Diagrams to Class Diagrams

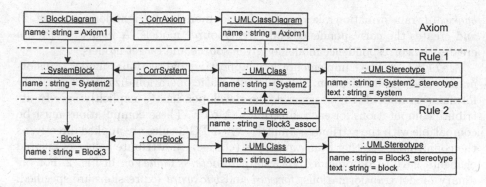

Fig. 3. A Block Diagram and Class Diagram connected by a correspondence model

Class Diagrams and a correspondence metamodel. Fig. 2 shows a TGG specifying a transformation between these languages.

A TGG consists of an *axiom* and several *rules*. Fig. 2 uses a shortened notation, which combines the Left-Hand-Side (LHS) and the Right-Hand-Side (RHS) of a rule. Elements occurring on both sides are black, elements occurring only on the RHS, i.e. which are created by the rule, are green and marked with $++$[1]. TGG rules never delete elements, therefore, the LHS is always a subset of the RHS. In addition, *attribute formulae* (ϕ_i) are specified to ensure consistency of attribute values.

The axiom in Fig. 2 transforms a *BlockDiagram* element to a *UMLClassDiagram* and a *CorrAxiom* node. Rule 1 transforms a *SystemBlock* to a *UMLClass* and a *UMLStereotype* with the *text* "system". Rule 2 transforms a *Block* to a *UMLAssoc*, *UMLClass* and a *UMLStereotype* with the *text* "block". Attribute formulae ensure equality of element names. Fig. 3 depicts instances of the metamodels resulting from the following *rule sequence*: Axiom, rule 1, rule 2.

A TGG rule can be applied on a host graph if there is an *injective morphism* from the rule's LHS to the host graph. In practice, type inheritance of the node types must also be respected, i.e. the matched nodes in the host graph must have the same type or a subtype of the node types in the rule. A graph morphism respecting type inheritance is formally defined in [7]. In addition, the rule's attribute formulae must hold. A TGG *rule sequence* is a sequence of the axiom and an arbitrary number of TGG rules. Each rule may appear multiple times in a sequence. A *rule sequence* is *applicable* on a host graph if one rule after the other is applicable starting with the host graph. This implies that all rules in the sequence must only use elements in their LHSs that are available in the initial host graph or are produced by previous rules. If the host graph is empty (as is the case when using the TGG to generate models, cf. Sec. 3), an applicable rule sequence must start with the axiom.

TGGs are relational model transformation specifications that cannot be executed directly to transform a given source model to a target model. Instead, operational rules have to be derived for each transformation direction: A *forward/*

---

[1] For better readability, only nodes in Fig. 2 are marked with $++$.

backward transformation takes a source/target model (left/right domain in Fig. 2) and creates the correspondence and target/source models. A *model integration* creates the correspondence model for given source and target models.

$MoTE^2$ is a TGG implementation supporting bidirectional model transformation and synchronization. Since the automatic operationalization of attribute formulae is difficult[13] in general, the developer has to explicitly specify attribute computations for each direction in MoTE. These computations must be compatible with the attribute formulae. When TGG rules are applied directly, as the conformance testing framework does (cf. Sec. 3), attribute values of created elements have to be provided via *rule parameters*, *nameVar* in Fig. 2. For ordinary model transformations, *forward* and *backward* expressions are specified, which compute a parameter's value based on the respective input model.

MoTE's algorithm has been formalized [6] and suitable criteria have been defined[3], which a TGG must satisfy so that MoTE can efficiently execute the transformation and so that conformance is not lost. In addition, these criteria play a crucial role in the *random* and *dependency-guided* test case generation approaches (cf. Sec. 3 and Sec. 4). Among these criteria, the following subset is especially important for the remainder of this paper:

1. Every TGG rule and the axiom create exactly one correspondence node.
2. Every TGG rule contains at least one correspondence node in its LHS.
3. Every model element in a TGG rule (a node or a link in the rule's source or target model domain) is connected to exactly one correspondence node via one correspondence link.
4. Every TGG rule and the axiom always create correspondence links along with their incident nodes.

These criteria have several implications: A single correspondence node in a TGG rule, its outgoing correspondence links and the correspondence links' model elements always form a pattern (criteria 3 and 4). The correspondence node can be used as a representative of that pattern. This is referred to as a *correspondence pattern*. It is denoted as $CorrP_c(r)$ when referring to the correspondence pattern of correspondence node c in rule r. Moreover, every rule and the axiom create exactly one correspondence pattern (criterion 1) and every rule contains at least one correspondence pattern in its LHS (criterion 2). Rule 2 (cf. Fig. 2) consists of three correspondence patterns: $CorrP_{ca3}(r_2)$, $CorrP_{cb3}(r_2)$ and $CorrP_{cb4}(r_2)$.

Furthermore, in an *applicable* TGG rule sequence, all correspondence patterns used in the LHS of a rule must be produced by previous rules. In addition to the aforementioned criteria and for the remainder of this paper, all TGGs are assumed to be well-formed according to the following *well-formedness* criterion:

Definition 1 (Well-Formed TGG). *A TGG is* well-formed *if each of its rules satisfies criteria 1 to 4 and an applicable rule sequence exists, which contains that rule.*

---

[2] http://www.mdelab.de/mote/

[3] Note, that MoTE has been developed further since [6] was published. In particular, link bookkeeping has been implemented. Therefore, all criteria demanding to always treat a transformed link along with a transformed node can be relaxed.

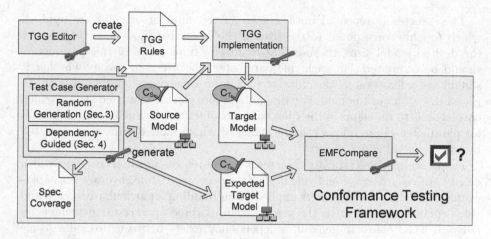

Fig. 4. Components of the automatic conformance testing framework for TGG implementations

A TGG is not well-formed if, for example, one of its rules uses elements that are not produced by any other rule. Such a TGG rule would obviously be unnecessary, comparable to unreachable code in a program. Test cases for such a TGG could never achieve complete *specification coverage*.

3   Automatic Conformance Testing with Random Model Generation

As explained in Sec. 1, a framework for *automatic conformance testing* of TGG implementations was already presented [10]. It is briefly explained in this section.

The testing framework is depicted in Fig. 4. The *Test Case Generator* generates pairs of a source and an expected target model, based on the TGG. This pair forms a test case. It can either use the existing *random* generation approach or the new *dependency-guided* generation presented in Sec. 4. The *TGG Implementation* under test transforms the source model to a second target model, which *EMFCompare* compares to the expected target model. This kind of comparison limits the framework to deterministic TGGs, i.e. there is only one target model per source model.

The existing *random* approach generates random applicable TGG rule sequences and applies them on the empty graph as follows: First, the TGG's axiom is applied to create the root nodes of the three models. The first correspondence node is put into a set. After that, a TGG rule is selected randomly. A match must be provided for each of the rule's LHS correspondence nodes (cf. criterion 2), and, therefore, for all required correspondence patterns. The nodes are selected randomly from the set of previously created correspondence nodes. Then, an attempt is made to apply the rule to extend all three models simultaneously. If this is successful, its created correspondence node is added to the set of previously created correspondence nodes (cf. criterion 1). If the attempt is not successful, another TGG rule is selected randomly and attempted to be applied.

This process is repeated until a user-defined number of rules are applied, which roughly corresponds to the sizes of the generated models. In addition to the desired model sizes, the user has to specify how values of rule parameters should be computed. For each rule parameter, the user can specify whether it should get a fixed value, the value of a counter, or a concatenation of both. In Fig. 3 the values of the *nameVar* rule parameters consist of a fixed string, which corresponds to the name of the rules, and a counter value. The use of rule names for parameter values allows easy retracing of which model element was created by which rule in which order.

Furthermore, the *Test Case Generator* computes *specification coverage*, which consists of *rule coverage* and *rule dependency coverage*. Rule coverage is the percentage of TGG rules that were applied when building a particular test case and rule dependency coverage is the percentage of covered *produce-use* dependencies between TGG rules. In general, a dependency exists between two rules if one rule uses elements in its LHS that are produced by the other rule. Of course, the coverage of a set of test cases should be as high as possible to ensure confidence in the quality of the tested subject. Theoretically, the random approach can achieve complete specification coverage for well-formed TGGs because all existing rule sequences (up to the predefined size) can be generated. However, complex TGG rules may appear only in a small fraction of all possible rule sequences. Therefore, generating such sequences and achieving complete coverage for complex TGGs in practice is unlikely.

Another drawback of the random generation approach is that the test models may become much larger than is actually necessary in order to achieve high coverage. This complicates debugging if a conformance error is found.

4   Dependency-Guided Test Case Generation

To achieve complete *specification coverage*, in particular *rule dependency coverage*, test cases have to be generated to specifically target dependencies present in a TGG. The presented approach analyzes the TGG and makes all dependencies explicit as *rule dependency graphs* (Sec. 4.1). Based on these graphs, *test case descriptions*, which are basically TGG rule sequences, are generated and executed to yield a test case (Sec. 4.2). These test cases achieve complete *specification coverage* and are *minimal* (Sec. 4.3).

4.1   Deriving Rule Dependencies from TGG Rules

The relevant dependencies are *produce-use* dependencies[4] [12]. Therefore, "dependency" will be used synonymously with this term in the remainder of this paper. According to the common definition of *produce-use* dependencies [12], a *produce-use* dependency exists if a rule produces an element that is used by another rule. Due to the criteria imposed on TGG rules (Sec. 2), a *produce-use* dependency between TGG rules can be defined as follows:

---

[4] Other kinds of dependencies, e.g. delete-forbid dependencies, do not occur because TGGs as presented in Sec. 2 do not delete any elements.

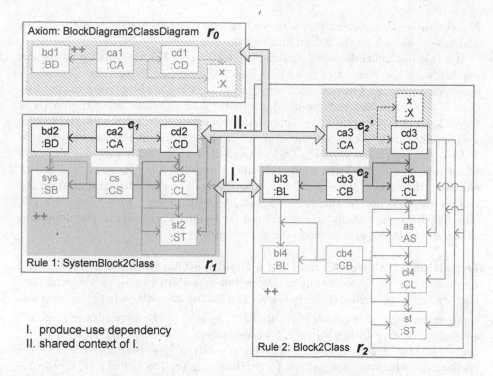

Fig. 5. Dependencies between TGG rules. Node types are omitted. The annotations in italics match the variables used in Definition 2 and Definition 3. Correspondence patterns with same backgrounds can be matched to each other.

Definition 2 (Produce-Use Dependencies between TGG Rules). *A produce-use dependency exists from a required TGG rule r_1 to a dependent rule r_2, and in particular to a correspondence node c_2 in the LHS of r_2, if there is an injective morphism respecting type inheritance between the correspondence pattern of c_2 and the correspondence pattern created by r_1. It is denoted $r_1 \rightarrow r_2^{c_2}$.*

Definition 2 is more specific than the general definition of *produce-use* dependencies, because a dependency only exists if the complete correspondence pattern on the LHS of one TGG rule is created by another rule. The classical definition of *produce-use* dependencies also considers the case in which only particular elements of the patterns are used, which would result in a large number of rule dependencies. However, due to criteria 2 and 3 a correspondence pattern is always created by a single rule so that Definition 2 filters out many, but not all (see Sec. 5), dependencies resulting in non-applicable rule sequences. Note, that a TGG rule may have a dependency to itself, e.g. in rule 2, the pattern $CorrP_{cb3}(r_2)$ matches $CorrP_{cb4}(r_2)$ (Fig. 2).

Every TGG rule is applicable in a certain *context*. The *context* of a rule r_2 is a set of TGG rules (or the axiom), which contains one required TGG rule (or axiom) r_i for each correspondence node c_j in the LHS of r_2 so that $r_i \rightarrow r_2^{c_j}$. A TGG rule may be applicable in multiple contexts. The context of rule 1 (cf.

Fig. 5, ignore dashed elements) is the axiom, the contexts of rule 2 are the axiom and rule 1, as well as the axiom and rule 2.

If a rule has multiple correspondence nodes on its LHS, the rule's context can overlap with the context of one of its required rules, i.e. both rules depend on some common rule. The pattern $CorrP_{ca3}(r_2)$ in rule 2 is also present in rule 1 as $CorrP_{ca2}(r_1)$ (dashed backgrounds). Moreover, the combination of the patterns $CorrP_{ca3}(r_2)$ and $CorrP_{cb3}(r_2)$ (grey background) in rule 2 can be found in rule 1. Therefore, rule 2 can only be applied in the context of the axiom and rule 1 if $CorrP_{ca2}(r_1)$ and $CorrP_{ca3}(r_2)$ are matched to the same instance elements when rule 1 and rule 2 are applied. If rule 2 matches $CorrP_{ca3}(r_2)$ to different elements than $CorrP_{ca2}(r_1)$, it is not applicable. The class diagram matched to *cd3* would then not be the class diagram, to which rule 1 added the class *cl2*. The link between *cd3* and *cl3* would not be found. This leads to the definition of a *shared context of a produce-use dependency*.

Definition 3 (Shared Context of a Produce-Use Dependency). *Given a dependency* $r_1 \rightarrow r_2^{c_2}$ *according to Definition 2, a third rule* r_0 *is a shared context of this dependency if the following conditions are satisfied: (1)* r_2 *contains another correspondence node* c'_2 *in its LHS,* $c_2 \neq c'_2$; *(2) a dependency* $r_0 \rightarrow r_2^{c'_2}$ *exists; (3) a dependency* $r_0 \rightarrow r_1^{c_1}$ *exists, where* c_1 *belongs to the LHS of* r_1; *and (4) there is an injective morphism respecting type inheritance[5] from the restricted correspondence pattern* $CorrPRes_{c'_2 \leftrightarrow c_2}(r_2)$ *to* $CorrP_{c_1}(r_1)$. *The restricted correspondence pattern* $CorrPRes_{c'_2 \leftrightarrow c_2}(r_2)$ *is* $CorrP_{c'_2}(r_2)$ *except those nodes that are neither source nor target of a link in* $CorrP_{c_2}(r_2)$ *and those links whose source and target are not in* $CorrP_{c_2}(r_2)$.

The restricted pattern is necessary to handle cases like the following: Assume the axiom creates an additional element x (drawn with a dashed line in Fig. 5) in the class diagram, which also appears in $CorrP_{ca3}(r2)$ but not in $CorrP_{ca2}(r1)$. Then, an injective morphism from $CorrP_{ca3}(r2)$ to $CorrP_{ca2}(r1)$ would not exist, although the dependencies would still be the same. Therefore, all elements in $CorrP_{ca3}(r2)$ not directly connected to an element in $CorrP_{cb3}(r2)$ have to be ignored in order to detect a shared context.

The dependencies and shared contexts of a TGG rule are made explicit in *Rule Dependency Graphs* (RDG). For each TGG rule, one RDG is generated. It contains all correspondence nodes on the LHS of that rule, denoted as rounded rectangles in Fig. 6. All dependencies to these correspondence nodes are depicted using solid arrows from circles representing rules that produce matches for these correspondence nodes. Shared contexts are depicted using a dashed arrow from the correspondence node in the required rule (c_1 in Definition 3, denoted by a

---

[5] As a consequence of the fact that both r_1 and r_2 have a dependency to r_0, elements created by r_0 must match $CorrP_{c_1}(r_1)$ and $CorrP_{c_2}(r_2)$ at the same time. Therefore, the morphism between $CorrP_{c_1}(r_1)$ and $CorrPRes_{c'_2 \leftrightarrow c_2}(r_2)$ matches nodes if they have the same type, one type is a subtype of the other, or both types have a common subtype.

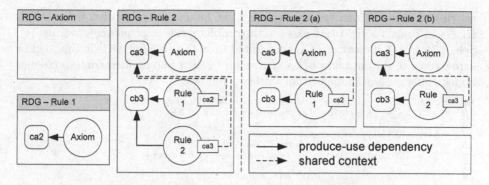

Fig. 6. Rule dependency graphs generated from the example TGG (Fig. 2)

rectangle) to the correspondence node in the current rule (c_2'). The RDGs of the example TGG are shown in the left half of Fig. 6.

Before generating *test case descriptions* from RDGs in the next step, the RDGs are simplified, so that only one dependency, i.e. one outgoing edge, is stored for each correspondence node. For example, *RDG - Rule 2* contains two dependencies for *cb3*. These are split to create *RDG - Rule 2 (a)* and *(b)*. If there are multiple correspondence nodes with more than one dependency, all combinations have to be built and the number of *simple* RDGs increases accordingly.

4.2 Deriving Test Cases from Rule Dependencies

A *Test Case Description* (TCD) is a sequence of TGG rules that also specifies the values of rule parameters and the bindings of LHS correspondence nodes to

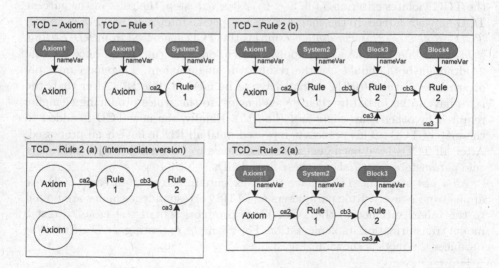

Fig. 7. Test case descriptions generated from the rule dependency graphs (Fig. 6)

previously created correspondence nodes. TCDs can be generated from *simple* RDGs in order to yield test cases with complete *rule dependency* coverage (cf. Sec. 4.3). Fig. 7 shows the TCDs generated from the *simple* RDGs in Fig. 6. The arrows denote the data flow of rule parameter values and created correspondence nodes. This generation algorithm works as follows:

```
1    Set RDGs = {Set of simplified rule dependency graphs}
2    Map TCDs = {} //maps TGG rules to their TCDs
3
4    while (RDGs is not empty) {
5      rdg := remove an RDG from RDGs, where
6        a TCD exists already for all required rules
7
8      tcd := create new TCD, add rule of rdg
9
10     for each (TGG rule r required by rdg) {
11       clone shortest TCD of r and insert into tcd
12     }
13     merge occurrences of rules according to RDG
14
15     sort rules by dependencies
16
17     add to TCDs
18   }
19
20   add values of primitive parameters to all TCDs
```

First, all simple RDGs are put into a set (line 1). Also, a map is created, which maps all TGG rules to their TCDs (line 2). Then, the TCDs are created in a loop. An RDG is selected, so that a TCD exists for all its required TGG rules (line 5).[6] A new TCD is created, which contains only the rule of the RDG. Then, rules have to be added to the TCD, which create the correspondence patterns required by the rule of the current RDG (lines 10-12). This is done by picking the shortest TCD from the map of already created TCDs and copying and inserting it into the current TCD. If no TCD has been created yet for a required rule, the TGG violates criterion 5 (cf. Sec. 2). After this step, the rules in the current TCD may not adhere to the shared contexts specified in the RDGs. For example, *TCD - Rule 2 (a) (intermediate version)* is the TCD generated from *RDG - Rule 2 (a)* after line 12. The axiom appears twice, once for rule 1 and once for rule 2, although both should use the result of a single axiom. Therefore, multiple occurrences of rules (or the axiom) have to be merged (line 13). After that, the rules have to be sorted by their dependencies, so that rules producing elements required by other rules come first (line 15). Finally, the new TCD is added to the map of TCDs. This process is repeated until all RDGs have been processed. After all TCDs have been generated, they have to be extended with values for rule parameters. Fig. 7 shows these final TCDs.

As a last step, the TCDs have to be executed. The rules in each TCD are applied successively. Rule parameters and LHS correspondence nodes are bound to the values specified in the TCDs. This produces sets of test cases to test a model transformation implementation. For example, executing *TCD - Rule 2(a)* produces the models shown in Fig. 3.

---

[6] In the first loop iteration, this is only the case for the axiom's RDG because it does not require any rules.

4.3   Completeness and Minimality of Test Cases

The test suite consisting of test cases specified by the TCDs generated from a TGG as described in Sec. 4.1 and Sec. 4.2 is complete w.r.t. rule dependency coverage. A test case *covers* a particular dependency $r_1 \rightarrow r_2^{c_2}$ if the rule sequence that built the test case contains at least r_1 and r_2, and the created elements of r_1 were bound to $CorrP_{c_2}(r_2)$ when r_2 was applied. Complete dependency coverage of generated test cases is ensured because the dependency analysis first finds all *produce-use* dependencies without considering shared contexts. If TCDs were then generated, all rule sequences with all possible rule dependencies would be generated. *TCD - Rule 2 (a) (intermediate version)* (cf. Fig. 7) would already be a final TCD. Then, all rules that occur multiple times would have to be combined in all possible ways to generate additional TCDs, *TCD - Rule 2 (a)* in the example. For more complex TGGs, a combinatorial explosion of the set of generated TCDs could be observed, e.g. if *TCD - Rule 2 (a) (intermediate version)* contains the axiom three times, this would result in four additional combinations. However, many combinations would not be applicable. By considering shared contexts, most non-applicable rule combinations are filtered out. If it is already known that a rule is only applicable in a certain context, all other contexts can be discarded.

A direct consequence of complete *rule dependency* coverage is complete *rule* coverage. If a test suite applies TGG rules so that all dependencies between rules are covered, then all rules of the TGG have to be applied, too, because every TGG rule depends on at least one other rule or the axiom (criterion 2).

Furthermore, each test case yielded from a generated TCD is *minimal* w.r.t. the rules required to test a particular dependency. *Minimal* means that if any rule except the last rule is removed from the TCD, the TCD would not be applicable anymore. This is ensured by the way in which TCDs are generated. Each TCD is generated for a rule and a particular context. Only those previously generated TCDs are added to this TCD, which contribute to the rule's context.

5   Evaluation

The presented algorithms for dependency analysis and test case generation have been implemented in QVT Operational and Java. They are available from the MDELab Update Site[7].

The new dependency-guided test case generation approach was verified by generating test cases for the same TGGs as in [10] and analyzing their specification coverage. The TGGs are: SDL2UML, which is slightly more complex than the example TGG (cf. Fig. 2); Automata2PLC, which is a transformation from automata models to a language for programmable logic controllers; and SystemDesk2AUTOSAR, which is a transformation from a tool-specific metamodel to AUTOSAR, a modeling standard from the automotive domain. Using the random test case generation approach (cf. Sec. 3), complete rule and rule

---

[7] http://www.mdelab.de/update-site

dependency coverage were achieved only for the SDL2UML and Automata2PLC TGGs. For SystemDesk2AUTOSAR, only 71% rule coverage and 19% rule dependency coverage were achieved using test models with more than 1000 model elements. With the new dependency-guided approach, complete rule and rule dependency coverage was achieved for all TGGs. Some of these test cases also uncovered previously unknown errors in the TGG.

Moreover, a weakness of the dependency analysis became visible. In the SystemDesk2AUTOSAR TGG, elements in the LHS of a rule have types that were too general. Several other rules produce elements that fit the correspondence pattern, which contains this general type. The dependency analysis detected these dependencies. However, due to the overall structure of the LHS of that rule, and in particular the connections between correspondence patterns, the rule was only applicable for particular subtypes. Not all dependencies detected by the dependency analysis yield applicable rule sequences. Still, one can argue that this is also an indication of a modeling error. Therefore, the rules were changed so that more concrete types are used and the problem disappeared. Another cause for non-executable test cases are OCL conditions, which are used to express structural application conditions or attribute constraints in a TGG rule. They may restrict applicability of a TGG rule but are not considered by the dependency analysis, yet. For these reasons, all non-applicable TCDs are also output by the testing framework. This assists the user in finding the reason why they are not executable.

Another advantage of the dependency-guided approach is that the generated test cases are minimal (cf Sec. 4.3). The largest test case for the SystemDesk2AUTOSAR TGG consists of only nine rule applications. Moreover, the rules are tested separately, i.e. there is a separate test case for each rule and each context. This helps in debugging the TGG implementation if errors are found. However, although the test cases themselves are usually small, the total number of test cases can be very large for complex TGGs. For example, 99 test cases were generated for the SystemDesk2AUTOSAR TGG. Yet, many test cases are already contained in others. In the example (cf. Fig. 7), *TCD - Rule 2(b)* contains all other TCDs. Therefore, it is possible to minimize the number of test cases by eliminating those test cases that are subsumed by others. This is done by a pairwise comparison of the generated test cases. The number of test cases for the SystemDesk2AUTOSAR TGG could be reduced from 99 to 68.

6   Related Work

A number of *conformance testing* approaches exists, which rely on graph transformation as a specification technique [2,8]. Instead of focusing on model transformation specifications and implementations, they are rather concerned with conformance testing of *behavioral specifications* w.r.t. (actual) behavior in refined models or (generated) code. There are some testing approaches proposed for *model transformation implementations*. Most *black-box* methods are concerned with generating qualified test input models (e.g. [15,4]) taking the input metamodel (and corresponding constraints) into consideration. For example, metamodel coverage is considered using data-partitioning techniques in [4]. It is required, for example, that models must contain representatives of association ends, which differ in their cardinalities. PaMoMo [1] is a high-level language for the specification of inter-model relationships, which can be used to check validity of models, derive model transformations, e.g. TGG rules, or derive transformation contracts for automated testing of transformation implementations. In contrast, *white-box* criteria are proposed in [11] to qualify test input models. The TGG conformance testing framework[10] generates conformance test cases using the model transformation specification as an "executable contract" generating not only test input models, but also expected results obtaining a complete oracle. In [3] the specification is used as partial oracle and no expected results are generated. Moreover, it proposes a new uniform framework, whereas the conformance testing framework [10] relies on TGGs as an existing model transformation specification technique for which several tools are already available.

Applicability criteria of graph transformation rule sequences are presented in [12]. If certain criteria are satisfied by the rules of a rule sequence, it can be decided statically whether the sequence is applicable or not. In general, though, the TGG rule sequences in the test case descriptions do not satisfy these criteria and, thus, their applicability cannot be checked statically using these results alone. Maybe specialized definitions can be formulated, which take the specific criteria of TGG rules (cf. Sec. 2) into account, but this is part of future work.

7 Conclusion

Model transformations play an important role in MDE. Triple graph grammars are an important representative of relational model transformations. The previously presented automatic conformance testing framework [10] can test conformance of a TGG implementation with its specification by automatically generating and executing test cases. Since this framework relies on a random generation approach, it cannot, in practice, achieve complete *specification coverage* for complex TGGs. The *dependency-guided* generation approach presented in this paper analyzes dependencies implicitly present in a TGG and generates test cases targeting these dependencies so that complete *specification coverage* is achievable in practice for well-formed TGGs. In addition, the generated test cases are minimal, which helps in debugging. The improved framework can now automatically generate high-quality test cases for conformance testing of TGG implementations.

In future work, the dependency analysis may be extended to analyze dependencies more thoroughly to cope with structural application conditions in TGG rules or even OCL constraints on the source and target metamodels.

References

1. de Lara, J., Guerra, E.: Inter-modelling with graphical constraints: Foundations and applications. EC-EASST 47 (2012)
2. Engels, G., Güldali, B., Lohmann, M.: Towards model-driven unit testing. In: Kühne, T. (ed.) MoDELS 2006. LNCS, vol. 4364, pp. 182–192. Springer, Heidelberg (2007)
3. Fiorentini, C., Momigliano, A., Ornaghi, M., Poernomo, I.: A constructive approach to testing model transformations. In: Tratt, L., Gogolla, M. (eds.) ICMT 2010. LNCS, vol. 6142, pp. 77–92. Springer, Heidelberg (2010)
4. Fleurey, F., Steel, J., Baudry, B.: Validation in model-driven engineering: Testing model transformations. In: Proc. of MoDeVa 2004, pp. 29–40. IEEE Computer Society Press (2004)
5. Giese, H., Hildebrandt, S., Lambers, L.: Toward bridging the gap between formal semantics and implementation of triple graph grammars. Technical Report 37, Hasso Plattner Institute at the University of Potsdam (2010)
6. Giese, H., Hildebrandt, S., Lambers, L.: Bridging the gap between formal semantics and implementation of triple graph grammars. Software and Systems Modeling, 1–27 (2012)
7. Golas, U., Lambers, L., Ehrig, H., Orejas, F.: Attributed graph transformation with inheritance: Efficient conflict detection and local confluence analysis using abstract critical pairs. Theor. Comput. Sci. 424, 46–68 (2012)
8. Heckel, R., Mariani, L.: Automatic conformance testing of web services. In: Cerioli, M. (ed.) FASE 2005. LNCS, vol. 3442, pp. 34–48. Springer, Heidelberg (2005)
9. Hermann, F., Ehrig, H., Golas, U., Orejas, F.: Efficient analysis and execution of correct and complete model transformations based on triple graph grammars. In: Proc. of MDI 2012, pp. 22–31. ACM (2012)
10. Hildebrandt, S., Lambers, L., Giese, H., Petrick, D., Richter, I.: Automatic Conformance Testing of Optimized Triple Graph Grammar Implementations. In: Schürr, A., Varró, D., Varró, G. (eds.) AGTIVE 2011. LNCS, vol. 7233, pp. 238–253. Springer, Heidelberg (2012)
11. Küster, J.M., Abd-El-Razik, M.: Validation of model transformations – first experiences using a white box approach. In: Kühne, T. (ed.) MoDELS 2006. LNCS, vol. 4364, pp. 193–204. Springer, Heidelberg (2007)
12. Lambers, L., Ehrig, H., Taentzer, G.: Sufficient Criteria for Applicability and Non-Applicability of Rule Sequences. In: de Lara, J., Ermel, C., Heckel, R. (eds.) Proc. GT-VMT 2008, vol. 10, EC-EASST, Budapest (2008)
13. Lambers, L., Hildebrandt, S., Giese, H., Orejas, F.: Attribute Handling for Bidirectional Model Transformations: The Triple Graph Grammar Case. In: Proceedings of BX 2012, vol. 49, pp. 1–16. EC-EASST (2012)
14. Schürr, A., Klar, F.: 15 years of triple graph grammars: research challenges, new contributions, open problems. In: Ehrig, H., Heckel, R., Rozenberg, G., Taentzer, G. (eds.) ICGT 2008. LNCS, vol. 5214, pp. 411–425. Springer, Heidelberg (2008)
15. Sen, S., Baudry, B., Mottu, J.-M.: Automatic model generation strategies for model transformation testing. In: Paige, R.F. (ed.) ICMT 2009. LNCS, vol. 5563, pp. 148–164. Springer, Heidelberg (2009)

Partial Test Oracle
in Model Transformation Testing

Olivier Finot, Jean-Marie Mottu, Gerson Sunyé, and Christian Attiogbé

LUNAM Université,
LINA CNRS UMR 6241 - University of Nantes
2, rue de la Houssinière, F-44322 Nantes Cedex, France
firstname.lastname@univ-nantes.fr

Abstract. Writing test oracles for model transformations is a difficult task. First, oracles must deal with models which are complex data. Second, the tester cannot always predict the expected value of all the properties of the output model produced by a transformation. In this paper, we propose an approach to create efficient oracles for validating part of the produced output model.

In this approach we presume that output models can be divided into two parts, a predictable part and a non-predictable one. After identifying the latter, we use it to create a filter. Before providing a (partial) verdict, the oracle compares actual output model with the expected output model, returning a difference model, and uses the filter to discard the differences related to the unpredictable part. The approach infers the unpredictable part from the model transformation specification, or from older output models, in the case of regression testing.

The approach is supported by a tool to build such partial oracles. We run several experiments writing partial oracles to validate output models returned by two model transformations. We validate our proposal comparing the effectiveness and complexity of partial oracles with oracles based on full model comparisons and contracts.

Keywords: Test, Partial Oracle, Model Comparison.

1 Introduction

Model transformations are among the key elements of Model Driven Engineering. Since a transformation is often implemented to be reused several times, any implementation error impacts on all the produced models. Therefore, it is important to ensure that the implementation is correct w.r.t. its specification.

Software testing is a well-known technique for ensuring the correctness of an implementation. In the precise case of model transformations, a test consists of a transformation under test (TUT), a test input model and a test oracle. The role of the oracle is to ensure that the output model, produced by the TUT, is correct w.r.t. the transformation specification. Two methods are mainly used to implement the test oracle: (i) comparing the output with an *Expected Model* or (ii) using constraints to verify *Expected Properties* on the output model.

K. Duddy and G. Kappel (Eds.): ICMT 2013, LNCS 7909, pp. 189–204, 2013.

The tester is often able to predict the expected value for part of the output model only. For instance when part of the specification is very complex. In this case, the tester can only predict the part corresponding to what she knows about the specification. In other cases, the specification may allow several different, or *polymorphic*, outputs for the same input model. Therefore, the tester can predict the expected value of the output model's part that does not change from one variant to another. Finally if the TUT performs a model refactoring, then the tester can predict the part that should not be modified by the transformation. We are interested in using this predictable part with a partial test oracle to partially validate the correctness of output models.

Several approaches exist to write oracles for model transformation testing [1]. Full model comparison requires the expected model to be comprehensive. Contracts express constraints between any input and output models but considering few properties each. Assertions or patterns are suited to individually validate properties of one output model. However, we need to entirely validate the predictable part of the output model, not just a compilation of properties.

The contribution of this paper is an approach to implement test oracles issuing partial verdicts when part of the output model is predictable. The approach relies on filtered model comparison with partial expected models.

The partial expected model is compared with the output model generated by the TUT. The observed differences are filtered in order to reject those concerning the unpredictable part of the output model. To create the filter we need to precisely identify the unpredictable part. Elements are considered as belonging to the unpredictable part based on the meta-elements they are instance of. Therefore, we propose to filter the comparison's result with a pattern extracted from the transformation's output meta-model.

Along with this approach, we propose a tool that automatically produces partial verdicts. The tool's inputs are an output model, a partial expected model, and patterns made of meta-model excerpts. We apply our approach to test two model transformations with polymorphic outputs. We create 94 test models; obtaining 94 partial verdicts with our partial oracles, detecting 4 bugs. We define 94 partial expected models with 2,632 elements, 70% less than for the classical model comparison approach.

Section 2 discusses the control of part of an output model by an oracle. Section 3 details our approach to define a partial oracle for part of the output model. Section 4 presents our implementation of the approach. Section 5 presents the experiments we ran on two case studies and discuss the results. Section 6 discusses existing contributions on the topic of the verification of model transformations.

2   Test Oracle for Models Transformations

In this section, we discuss the situation where the tester is able to predict part of an output model but she does not have any oracle function suited to use it.

2.1   Test Oracle for Model Transformations

Figure 1 depicts the process of model transformation testing. The input and output data are models that conform to meta-models. The tester selects an input model, then the TUT transforms it, obtaining an *output model*. Finally, she writes test oracles aimed at validating the output model, ensuring that it is correct w.r.t. the TUT's specification.

A test oracle consists of two elements: *oracle function* and *oracle data* [1]. The oracle function analyses the output model and uses the oracle data to produce the verdict. For instance when comparing the actual result with the expected one, the oracle function is the comparison and the oracle data is the expected result. In previous work [1], we have defined several oracle functions to test model transformation. These oracle functions use *comparison* with an *expected model* or *constraints* expressed either between the input and output models or on the output one only.

2.2   Partial Verdict for Model Transformation Testing

A test oracle may produce a partial verdict when only part of the specification is considered or part of the output data is validated. In model transformation testing, one may want to write partial oracles because the tester can only or easily predict part of the expected output model in many situations. We distinguish three such situations:

1. The transformation's specification can be large and output models are complex data. The tester could predict only the part for which she can handle the complexity.
2. The transformation can be endogenous, modifying partially the input model, e.g., model refactoring. Therefore, part of the input model remains unchanged and could be used as oracle data to check that the transformation is side-effect free.
3. The transformation can return polymorphic outputs: instead of a unique output solution, several variants of the expected model exist. Most of the time, those variants are semantically equivalent, but syntactically different. This variability usually comes from the model transformation's specification. The tester cannot predict which variant should be produced by the transformation's implementation and she should consider them all.

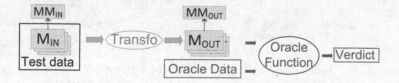

Fig. 1. Model Transformation Testing

The flattening of a state machine is an example of such a transformation. Its input is a hierarchical state machine, the output is another state machine expressing the same behavior without any composite state. The input model presented in Figure 2 can be transformed into the output model presented in Figure 3(a). With such state machines, the number of final states is not limited to only one. Thus, the model presented in Figure 3(b) is also a correct output for the transformation of the input presented in Figure 2.

In such situations, the tester is able to predict the expected value for part of the output model with limited effort, while the remaining part is unpredictable or too difficult to be predicted. We envisage being able to write a partial oracle, using predictable part of the expected model as oracle data.

2.3   Existing Oracle Functions and Partial Verdict

Considering *partial expected model* as oracle data requires a suitable oracle function. Several oracle functions have been proposed for model transformation testing [1], but are they suitable for partial verdict?

A first set of oracle functions considers *model comparison*. Testing frameworks implement such approach: (i) Lin et al. developed a testing engine [2] based on DSMDiff, a model comparison engine, (ii) EUnit [3] compares models with EMFCompare (compliant with the principles exposed by Cicchetti et al. [4]). They compare the output model with an expected model. The latter is obtained manually by the tester, or from a reference transformation (e.g., previous version or regression testing), or a reverse transformation returns an input model from the output model to be compared with the test model (this last approach is limited to injective transformations which are rare and require the existence of such a transformation, which cannot be developed only for testing, especially when the transformation returns polymorphic outputs).

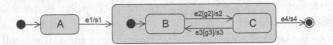

Fig. 2. Example M^{in}, of Hierarchical State Machine

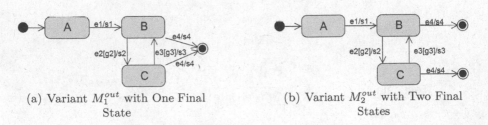

(a) Variant M_1^{out} with One Final State

(b) Variant M_2^{out} with Two Final States

Fig. 3. Possible Results for the Flattening of M^{in}

Hence, using such comparison approaches is not suited to get partial verdict from part of an expected model. The comparison would identify differences concerning the unpredictable part of the output model: (1) when this part is too complex to be predicted by the tester, (2) when it concerns part transformed by a refactoring, (3) when it is a polymorphic model with many variants.

Those differences should be manually analyzed to get the verdict of the test. We face this issue considering the three situations where we want to use partial expected models as oracle data. Such complete model comparison requires comprehensive expected models. Moreover, in case of polymorphic output models, it requires all the variants to be compared with the output model because only one of them could be equal to it. Therefore this oracle function is not effective to write partial oracle.

A second set of oracle functions considers *properties to be checked* on the output model. Contracts are constraints between input and output models. Cariou et al. [5], verify model transformations using contracts. Their contracts are composed of constraints (i) on the output model, (ii) on the evolutions of model elements from the input model to the output model. Defining contracts between input and output model is at least as complex as writing the transformation itself; thus they are as error prone as the transformation. Contracts are not suited to provide the partial verdict we envisage. They are only appropriate to control a few requirements of the specification: no output with composite states for instance. Vallecillo et al. [6] reach the same conclusion and present Tracts, partial contracts for this purpose.

A third set of oracle functions considers *assertions or patterns* (e.g., OCL constraints on the output model of one test case). It would allow controlling dedicated properties of one model. However a model is not just a big set containing many properties, the organization of these properties, i.e., their structure, is also important. Our goal is to globally control the predictable part and not a compilation of properties, thus assertions are not suited to our needs.

To sum up, existing oracle functions are not suited to our needs: controlling part of the output model using a partial expected model as oracle data.

3   Filtered Model Comparison for a Partial Verdict

We propose a new approach to obtain a partial verdict for the test of model transformations. We define a partial oracle function considering part of the output model, the one the tester can predict.

The obtained verdict is only partial but it is still a good piece of information for the tester. Using this oracle function she is able to detect bugs in the transformation under test. Furthermore, this partial verdict requires less effort to be obtained and consumes less resources than a complete one.

3.1   Partial Oracle Data to Focus on Part of the Output Model

The oracle data, which is provided by the tester, consists of two elements: a partial expected model and a set of patterns defining which part of the model is

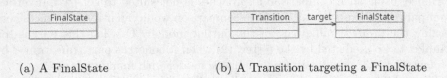

(a) A FinalState   (b) A Transition targeting a FinalState

Fig. 4. Patterns defining the Unpredictable Part for our Flattening Transformation

not considered by the oracle. The *partial expected model* conforms to a relaxed version of the meta-model as in [7]. It can be a comprehensive output model if the tester can provide it. In particular, when the output model is polymorphic, she may provide one comprehensive variant of the model; this is especially interesting when such a variant is available (e.g. from a reference transformation).

The patterns define which elements of the output model are not considered in the models to produce the partial verdict. Elements belong to the unpredictable part based on the meta-elements (EClass, EAttribute, EReference) they are instance of. Those meta-elements are extracted from the output meta-model, thus our patterns are *meta-model fragments*.

In the example presented in Figure 3, several variants exist, expressing the same semantics; the output model is polymorphic. In Figure 3(a), both transitions have the same target, while in Figure 3(b) each one has a different target. The final states as well as the transitions targeting them, change from one variant to another, they are not predictable. We express this unpredictable part in a pattern presented in Figure 4. It combines two patterns to filter the instances of FinalState and those of Transition targeting a FinalState[1].

3.2   Comparison and Filtering to Control the Predictable Part

We define a partial oracle function by entirely comparing the output model with one partial expected model, then filtering the result of this comparison. Model comparison is already implemented by several tools (e.g. EMFCompare), our proposal focuses on filtering the comparison's result.

In our proposal, any observed difference concerning the unpredictable part is taken off the comparison's result. The verdict is "pass" if the filtered comparison's result is empty, because in this case, there is no difference between produced and expected models' predictable part. Otherwise, the test fails and reveals a fault in the model transformation.

This result is interesting because the tester detects faults with only a partial expected model when the classical model comparison approach (see Section 2.3) needs at least a comprehensive one before detecting any fault. The filtering patterns, which are written once, are used for every test of a given transformation. Additionally, they are built in a familiar way for a MDE tester, extracted from meta-models. Thus, unlike using specific matching language like ECL (Epsilon

---

[1] we also consider the guards, actions and events in the experimentation (Section 5).

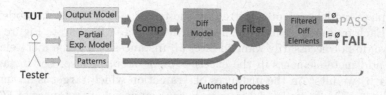

Fig. 5. A synoptic of our Approach to Produce a Partial Verdict

Comparison Language) [8], or specializing the model comparison engine for each transformation, she does not have to learn additional language.

Figure 5 summarizes our approach. The tester identifies the unpredictable part, and writes patterns defining it. She provides partial expected models which are compared with TUT's output models. The result of this comparison is then filtered using the patterns. The verdict is produced after observation of this filtered comparison's result.

Pattern could be empty to only check if the partial expected model is included in the output model. However, such an oracle would not detect when elements are wrongly generated in the predictable part of the model. For instance, a wrong state "BC" erroneously linked to state "A" in Figure 3(a) would not be detected. Using pattern to express unpredictable part, we completely validate the predictable part.

4   Implementation

In this section, we describe the implementation of the proposed approach and its application to the running example of the paper.

4.1   The Technical Framework

Technically, our oracle function allows testing transformations generating XMI[2] models, as in the Eclipse Modeling Framework[3]. We choose EMF framework because it is widely used and it has many tools.

We use EMFCompare[4] to compare our models. For each comparison, EMFCompare produces two result models: the *Match model* for the elements matched between the two models, and the *Diff model* for the differences. In the Diff model, an observed difference is defined as an instance of `DiffElement`. It can concern an `EClass`, an `EAttribute` or an `EReference`.

For the filter activity (Figure 5), we perform pattern matching on the Diff model returned by EMFCompare. We look for any difference concerning elements of the unpredictable part and reject them. The test passes if the rest of the Diff model concerning the predictable part is empty.

---

[2] http://www.omg.org/spec/XMI/
[3] http://www.eclipse.org/emf/
[4] http://www.eclipse.org/emf/compare/

The meta-model excerpts, written by the tester, are Ecore meta-model fragments. Each fragment defines one meta-element (e.g. a final state Figure 4(a)). Since, we do not necessarily want to filter all instances of a given meta-element, we can add meta-elements in the excerpts to be more precise. For instance in Figure 4(b) we filter on the instances of Transition which target is an instance of FinalState. Our meta-model fragments are composed of instances of EClass, EAttribute or EReference. There is at most one attribute in each fragment, the one we want to filter. Therefore, we are able to filter any element that can be concerned by a difference observed by EMFCompare.

The pattern matching engine used is EMF Incquery[5]. With Incquery, patterns are written in a textual form. Thus, we transform our meta-model fragments into Incquery patterns. We wrote a Java transformation, available on a public repository [9], for this purpose. The transformation is integrated into the filter (Figure 5). It takes as input the meta-model fragments defining the unpredictable part of the output model, along with the name of the element the tester wants to be filtered, as well as the root meta-class of the fragment. The root meta-class is the one from which the transformation starts browsing the fragment. For instance, in the fragment from Figure 4(b), Transition is the element the tester wants to filter as well as the fragment's root meta-class. It produces Incquery rules that can be automatically applied on the result of the comparison to return the differences concerning the predictable part only.

4.2   Automatic Treatment of the Patterns in Three Steps

First Step. Since we look for differences between two models, we need to define how a difference is represented in the Diff model. This is the role of the pattern *isDifference*. It basically matches any element for which a difference was observed (an element referenced in a instance of DiffElement). This pattern is generic and is generated independently from the TUT.

Second Step. In the second step, we generate the Incquery patterns corresponding to the fragments defined by the tester, one pattern for each of the fragments. For instance, the fragments of Figure 4 are transformed into the Inquery patterns presented in Listing 1.1. For each fragment, we create the header of the pattern with its name (the fragment's name) and its parameter (where the matched elements are collected).

The instances of EClass are transformed into a rule to match in the model those elements. For instance, the EClass FinalState in the pattern of the Figure 4(a) is transformed into the rule FinalState(F) to collect in the model the instances of FinalState into the variable F. When the patterns express more constraint, additional rules are generated in Inquery. For instance, the pattern of the Figure 4(b) is transformed into the pattern finalTransition(T): (i) the EClasses Transition and FinalState are transformed into rules Transition(T)

---

[5] http://viatra.inf.mit.bme.hu/incquery

and FinalState(F) to collect in the model the instances of Transition and Final-State into the variables T and F, (ii) in addition the EReference target linking Transition and FinalState is transformed into the rule Transition.target(T, F) to reject from T the transitions not targeting a final state.

```
// A FinalState F
pattern finalState(F) = {
    FinalState(F);
}

// A transition targeting a final State
pattern finalTransition(T) = {
    Transition(T);
    FinalState(F);
    Transition.target(T, F);
}
```

Listing 1.1. Expression of the Non Considered Part with Incquery

Third Step. In the third and last step, we generate the pattern that provides the result of the filtered comparison. In the first step, we defined an element about which a difference is observed. In the second step, we defined the un-predictable part's elements. In this final step, we are looking for any of the unpredictable part's elements about which a difference is observed. Therefore, we need to combine the previous steps' patterns into a new one. In Listing 1.2 we are looking for any elements for which a difference is observed but which are not instance of FinalState or of Transition targeting a FinalState. This last pattern finding nothing means that there is no difference in the predictable part: the test passes.

```
/* A is a Difference which is not about a FinalSate
   or a Transition targeting one FinalState
   If the result is empty then the test pass for the common part */
pattern verdictPassIfAEmpty(A) = {
    find isDifference(A);
    neg find finalState(A);
    neg find finalTransition(A);
}
```

Listing 1.2. Pattern for the Verdict of the Considered Part

5   Experiments and Discussion

We validate our approach by running several experiments. We build partial test oracles for two model transformations. After describing the case studies, we detail the test protocol set up for these experiments. Afterwards, we discuss the obtained experimental results and potential threats to the validity of our experiments and approach.

5.1   Case Studies

State Machine Flattening transformation. This transformation, which flattens UML state machines to remove composite states, is used as an illustrative example throughout this paper. It was implemented by Holt et al. [10] in Kermeta. We specify that input model is valid only with no orthogonal state, no pseudostate other than initial state, no hyper-edge, and transitions leaving a composite state containing a final state have no trigger.

UML Activity Diagram to CSP transformation. This transformation transforms UML activity diagram into model of CSP[6] program.

Part of the output models is unpredictable since models of CSP programs are polymorphic. Indeed, from the specification proposed by Bisztray et al. [12], we identify two elements, which can introduce variations in the output model:

- A decision node is transformed into an n-ary condition. In this situation, the operands can be permuted and several links can be combined. According to the authors, provided that the guards' conditions are distinct, for the UML norm, several syntactic combinations are semantically equivalent.
- A fork node becomes a combination of concurrency operators which are commutative; changing the order of operands does not modify the program's semantics.

For instance, let us consider a fork node transformed into three parallel processes (F1, F2, F3), they can be organized in twelve variants of the same polymorphic model. Firstly, they can be permuted in six different ways:

F1‖F2‖F3   F1‖F3‖F2   F2‖F1‖F3   F2‖F3‖F1   F3‖F1‖F2   F3‖F2‖F1

Secondly, the concurrency being a binary operator, to compose three processes, one of the two operands is the composition of two processes:

- (Fi ‖ (Fj ‖ Fk))   - ((Fi ‖ Fj) ‖ Fk)

We have implemented this transformation in ATL[7].

Writing partial oracles, the unpredictable part of these CSP models is composed of the binary operators (conditions and concurrencies) and their operands. Therefore, we create 3 patterns which are excerpts of the CSP meta-model. For space reason they are available on [9].

5.2   Testing Protocol

In this experimental section, we want to answer several questions:
Question 1: Can a tester write partial expected models and patterns?

---

[6] CSP = Communicating Sequential Processes [11].
[7] http://www.eclipse.org/atl

Question 2: Do the patterns and part of expected models can be processed by partial oracle function to produce partial verdict?

Question 3: Is the proposal more appropriate than other oracle functions to produce partial verdict considering part of expected model?

Answering the first question, we produce a set of test models for our cases studies, then we write corresponding partial expected models, and patterns.

Answering the second question, we transform the test input models with the two TUT and we check that partial oracle return partial verdicts.

Answering the third question, we compare the size of the partial expected models with comprehensive models that would have been written without our proposal. Moreover, we check that it would be simpler to get the same partial verdicts with our proposal than with contracts.

The test model creation method was introduced by Fleurey et al. [13] and validated by Sen et al. [14][7], it relies on the partition of the input domain. We define partitions of the values of each attribute and reference of the input meta-model. Then, different strategies combine those partitions defining model fragments. Finally, for each model fragment, at least one correct input model is created.

We create 94 test models: 30 for the first transformation, 64 for the second. For the first case study, we create 10 fragments using the IFClassΣ strategy, then create 3 test models for each model fragment. For the second case study, using IFCombΠ strategy we create 8 model fragments. We define all the possible combinations, eliminate invalid ones, and produce the models.

5.3   Results

In this subsection, we present results answering the three previous questions. We already answer partially **Question 1** in Section 4.2 when we introduce the patterns for one case study.

Part of the experiments' results is shown in Table 1. For each partial expected model, we present the number of its elements, the number of elements in the complete expected model, the proportion of the predictable part in the model, as well as the number of existing variants and the partial verdict of the test.

UML State Machine Flattening. The second result answering **Question 1** is the writing of the partial expected models and the patterns for the filter rejecting unpredictable part of the models. This transformation returns polymorphic models, therefore we can create comprehensive expected models but some of them are only one variant among several possibility. Out of the 30 input models created, 10 do not have any composite state to be transformed. Therefore, their corresponding expected models are exactly the ones we expect. In the opposite, each of the 20 other expected models is only one variant: for instance, we can use the one of the Figure 3(b). Those models are available in [9].

Answering **Question 2**, four test cases produce a failure partial verdict, two of them because of a missing transition in the output model. The other two failed for a missing guard on a newly created transition; more precisely, the guard was created but not linked to the transition.

The three following paragraphs answer **Question 3**. While with most of our test models the number of variants for the transformation is quite small (1, 2 or 5), we can see that one of the output models has 93 variants (model 9 in the table). In this case without our approach, using the classical model comparison approach would require 93 expected models (about 3,906 elements), along with 93 model comparisons to obtain a verdict.

One could argue that since the majority of the output model elements belong to the predictable part, the tester should just create one model with the predictable part then copy it as much as needed, and then only add the unpredictable part. However in this case with 93 variants, the tester still would have to create 1,238 model elements (29 + (42 - 29) * 93) and 93 comparisons would still be needed, before getting the least verdict.

Whereas the transformation is 500 lines, we write 510 lines worth of contracts. Three of them concern the unpredictable part of the output model. With these contracts we detect the same errors as with our approach. Even though the contracts are more complex than the transformation, they do not cover the whole output models' predictable part. For instance, the transitions' effects are not controlled with the contracts. On the contrary, our approach permits to entirely control the predictable part, which is present in our partial expected models.

Activity Diagram to CSP. The experiment on this second transformation answer the **three questions** again. Four test cases produce a failure partial verdict, when two or more join nodes are present in the input model only the first is correctly transformed. The maximum number of variants is 96 for 3 models. Without our approach, the tester would have to create the 96 expected models: 4,800 elements or 715 elements (43 + (50 - 43) * 96) by copying the predictable part elements.

Once again, we write contracts which are as complex as the transformation (218 lines of contracts and 210 of transformation) and detect the same errors as our approach , but do not entirely control the output models' predictable part. For instance they do not control the order in which the instances of ProcessAssignment are defined, when our partial expected models do. Two of the contracts we write partially control the unpredictable part.

Discussion We obtain partial verdicts from the use of partial expected models and patterns with our oracle function, thus answering Question 2. To obtain partial verdicts we create only 94 partial expected models (2,632 elements) and 8 patterns (18 elements) and perform 94 model comparisons, instead of 835 models (36,184 elements or 8,677 elements by copying the predictable parts) and 835 model comparisons for the classical model comparison approach. The gain here is of 93% in terms of model elements (70% if copy of the predictable part) and of 89% in terms of model comparisons. Our case studies handle simple models with an average of 35 and 37 elements per model. The gain for the tester would be greater with transformations handling more complex models. It would be decisive if she would manually write those models' variants.

Table 1. Observed Results for our Case Studies

(a) State Machine Flattening

expected model	#considered part elements	#elements in a comprehensive variant	%considered part	#variants	partial verdict
1	32	36	89%	1	pass
4	35	42	83%	2	pass
5	31	35	89%	1	fail
7	32	42	76%	5	pass
8	32	39	82%	2	fail
9	29	42	69%	93	fail
14	12	17	71%	2	fail
17	18	25	72%	5	pass
...					
avg	28	35	79%	6.71	
sum	582	734		157	

(b) UML To CSP

expected model	#considered part elements	#elements in a comprehensive variant	%considered part	#variants	partial verdict
4	32	38	84%	2	pass
7	36	42	86%	4	fail
8	36	42	86%	4	fail
10	35	42	83%	6	pass
13	29	34	85%	12	pass
16	40	48	83%	24	fail
17	40	48	83%	24	fail
18	43	50	86%	96	pass
...					
avg	32.03	37.3	87%	10.6	
sum	2050	2338		678	

We write incomplete contracts that are as complex as our transformations. However, these contracts do not detect any error in the predictable part of the output models that our approach has not already found. Also they do not entirely control the predictable part. Contracts controlling a whole transformation are at least as error-prone as the transformation's implementation. Thus global contracts are not suited for our needs. Answering the third question, we can conclude that our proposal is more appropriate than the other oracle functions to provide a partial verdict considering part of an output model.

One could argue that we do not control the correctness of the whole output model. However, first, our partial oracles find errors in those transformations, one of them not being ours [10]. Second, the predictable part is a significant part of our output models (over 61%). Third and last, in both case studies, elements in the predictable part are transformed. The transformations do not only act on the unpredictable part of a model. In the first transformation, simple states are not modified, but incoming or outgoing transitions of the composite states are (relation between A and B in Figure 3). In our second transformation, we transform from one language to another, the input and output meta-models are different. So this partial verdict is a good piece of information for the tester.

Also to fill the gap of our only partial verdict, we could use contracts. While global contracts are too complex, we could use smaller ones to control the unpredictable part. This way we could benefit from our approach and add simple contracts to obtain a complete verdict.

5.4   Threats to Validity

We have successfully applied our approach to build partial test oracles for two model transformations. A major threat to the validity of our experiments is the question of the representativity of our case studies. While with our case studies we do not cover the whole range of possibilities of model transformations, they still are quite distinct from one another. One, a refactoring transformation, modifies only part of the input model; the other transforms the input model into a completely different one. Also the first one directly transforms UML models, its inputs and outputs conform to the UML model.

Another threat, this time to the global usability of our approach is the problem of the identification of the predictable part. Unfortunately this step is still manual, with the tester having to understand the transformation's specification. Yet she can find clues, for instance elements that indicate possible polymorphism, such as binary operators for polymorphic outputs, like in our second case study. If part of the specification is too complex for her to handle, then she should be able to describe it. When performing regression testing of a refactoring transformation, the part of the meta-model appearing in the specification is the one modified by the transformation, therefore this part is the unpredictable part.

6   Related Work

Model transformation testing has been studied several times.

Model transformations can be seen as graph transformations, Darabos et al. [15] tested such transformations. They identified and classified most common faults in erroneous transformations.

In Section 2.3, we discussed the use of generic contracts for the oracle. Braga et al. [16] [17], specify a transformation using a meta-model. In order to verify a transformation they use contracts expressed as a transformation meta-model along with a set of properties over it. Similarly, Büttner et al. [18] model an ATL transformation for its validation. Cabot et al. [19] also build on this concept of transformation model, to which they add an invariant. Guerra et al. [20] developed transML, a family of modeling languages for the engineering of transformations. They generate both test inputs and oracles, relying on a transML specification of the TUT. This specification can be seen as contracts. As we already mentioned the main drawback of contracts is that they are as complex to write as the transformations and thus as error prone.

Tiso et al. [21] are particularly interested in testing model to text transformations. They use assertions to check properties on the produced output. They argue that the assertions' writing should be white box, because they have to know of some choice made by the developer. Several syntaxes exists for the same semantics, this is a case of polymorphic outputs. As discussed in Section 2.1, the oracle is strictly black box, thus their approach is not suited.

7   Conclusion and Future Work

In this paper, we presented an approach to write a partial oracle to validate a part of output models. This approach produces a partial verdict by comparing the output model with an expected one. Running experiments on two transformations with polymorphic outputs, we measured our approach against two classical oracle functions, global model comparison and contracts. These experiments showed that our approach is more appropriate to produce a verdict when considering part of the output model.

Our experiments are a first step towards the validation of our approach. We plan to study case studies concerned with regression testing. Moreover, we plan to evaluate the fault detecting effectiveness of such test oracles using mutation testing. In the future we want to evaluate how we can assist the tester in the identification of the unpredictable part.

References

1. Mottu, J.-M., Baudry, B., Le Traon, Y.: Model transformation testing: oracle issue. In: MoDeVVa 2008 (2008)
2. Lin, Y., Zhang, J., Gray, J.: A testing framework for model transformations. Model-driven software development, 219–236 (2005)
3. García-Domínguez, A., Kolovos, D.S., Rose, L.M., Paige, R.F., Medina-Bulo, I.: EUnit: A unit testing framework for model management tasks. In: Whittle, J., Clark, T., Kühne, T. (eds.) MODELS 2011. LNCS, vol. 6981, pp. 395–409. Springer, Heidelberg (2011)
4. Cicchetti, A., Di Ruscio, D., Pierantonio, A.: A Metamodel Independent Approach to Difference Representation. JOT (2007)
5. Cariou, E., Belloir, N., Barbier, F., Djemam, N.: Ocl contracts for the verification of model transformations. ECEASST (2009)
6. Vallecillo, A., Gogolla, M., Burgueño, L., Wimmer, M., Hamann, L.: Formal specification and testing of model transformations. In: Bernardo, M., Cortellessa, V., Pierantonio, A. (eds.) SFM 2012. LNCS, vol. 7320, pp. 399–437. Springer, Heidelberg (2012)
7. Sen, S., Mottu, J.-M., Tisi, M., Cabot, J.: Using Models of Partial Knowledge to Test Model Transformations. In: Hu, Z., de Lara, J. (eds.) ICMT 2012. LNCS, vol. 7307, pp. 24–39. Springer, Heidelberg (2012)
8. Kolovos, D.S.: Establishing correspondences between models with the epsilon comparison language. In: Paige, R.F., Hartman, A., Rensink, A. (eds.) ECMDA-FA 2009. LNCS, vol. 5562, pp. 146–157. Springer, Heidelberg (2009)
9. Finot, O., Mottu, J.-M., Sunyé, G., Attiogbe, C.: Experimentation material, https://sites.google.com/site/partialverdictmt/
10. Holt, N., Arisholm, E., Briand, L.: An eclipse plug-in for the flattening of concurrency and hierarchy in uml state machines. Tech. Rep. (2009)
11. C. A. R. Hoare: Communicating sequential processes (1978)
12. Bisztray, D., Ehrig, K., Heckel, R.: Case study: Uml to csp transformation. AGTIVE (2007)
13. Fleurey, F., Baudry, B., Muller, P.-A., Le Traon, Y.: Qualifying input test data for model transformations. SOSYM (2009)
14. Sen, S., Baudry, B., Mottu, J.-M.: Automatic model generation strategies for model transformation testing. In: Paige, R.F. (ed.) ICMT 2009. LNCS, vol. 5563, pp. 148–164. Springer, Heidelberg (2009)
15. Darabos, A., Pataricza, A., Varró, D.: Towards testing the implementation of graph transformations. ENTCS 211 (2008)

16. Braga, C., Menezes, R., Comicio, T., Santos, C., Landim, E.: On the specification, verification and implementation of model transformations with transformation contracts. In: Simao, A., Morgan, C. (eds.) SBMF 2011. LNCS, vol. 7021, pp. 108–123. Springer, Heidelberg (2011)
17. de, C., Braga, O., Menezes, R., Comicio, T., Santos, C., Landim, E.: Transformation contracts in practice. IET Software 6(1), 16–32 (2012)
18. Büttner, F., Cabot, J., Gogolla, M.: On validation of atl transformation rules by transformation models. In: MoDeVVa (2011)
19. Cabot, J., Clarisó, R., Guerra, E., De Lara, J.: Verification and Validation of Declarative Model-to-Model Transformations through Invariants. JSS 83 (2010)
20. Guerra, E.: Specification-Driven Test Generation for Model Transformations. In: Hu, Z., de Lara, J. (eds.) ICMT 2012. LNCS, vol. 7307, pp. 40–55. Springer, Heidelberg (2012)
21. Tiso, A., Reggio, G., Leotta, M.: Early experiences on model transformation testing. In: Huang, R., Ghorbani, A.A., Pasi, G., Yamaguchi, T., Yen, N.Y., Jin, B. (eds.) AMT 2012. LNCS, vol. 7669, Springer, Heidelberg (2012)

Systematic Testing of Graph Transformations: A Practical Approach Based on Graph Patterns

Martin Wieber and Andy Schürr

Technische Universität Darmstadt,
Real-Time Systems Lab,
Merckstraße 25, 64283 Darmstadt, Germany
{martin.wieber,andy.schuerr}@es.tu-darmstadt.de

Abstract. Correctness is an essential property of model transformations. Although testing is a well-accepted method for assuring software quality in general, the properties of declarative transformation languages often prevent a direct application of testing strategies from imperative programming languages. A key challenge of transformation testing concerns limiting the testing effort by a good *stop criterion*. In this work, we tackle this issue for *programmed graph transformations*, and present a practical methodology to derive *sufficient test suites* based on a new *coverage notion* inspired by mutation analysis. We systematically generate *requirement (graph) patterns* from the transformation under test, applying different requirement construction strategies, and analyze the approach in terms of practicability, test suite quality and the ability to guide and support test case construction.

Keywords: Testing, Coverage, Programmed Graph Transformations.

1 Introduction

One goal of software engineering is to develop *high quality* software. Testing is widely accepted as a practical, effective, and efficient approach to ensure and maintain software quality. It can help to find *defects* and to gain confidence in an implementation. Model transformations (MT) are a core building block in MDE [25], and thus must be tested like any other piece of software. Unfortunately, the plethora of transformation languages in conjunction with their properties (e.g. declarative, rule-based) hinder the direct application of well-established testing techniques for programs written in general-purpose programming languages [5,6].

Testing is generally not able to *prove* the correctness of a program, since *exhaustive* testing is not feasible. Methods are needed to derive a *representative test suite*. Consequently, an important issue of MT testing is to restrict testing effort by means of an objective *stop criterion*. This criterion must ensure that a test suite comprises enough tests to stimulate the transformation *sufficiently*, thus increasing chances of fault manifestation.

Existing literature on MT testing lists different *coverage criteria*, mainly for *specification*-based (*black-box*) testing [16,18]. In this case, the abstract specification (use-cases, typical input values etc.) is used to test for correctness in terms

K. Duddy and G. Kappel (Eds.): ICMT 2013, LNCS 7909, pp. 205–220, 2013.

of input-output-behavior. Such coverage criteria are relatively straightforward to comprehend, existing techniques (e.g. *input partitioning* [1]) can be applied, and the choice of implementation language does not matter.

We focus on *structure*-based (*white-box*) testing, because we want to develop a specific technique for *programmed graph transformations* (PGT) which must be able to consider and test *pattern matching* and control flow aspects thoroughly. White-box coverage criteria are defined via properties of the implementation structure (control flow, conditions, etc. [1]). For *graph transformations* (GT), only few such approaches exist, and though very sophisticated, they cannot be applied here (cf. Sec. 2). *Mutation analysis*, on the other hand, is a powerful technique to evaluate the quality or (relative) *adequacy* of a test suite [12]: A system under test is repeatedly modified/*mutated* whereby each resulting *mutant* contains a typical fault. A test suite *kills* a mutant, if it unveils the corresponding bug, and can be considered the better the more it unveils. *Mutation testing* is a promising but expensive approach [1]. To the best of our knowledge, no one has studied it for PGTs yet. Works have been published classifying typical programmer errors for MT [23] or GT [11], but *mutation operators* are inherently language specific. Killing a mutated PGT would be tedious, since non-deterministic pattern matching hinders reliable decisions, at least when using model-diffs as oracle. Our approach (re)uses several mutation strategies for graph patterns. The mutants are used differently than in mutation testing, though.

In this paper, we present a new white-box coverage notion based on mutated graph patterns, called *requirement pattern coverage*. A tool is presented that can automatically derive requirement patterns from a given transformation implementation (written in the transformation language of choice) and instrument the original transformation under test to produce a coverage report. We evaluate the approach w.r.t. properties of relevance for application and report on first experiment results obtained during testing a real-world transformation in part.

The remainder of the paper is structured as follows: Section 2 reviews related work on model/graph transformation testing. We introduce and outline the problem domain in Sect. 3. In Sect. 4, we describe how to derive and use the test requirements, relating the used strategies to typical faults. Section 5 presents first evaluation results. Section 6 concludes the paper.

2   Related Work

Testing model transformations is a challenging task [5,6]. As for general MT testing, prevalent approaches use specification-based coverage based on meta-model coverage and input data partitioning, e.g. [16,7]. The main advantage of black-box testing is general applicability due to language independence; the main disadvantage is that the implementation is not exploited as a proper source of information. Since our use case defines a language class as given, we want to use such information. Some white-box coverage criteria for textual languages exist [10,22]. [21] presents a white-box approach where the authors derive "metamodel templates" (somehow resembling graph patterns) from concrete rules. Instantiating the templates in such a way that the metamodel is covered, yields the tests. Constraints and rule pairs are used to find additional tests. Covering the metamodel is only one possible option, and programmed graph transformations have explicit rule (resp. pattern) interdependence in our case.

Other approaches rely on constraints derived from the transformation to generate test cases [9,18]. Automatically deriving tests is intriguing, and coverage can be used to guide the process and limit test suite size. Nevertheless, we do not consider this for two reasons: (1) generation can be computationally hard and resulting models limited in size, and (2) focus rests on the problem of deciding whether a test suite can be considered complete. A similar goal is pursued in [23], where mutation analysis [12] is applied to evaluate test suite adequacy [13]. We adapt and reuse some of the described (generic) mutation operators in our setup, but we choose not to base our coverage notion on mutation score (cf. [26]).

Graph transformation testing has also been examined. The authors of [11] focus on testing the (code-based) implementation of a graph transformation. They classify typical programmer faults in an effort to derive test data that is sensitive enough to detect resulting flaws. They simulate the latter by mutating patterns. We refer to this work later on (Sect. 4) when treating the classification of faults. In [20], the language generating property of TGGs is used to address the oracle and the test generation problem. Test suite size is limited by production steps. Other groups reported on using graph transformations for model-based testing, e.g. for testing optimizing code generators [4] or web services [19]. Tests are derived by graph unfolding or input partitioning.

Closest to our scenario is [17]. The author reports on the *testing* of *SDM*-transformations (cf. Sect. 3) among other things. Despite using the same transformation language, and thus struggling with related problems, our testing approaches share minor commonalities. [17] uses code coverage which is mapped back to coverage of transformation level concepts, whereas we define coverage on the modeling level.

3 Testing Programmed Graph Transformations

This section provides an overview of programmed graph transformations and the concrete transformation language in use. Additionally, we describe an exemplary transformation serving as a running example in the remainder. We also introduce necessary testing terminology and discuss relevant testing challenges.

3.1 Programmed Graph Transformations

Graph transformations are a well-researched MT paradigm [24,14]. In this context, a *model* (M) is represented by a graph (*instance graph*) which is *typed*, meaning that each node and edge has a resp. type, over a *type graph* or *metamodel* (MM). The core building blocks of a GT specification are *rules* consisting of (graph) *patterns* (GP) and modifying *rewrite operations*. The semantics of both follow from a stringent formal theory [14]. Rules comprise typed nodes and edges to which we refer to as *object variables* and *link variables*, respectively. The modifying operations usually follow from the GP specification: the *left hand side* (LHS) of a rule represents the application condition (situation before the rewriting step); the *right hand side* (RHS) represents the situation after the modification. Model elements which are mapped to object and link variables occurring only on the LHS are deleted; elements mapped to variables which occur only on the RHS are created. The remaining variables, resp. the model elements that are mapped to them, remain unchanged. Regularly, LHS and RHS are combined in one single artifact for brevity of presentation.

Transforming a model by a GT involves the following steps: (1) select a GP, (2) find (at least) one *match* in the model by solving the *subgraph isomorphism problem*, (3) iff a match has been found and all preconditions are met, perform the rewritings, (4) if required, restart from beginning, (5) quit. Selecting the pattern in step (1) can be performed differently depending e.g. on the concrete GT language (options: choose a pattern randomly, in a round robin fashion or based on some dependency relation). In our case, we rely on a control flow algorithm, thus *programmed* GT. Depending on the transformation language and the used constructs, step (2) must find a single match or all existing matches at the same time. Of course, this decision heavily influences step (3), where manipulation is either performed on an isolated match, on several matches one at a time, or on all matches in parallel. The decision in step (4) depends on some arbitrary, potentially external condition.

In the remainder, we use the *Story Driven Modeling* (SDM) language [15] as our prototypical representative for PGT languages. It is an integral part of Fujaba (www.fujaba.de) and its spinoffs: one SDM dialect is part of our eMoflon [2] tool suite. The language consists of a control flow part and a declarative graph transformation part, whereby the concrete syntaxes are based on UML activity diagrams and object diagrams respectively. A detailed tutorial to the language and the toolkit can be obtained from the project homepage www.emoflon.org.

3.2   Exemplary Transformation

We use a slightly simplified excerpt of the `flattening` algorithm [3] for feature models (FM) [8]. The reasons for choosing this example are availability of the implementation and the intuitive semantics of simple feature models. The purpose of the `flattening` algorithm is to optimize the structure of a given feature model, by reducing the height of the rooted tree, without changing the semantics of the FM. Figure 1a depicts the FM metamodel. A `FeatureModel` contains one root `Feature` and an arbitrary number of child `Features` organized in a tree hierarchy (cf. the containment relations). Each `Feature` references zero or more child `Dependency` instances which themselves contain child `Features` (`childF`). The opposite direction is modeled by the reference `parentDep`. The concrete subclasses of `Dependency` model the different semantics of the relation types between child and parent `Features`. `Flattener` is a helper class and comprises the transformation logic in form of operations. Figure 1b depicts a simple FM instance in concrete syntax (as used in [8]). A valid product (here: a concrete mouse) comprises all required features, some or none optional features, exactly

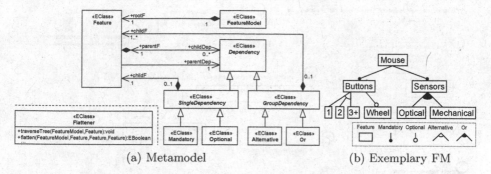

(a) Metamodel   (b) Exemplary FM

Fig. 1. Feature models – abstract and concrete syntax

one feature out of an alternative group of features, and at least one feature from an `Or` group.

Figure 2 depicts one operation of the `flattening` algorithm. It serves as our transformation under test for the remainder, and represents an ideal example for testing *pattern matching* aspects, since it does not define any rewriting steps itself (explicit testing of rewriting steps is not in focus here). One can distinguish four different types of activity nodes: (1) *start nodes* which mark the resp. entry point of the operation, (2) *story nodes* (all nodes except 4, 6, 9, and 10) which carry GT rules, the latter may be hidden, indicated by the ⊞ symbol, (3) *statement nodes* (gray background) which represent operation invocations, and (4) *end nodes* which mark exit points of operations. Story nodes can be sub-divided in terms of their semantics: (a) *regular patterns* (white background) that imply normal searching for a match (e.g. "check flattening precondition A. . . "), and (b) *for-each nodes* (dotted background) that imply iterating through the list of all distinct matches in the model, whereby each match results in a loop along the outgoing "`Each time`" labeled edge; eventually control is returned to the pattern again. For-each nodes are left via the "`end`" edge. Regular nodes can be left via "`success`" (→match found), "`failure`" (→no match found) and unlabeled (→don't care) edges.

The basic idea of the provided operation is to find flattenable sub trees and apply one of several well-defined graph rewritings to each of them. Repeatedly used, those basic rewritings condense the original tree and the algorithm converges. We removed most of the complexity from the example for the sake of brevity. The operation comprises three main steps, namely to search for a flattenable sub tree, performed as a top-down tree traversal, to delegate a sub tree to the actual flattening operation (which is also implemented as SDM transformations but omitted here, cf. [3]), whereby the direction of the shrinking is from leaves to root, and to re-evaluate the resulting tree after changes. All steps can be identified in the operation shown in Fig. 2: Starting from a given (nodes featuring a thick border are bound) feature `curF`, all its child `Dependency` objects are processed. Depending on whether the object is of subtype `SingleDependency` or `GroupDependency` the single child `Feature` or each of the group's children gets processed by a recursive call to this operation. In the left lower part of Fig. 2

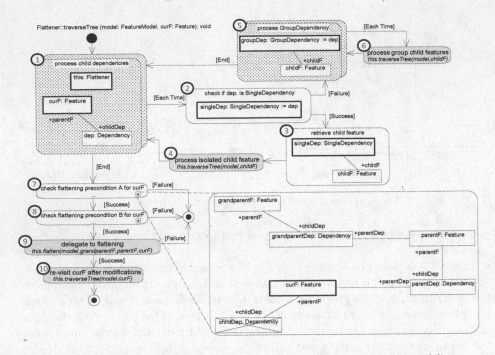

Fig. 2. Example SDM transformation (traversal of a feature tree, cf. [3])

two more complex patterns are located which check necessary conditions for the rewriting. In case the rewriting functionality gets invoked, the result has to be re-checked, indicated by the last recursive call before the stop node.

3.3   Testing SDMs

Dynamic testing means that one runs and observes the behavior of the transformation under test with different and representative input data. The goal is to provoke incorrect behavior that eventually hints to faults in the program. As mentioned before, it is usually impossible to prove the absence of faults by testing, because of the absurdly high number of required tests.

A *test (case)* (as defined by [1] and adapted to our case) is a tuple $T = (m_i, m_o, I, V, E)$, consisting of an input model m_i, an expected output model m_o, a set I of prerequisite initial steps to prepare the system for the actual test, a set V of post-processing verification steps, and a set E of exit/tear-down steps. The sets I, V, and E can be empty. One can also replace m_o by other artifacts, or might even be able to neglect it completely, if other means than e.g. output model comparison are available to reach a verdict on the test outcome. Consider, for example, the case of models with a runtime semantics serving as inputs and outputs for a refining, semantics preserving transformation. This allows for comparing the output directly to the input in terms of *bisimilarity*. As in the case of FMs as inputs and outputs and a semantics preserving transformation like in our example, it is possible to compare the transformation output directly to the input based on an equivalence relation. Thus we use the terms input model and test interchangeably in the following.

A collection of test cases is called a *test set/suite*. The construction of a test set is not done randomly but it is usually guided by a set of *requirements*. We borrow two definitions from [1]: a *test requirement* is "[...]a specific element of a software artifact that a test case must satisfy or cover." and a *coverage criterion* is a "rule or collection of rules" to derive such requirements. In the next section, we will refine this generic test requirement notion to the notion of *requirement patterns*. The algorithm for creating such requirement patterns from the given transformation specification forms the basis of our coverage criterion for testing programmed graph transformations.

Adequacy of Tests. A test suite can be considered fit for purpose, if it is able to unveil faults. To be able to detect an existing fault, the test set must contain at least one test that leads to a differing (incorrect) output of the program under test compared to the solution deemed correct (cf. [13,12]). An *adequate* test suite can, by definition, distinguish a correct program from any erroneous program [13]. This represents a highly intractable requirement for any real test suite which is why the notion of *relative* or *mutation adequacy* was introduced [12,13]. A test suite for a program is called adequate relative to a finite set of other programs, iff every incorrect version in the set can be detected by at least one test. This requirement is at the basis of mutation analysis and mutation testing.

Patterns as Basic Units. When testing an SDM transformation, one first needs to think about the scope of the tests. Testing a complete transformation is too coarse-grained, and would only fit a black-box approach. At a first glance, a complete operation seems to be a natural candidate for a unit under test. It corresponds to a single method in the generated code and comprises all "statements" (=activity nodes) that belong together to perform a basic functionality. On the other hand, these "statements" encapsulate pattern matching and rewriting steps, both complex and non-atomic at a technical level. Implementing the pattern matching itself is an error-prone task and demands for dedicated testing [11,27]. This rationale fosters the interpretation that testing a complete SDM operation shares more commonalities with the task of classical systems or integration testing rather than unit testing. The fact that story nodes (partially) depend on each other – subsequent nodes depend on preceding ones – supports this finding even further. It implies that story nodes are the basic units for testing and that a sound testing approach should respect this by defining coverage on a per pattern basis. Nevertheless, preference should be given to testing patterns in their actual context over testing them in isolation (which could be done in addition). The reason for this is twofold: (1) the control flow can have a strong influence on the result, and (2) thorough pattern testing can yield certain forms of structural coverage as by-product as explained later.

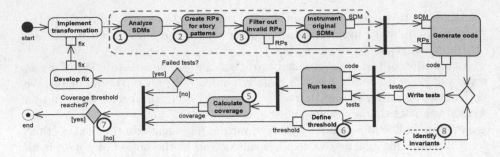

Fig. 3. Development and test process based on requirement patterns

4   Requirement Patterns and Coverage

In this section, we will provide an overview of the development and test process, discuss typical implementation errors that are likely to occur during the development, and define our new coverage notion.

4.1   Architectural Overview

Figure 3 provides an overview of our proposed development and testing process incl. relevant artifacts in standard UML activity diagram notation (cf. [1] for a general mutation testing process). The process comprises two intertwined cycles which could be characterized as *"code-test-fix"* and *"test-measure-optimize"*. The gray, highlighted actions represent steps that can be automated; the other tasks require user interaction. The four specially outlined actions form the core functionality: in step 1 all the graph patterns are collected from the transformation. In step 2 *requirement (graph) patterns* (RPs) are created by a component named *RP-licator* which builds on the metamodel and the relevant patterns (infeasible cases can be avoided proactively). The generated patterns can be further analyzed and filtered in step 3, before handed to the code generator of eMoflon. Step 4 takes care of instrumenting the original transformation. This ensures that RPs are evaluated during run-time.

The code generation then yields two code fractions: (a) code representing the original instrumented transformation incl. code for the metamodel, and (b) code derived from the requirement patterns and a simple container metamodel used for coverage measuring. To run a test means to execute code set of (a) stimulated by the test inputs which invokes the code of set (b). The task of writing actual tests can be challenging. Nevertheless, further details are problem specific and thus omitted. It should be noted that the obtained coverage information can be used to guide this task, although feedback is restricted to non-covered requirements. If a test fails, it is reasonable to fix the bug before writing further tests. The rationale is that altering the transformation will likely lead to a modified set of coverage items. If testing does not discover unexpected behavior, one has to compare measured coverage to a predefined threshold (cf. steps 5, 6, and 7).

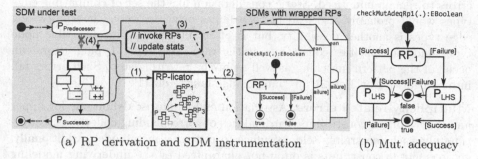

(a) RP derivation and SDM instrumentation   (b) Mut. adequacy

Fig. 4. Derivation of RPs and their application

Figure 4a sketches the RP derivation process complementing the description of the outlined actions depicted in Fig. 3. Based on a pattern P, the RP-licator component uses the pattern's LHS, P_{LHS}, to derive a collection of RPs ($RP_1, \ldots$) by exhaustively applying parameterized mutating operators to P_{LHS}, cf. step 1. Each generated RP is embedded into an evaluation operation in step 2. The operation's parameters correspond to the set of bound object variables whose values are forwarded to the helper operation. This set needs to be deduced from the preceding patterns of P and the parameters of the original operation. A return value of `true` indicates that the pattern has matched; otherwise `false` is returned. To include the evaluation of the generated patterns into the original control flow, a new evaluation node gets created in (3). It is embedded into the flow of control in (4), and its purpose is to invoke the operation and to update the statistics. Step 4 includes inserting one new edge from the evaluation node to P, and changing all incoming edges of P to point to the new predecessor. Note that "for-each" nodes require a second copy of the evaluation node, since the set of entering edges of the former nodes can be partitioned depending on whether an edge is part of a corresponding "each-time" loop, or not.

4.2   Typical Faults

We now analyze typical errors in SDMs. Results are similar to [11] in that several of our error types coincide with their fault classes, although focus of testing and languages differ. Another fault model is [21], but parallels are rather small.

Type-related errors. A common error is to choose wrong node or edge types. Such errors are likely to occur, if the type hierarchy is complex (many inheritance relations, great type count) or many different edge types exist. There are three possibilities to err when choosing a node type: (1) choose a superclass over of a subclass (2) select a subclass instead of a superclass (3) choose a completely unrelated (w.r.t. inheritance) class. In case of pattern matching (and despite of the concrete semantics), case (1) results in a less restrictive pattern, potentially matching too often, case (2) restricts the pattern, potentially excluding relevant matches. Case (3) might either lead to a higher or lower number of matches but most certainly results in totally wrong behavior which makes it less likely for such errors to remain unnoticed. Static consideration like the set of compatible edge types would probably also lead to such faults being noticed. Choosing wrong edge types is another possibility, but is often hindered by incompatible node types and multiplicities constraints at the respective ends. Typing errors can occur in the pattern matching as well as in the rewriting step. Such errors fall into categories 1 or 3 of [21] or "interchange faults" of [11].

Multiplicity-related errors. Association ends comprise definitions for upper and lower bounds constraining cardinalities of corresponding collections. Unfortunately, such constraints seldom suffice to restrict a metamodel. Additionally, enforcement of constraints is often not guaranteed by the underlying modeling layer. EMF (Eclipse Modeling Framework) is one popular example where code generation considers only upper limits and distinguishes two cases (upper bound "=1" and ">1"). Thus, programs based on an EMF repository, like our transformation, might be prone to multiplicity-related errors. For example, too many elements might get added to a container, or a developer might expect that multiplicity preconditions are always met, even when they are not. Errors concerning multiplicities might result in "omission" and "side effect faults" as in [11].

Graph isomorphism errors. One of the more subtle sources of faults is related to the way how object variables are bound to nodes in the model. Graph pattern matching semantics usually prevents that two variables of a pattern and of compatible type are bound to exactly the same node in the model (unless instructed to do so). Certain cases might require disabling isomorphic bindings for some object variables. Failing to do so might result in missed matches. On the other hand, enabling non-isomorphic bindings can also be erroneous and result in undesired matches. [11] refers to such faults as "violation of injectivity".

Errors related to the context of a match. A graph pattern should neither contain superfluous (context) elements potentially leading to a too restrictive pattern, nor omit necessary (context) elements potentially resulting in a too liberal pattern. Several pattern variants differing in element count exhibiting similar functionality for most cases might exist, making it easy to overshoot in both directions. Again, cf. "omission" and "side effect faults" of [11].

Control-flow errors. The control flow of SDMs is prone to typical bugs in that regard (unreachable activity nodes, wrong interconnections, or loop and branching errors), although the code generator can detect some problems statically. Similarities to traditional control flow testing are apparent. Obviously, the interdependency among story nodes prevents this language part to be completely neglected even when testing the pattern matching.

4.3   Test Requirements

Our approach is based on the derivation of requirement patterns from the LHS of the resp. original patterns. We use a set of mutation operations, comparable to the ones in [23] but adapted to the SDM language, to derive mutated patterns as in mutation analysis [12]. If combined correctly with the original patterns, as in Fig. 4b, RPs can also be used to evaluate a test suite's adequacy. A test can be considered adequate, if it discriminates the mutated pattern (RP_1) from the original pattern (P_{LHS}) w.r.t. matching behavior. Nevertheless, we do not strive to perform a mutation analysis here, but to develop a variable test suite to observe untested situations. Also, concerning entire operations, mutation analysis can even exhibit practical problems (equivalent mutants, non-deterministic pattern matching, etc.). It represents an adaption of a best practice (negative testing) to construct a test suite which trigger both cases of "match" and "no match" w.r.t. a pattern (cf. e.g. the "closed" criteria of [18], or [27]). We think this principle which can also be interpreted as a form of *predicate coverage* from logic coverage (cf. [1]) should be applied to the requirement patterns as well. On the level of testing isolated patterns, mutation testing can not guarantee this sort of coverage either.

Deriving meaningful Coverage Items. In general, one could derive coverage items in form of RPs based on any available information, e.g. specification documents, a tester's intuition/experience, or input value partitioning. Here, we advocate the automatic derivation of RPs from the SDMs and the metamodel.

The RP-generating algorithm takes a given metamodel mm and the relevant SDM transformation under test as input. The latter, though actually being models conforming to the SDM metamodel on their own, can be interpreted as being part of mm, both in a technical way, since they are actually filed within in the metamodel serialization, and a conceptual way, since they define the dynamic semantics of the modeled language. The algorithm thus outputs mm' which differs from mm only in that the comprised SDM transformations under test are instrumented according to steps 3 and 4 of Fig. 4a. Additionally, the algorithm outputs a second metamodel mm_{test}, representing the testing infrastructure. It comprises classes to store the coverage data and the generated operations resp. the SDMs containing the derived RPs as story patterns (cf. step 2 in Fig. 4a).

We continue by sketching the functioning of the algorithm which is as follows: iterate over all packages, classes, and operations in mm. For each class c in mm that defines at least on operation, two classes in mm_{test} are created: a statistics carrying counterpart c'_{stat}, with one Boolean variable for each coverage item, and a class c'_{test}. For each operation o of c retrieve the corresponding SDM – note that in our case an operation "comprises" the SDM implementation – and iterate over all contained graph patterns, to create (1) the set of requirement patterns, (2) the RP-wrapping evaluation SDMs and operations which are contained by c'_{test}, (3) the operations to update the coverage statistics (members of c'_{stat}), and (4) the instrumentation statements which are added to o. Step 1 modifies copies of LHSs, $P_{LHS,x}$, for each pattern P_x and applies the following generation strategies:

(a) Unmodified copy - UC. The unmodified P_{LHS} is used as a requirement pattern. Meeting this requirement which means that the RP does and does not match at least once and implies that the control flow reaches the original pattern. Additionally, it implies that all outgoing control flow edges leaving the story node to another story node are traversed, yielding a form of *weak edge coverage* which subsumes a form of *node coverage*. This notion of edge coverage is *weak*, because statement nodes which might branch the control flow are neglected here.

(b) Require all NAC elements - RAN. NAC elements of P are converted to mandatory elements. This requires one test where the NAC prevents P from matching. An example would be `childDep:Dependency` in pattern 7, Fig. 2.

(c) Require an optional element - RO. One optional element of P is converted to be mandatory. When met, at least one test exists where the optional element is present in the model.

(d) Exclude a mandatory object - EO. This strategy converts mandatory object variables to a NAC element (one per mutant). Each conversion is constrained by connectivity considerations, ensuring connectivity of the resulting pattern graph (w/o the new NAC element and adjacent edges). If met, the requirement guarantees that test models comprise situations where single nodes are missing to form a complete match. In our example (P_7, Fig. 2): `grandparentF` is the only variable that can be converted in such a way.

(e) Change object variable types - COT. The strategy requires that original types of each and every unbound object variable are changed in every possible manner. Each type substitution yields a new requirement pattern (only one substitution per mutant). But types can only be changed if requirements due to adjacent edges are not violated. Substituting with sub-types is without problems. But super-types are partitioned into compatible and incompatible types. The rationale behind the strategy is to test for wrong type decisions. In terms of our example a variable of type `SingleDependecy` could be altered to be a variable of type `Optional`. The type `Dependency` could not be chosen, if a `childF`-edge is an adjacent edge.

(f) Change link variable type (simple) - CLTS. Comparable to the previous strategy, this strategy alters P_{LHS} by replacing a link by a differently typed link. The link type can only be changed within the boundaries determined by the object variable types. (Note that *link type* refers the type of the link rather than the *reference*/object variable type). Additionally, the originally typed link is retained in NAC-form. When the corresponding requirements are met, potential linkage errors should become apparent. In our example (P_3, Fig. 2): connect `singleDep` and `childF` via `parentDep`-edge instead of `childF`-edge.

(g) Change link variable (complex) - CLTC. This strategy differs from the previous one in that not only the link variable type gets altered, but also the object variable type at one end of the link is changed as well. This implies rather complex checks on legal node types due to limitations implied by other, indirectly involved edges.

4.4   Requirement Pattern Coverage

Let $p \in P$ be one pattern out of the set P of all patterns selected for testing, and $S = \{t_1, \ldots, t_n\}$ be a test suite (comprising n tests) out of the set $\mathcal{S}$ of all possible test suites. Additionally, R denotes the complete set of requirement patterns generated for the transformation under test, and R_p refers to the set of requirement patterns due to p, whereby $\bigcup_{\forall p \in P} R_p$ is a partition of R (neglecting the case $\exists p \in P : R_p = \emptyset$).

We define a function $f : R \times S \to \mathbb{N}_0$ that maps a pattern-test-suite-pair onto the number of satisfied requirement patterns after testing with a test suite. "Satisfied" means that there exists at least one situation during testing, where the requirement pattern check evaluates to `true`. Analogously we can define function g that counts the number of unsatisfied requirement patterns, being those RPs that never match during testing (evaluation operation always returns `false`).

Now we can define the *positive* (c^+) and the *negative* (c^-) and *combined* (c) *RP-coverage* (RPC) for a pattern and a test suite as follows:

$$c^+(p, S) := \frac{f(R_p, S)}{|R_p|}, \quad c^-(p, S) := \frac{g(R_p, S)}{|R_p|}, \quad c(p, S) := \frac{f(.) + g(.)}{2\,|R_p|} \qquad (1)$$

Equation 2 extends this to the RPC of an operation o comprising a set P_o of patterns. And Eq. 3 defines the RPC of a transformation t, comprising a set O_t of operations. Respective negative and combined cases are omitted for brevity.

$$c^+(o, S) := \frac{\sum\limits_{\forall p \in P_o} f(s, R_p)}{\sum\limits_{\forall p \in P_o} |R_p|} \qquad (2) \qquad c^+(t, S) := \frac{\sum\limits_{\forall o \in O_t} \sum\limits_{\forall p \in P_o} f(s, R_p)}{\sum\limits_{\forall o \in O_t} \sum\limits_{\forall p \in P_o} |R_p|} \qquad (3)$$

5   Evaluation and First Results

We conclude our contribution by providing some details on our prototypical tool, and present important first findings during its practical proving.

5.1   Implementation

Creating the RPs manually is practically infeasible, esp. when experimenting with different strategies to derive them. This coincides with the statement of Ammann et al. that "[...]mutation yields more test requirements than any other test criterion" (cf. [1, p. 175]). Consequently, we implemented the outlined steps of Fig. 3 and Fig. 4a in a prototypical tool written in Java. Although possible, we refrained from using higher order transformations (building and manipulating SDM models by means of transformations specified in the SDM language) to exploit agility due to more elaborated Java editors. Most of the implementation effort was spent on static analysis (to prevent the generator from creating obviously unsatisfiable requirements), and on general automation of the process. The output of the prototype serves as input for our code-generation toolchain eMoflon. The generated code was then incorporated into an existing test-bench, and a rudimentary visualization view was used to analyze the resulting coverage reports. Currently, the prototype considers only structural constraints of the metamodel, OCL and attribute constraints within the patterns are not considered yet.

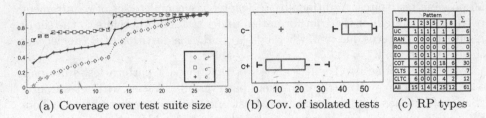

(a) Coverage over test suite size   (b) Cov. of isolated tests   (c) RP types

Type	Pattern						Σ
	1	2	3	5	7	8	
UC	1	1	1	1	1	1	6
RAN	0	0	0	0	1	0	1
RO	0	0	0	0	0	0	0
EO	1	0	1	1	1	1	5
COT	6	0	0	0	18	6	30
CLTS	1	0	2	2	0	2	7
CLTC	6	0	0	0	4	2	12
All	15	1	4	4	25	12	61

Fig. 5. Test

5.2   Evaluation Results

We used the described transformation of Sect. 3 to evaluate the general applicability of our approach and to collect first impressions during its application. A first finding is that the approach can be applied to the real-world example without further adaptions. The time required for deriving the RPs for the full transformation (including not presented parts) and the generation of the testing infrastructure model amounts to approx. 400ms (Intel Core2Duo @2.4GHz). Code generation for the instrumented version of the transformation required virtually no additional time compared to the not-instrumented version. It is considerably exceeded by the time required for generating the code for the testing infrastructure model (which is of the order of tens of seconds). Nevertheless, these time penalties occur only once every time code needs to be regenerated. Unfortunately, we did not evaluate the run-time overhead due to instrumentation in detail, but we deemed it negligible during testing, also because of the rather small input models used during testing.

For the given transformation the RP-licator produced a total of 61 RPs yielding a total of 122 coverage items. We incrementally constructed a test suite for the given operation comprising 27 tests; each test comprises a single input model. It took us approx. half to one person day to derive the test suite, and the required effort (time, model complexity) necessary to increase coverage rose over time. The resulting test suite leads to near optimal results: a c^+-value of 0.97 and a c^--value of 0.98. Figure 5a depicts corresponding coverage plots for the operation over test suit size (tests were combined in the order of appearing during the test creation). Figure 5b depicts two box plots for the number of covered (positive/negative) requirements by single tests. Obviously, it is easier to satisfy a higher number of requirements that demand patterns to not match. Figure 5c lists the numbers of RPs by type for the story patterns of Fig. 2.

The test suite helped to uncover an imperfection concerning pattern 3: there is no distinction between match and no match (cf. missing edge guards). Although not obvious from the metamodel, it is possible that singleDep does not reference a childF in which case the transformation can end up in a (non-obvious) infinite loop. Fixing the issue resulted in a drop of coverage (0.63 for c^+ and 0.97 for c^-) due to the changed control flow. The example led to further findings: (1) it is possible to achieve high coverage for our example which means that we mostly generate satisfiable RPs (3 out of 122 item were infeasible), (2) pattern interdependency rendered the items infeasible which hints to a general issue, (3) some requirements led to rather artificial test inputs which do not match intuition (but are valid due to missing constraints or at least possible due to missing checks), (4) all in all the approach is able to produce test suites with higher diversity. The iterative nature of the process can be motivational to a tester. The approach requires a certain insight in the transformation, but also guides the tester to untested section. RPs that cannot be covered can help to clarify the specification or unveil overlook constraints.

6 Conclusion

We have presented an approach to systematic testing of programmed graph transformations based on the new RPC coverage notion defined over *graph (requirement) patterns*. We showed that the approach is practical, and vital parts of a corresponding testing process can be automated. We also reported on applying our approach to a real world transformation, where it helped in finding a potential flaw. Important aspects like generalizability and test adequacy were evaluated. Future work includes the development of additional coverage requirement generation strategies, researching intelligent ways to combine the generated patterns, and an expansion of tooling. Test data generation and its interplay with the presented approach is another interesting option for future work.

References

1. Ammann, P., Offutt, J.: Introduction to Software Testing, 1st edn. Cambridge University Press, New York (2008)
2. Anjorin, A., Lauder, M., Patzina, S., Schürr, A.: eMoflon: Leveraging EMF and Professional CASE Tools. In: INFORMATIK 2011. LNI, vol. 192, p. 281. GI (2011)
3. Anjorin, A., Oster, S., Zorcic, I., Schürr, A.: Optimizing Model-Based Software Product Line Testing with Graph Transformations. In: Margaria, T., Padberg, J., Taentzer, G. (eds.) Proc. GT-VMT 2012. Electr. Comms. of the EASST, vol. 47, EASST (2012)
4. Baldan, P., König, B., Stürmer, I.: Generating Test Cases for Code Generators by Unfolding Graph Transformation Systems. In: Ehrig, H., Engels, G., Parisi-Presicce, F., Rozenberg, G. (eds.) ICGT 2004. LNCS, vol. 3256, pp. 194–209. Springer, Heidelberg (2004)
5. Baudry, B., Dinh-Trong, T., Mottu, J.M., Simmonds, D., France, R., Ghosh, S., Fleurey, F., Le Traon, Y.: Model transformation testing challenges. In: Proc. ECMDA workshop on Integration of MDD and MDT, Bilbao, Spain (2006)
6. Baudry, B., Ghosh, S., Fleurey, F., France, R., Le Traon, Y., Mottu, J.M.: Barriers to Systematic Model Transformation Testing. Commun. ACM 53(6), 139–143 (2010)
7. Bauer, E., Küster, J.M., Engels, G.: Test Suite Quality for Model Transformation Chains. In: Bishop, J., Vallecillo, A. (eds.) TOOLS 2011. LNCS, vol. 6705, pp. 3–19. Springer, Heidelberg (2011)
8. Benavides, D., Segura, S., Ruiz-Cortés, A.: Automated analysis of feature models 20 years later: A literature review. Inf. Syst. 35(6), 615–636 (2010)

9. Cabot, J., Claris, R., Guerra, E., de Lara, J.: A UML/OCL framework for the analysis of graph transformation rules. SoSyM 9, 335–357 (2010)
10. Ciancone, A., Filieri, A., Mirandola, R.: MANTra: Towards Model Transformation Testing. In: QUATIC 2010, pp. 97–105. IEEE (2010)
11. Darabos, A., Pataricza, A., Varró, D.: Towards Testing the Implementation of Graph Transformations. ENTCS 211, 75–85 (2008)
12. DeMillo, R., Lipton, R., Sayward, F.: Hints on Test Data Selection: Help for the Practicing Programmer. Computer 11(4), 34–41 (1978)
13. DeMillo, R., Offutt, J.: Constraint-based Automatic Test Data Generation. Software Engineering, IEEE Transactions on 17(9), 900–910 (1991)
14. Ehrig, H., Ehrig, K., Prange, U., Taentzer, G.: Fundamentals of Algebraic Graph Transformation. Springer (2006)
15. Fischer, T., Niere, J., Torunski, L., Zündorf, A.: Story Diagrams: A New Graph Rewrite Language Based on the Unified Modeling Language and Java. In: Ehrig, H., Engels, G., Kreowski, H.-J., Rozenberg, G. (eds.) TAGT 1998. LNCS, vol. 1764, pp. 296–309. Springer, Heidelberg (2000)
16. Fleurey, F., Baudry, B., Muller, P.A., Traon, Y.: Qualifying input test data for model transformations. SoSyM 8, 185–203 (2009)
17. Geiger, L.: Fehlersuche im Modell – Modellbasiertes Testen und Debuggen. Ph.D. thesis, Universität Kassel (2011)
18. Guerra, E.: Specification-driven test generation for model transformations. In: Hu, Z., de Lara, J. (eds.) ICMT 2012. LNCS, vol. 7307, pp. 40–55. Springer, Heidelberg (2012)
19. Heckel, R., Mariani, L.: Automatic Conformance Testing of Web Services. In: Cerioli, M. (ed.) FASE 2005. LNCS, vol. 3442, pp. 34–48. Springer, Heidelberg (2005)
20. Hildebrandt, S., Lambers, L., Giese, H., Petrick, D., Richter, I.: Automatic Conformance Testing of Optimized Triple Graph Grammar Implementations. In: Schürr, A., Varró, D., Varró, G. (eds.) AGTIVE 2011. LNCS, vol. 7233, pp. 238–253. Springer, Heidelberg (2012)
21. Küster, J.M., Abd-El-Razik, M.: Validation of Model Transformations – First Experiences Using a White Box Approach. In: Kühne, T. (ed.) MoDELS 2006. LNCS, vol. 4364, pp. 193–204. Springer, Heidelberg (2007)
22. McQuillan, J., Power, J.: White-Box Coverage Criteria for Model Transformations. In (prel.) Proc. MtATL 2009, pp. 63–77. AtlanMod INRIA & EMN (2009)
23. Mottu, J.-M., Baudry, B., Le Traon, Y.: Mutation Analysis Testing for Model Transformations. In: Rensink, A., Warmer, J. (eds.) ECMDA-FA 2006. LNCS, vol. 4066, pp. 376–390. Springer, Heidelberg (2006)
24. Rozenberg, G. (ed.): Handbook of graph grammars and computing by graph transformation: volume I. foundations. World Scientific, River Edge (1997)
25. Schmidt, D.: Guest Editor's Introduction: Model-Driven Engineering. IEEE Computer Society Computer 39(2), 25–31 (2006)
26. Sen, S., Baudry, B., Mottu, J.-M.: Automatic Model Generation Strategies for Model Transformation Testing. In: Paige, R.F. (ed.) ICMT 2009. LNCS, vol. 5563, pp. 148–164. Springer, Heidelberg (2009)
27. Wieber, M., Schürr, A.: Gray Box Coverage Criteria for Testing Graph Pattern Matching. In: Krause, C., Westfechtel, B. (eds.) Proc. GraBaTs 2012. Electronic Communications of the EASST, vol. 54, EASST (2012)

Author Index